WHEN GOD CALLS, EXPECT ADVENTURE

LESTER HAWKES with BRAD WATSON

Printed and published by
SIGNS PUBLISHING COMPANY
Victoria, Australia

Copyright © 2012 by Lester Hawkes and Brad Watson.

The authors assume full responsibility for the accuracy of all facts and quotations as cited in this book.

Unless otherwise indicated, all Bible quotations are taken from the Holy Bible, New International Version. Copyright © 1973, 1978 by the International Bible Society, used by permission of Zondervan Bible Publishers.

Proudly published and printed in Australia by
Signs Publishing Company
Warburton, Victoria.

This book was
Edited by Nathan Brown, Kerry Arbuckle and Lindy Schneider
Designed by Kym Jackson
Cover photographs and internal photographs provided by Lester Hawkes
    and Adventist Heritage Centre, South Pacific Division
Cover design by Shane Winfield
Typeset in Berkeley Book 11/14.5

ISBN 978 1 921292 69 9

You have searched me, Lord, and you know me. You know when I sit and when I rise; you perceive my thoughts from afar. You discern my going out and my lying down; you are familiar with all my ways. Before a word is on my tongue you, Lord, know it completely. You hem me in behind and before, and you lay your hand upon me. Such knowledge is too wonderful for me, too lofty for me to attain.

Where can I go from your Spirit? Where can I flee from your presence? If I go up to the heavens, you are there; if I make my bed in the depths, you are there. If I rise on the wings of the dawn, if I settle on the far side of the sea, even there your hand will guide me, your right hand will hold me fast. If I say, "Surely the darkness will hide me and the light become night around me," even the darkness will not be dark to you; the night will shine like the day, for darkness is as light to you.

For you created my inmost being; you knit me together in my mother's womb. I praise you because I am fearfully and wonderfully made; your works are wonderful, I know that full well. My frame was not hidden from you when I was made in the secret place, when I was woven together in the depths of the earth. Your eyes saw my unformed body; all the days ordained for me were written in your book before one of them came to be. How precious to me are your thoughts, God! How vast is the sum of them! Were I to count them, they would outnumber the grains of sand —when I awake, I am still with you.

(Psalm 139:1–18)

Dedicated . . .

To my precious wife, without whose commitment and support, many of the events recorded here would not have succeeded,

and

To our many missionary friends, both indigenous and expatriate, who gave—and are giving—so much honour and glory to the name of our Lord and our God.

FOREWORD

It is now more than 30 years since Julie and I, together with our little family, boarded a plane to travel from Sydney to Port Moresby to begin one of the most exciting and challenging periods of our ministry. We were "missionaries" to Papua New Guinea. Since before I can remember I had listened to stories told by missionaries on furlough. They were stories of crocodiles and precarious bridges constructed over raging rivers; of tribal wars and medical miracles; of Highland baptisms and coastal cyclones. As a small boy, I had been spellbound. I had learnt of places such as Fulton, Sopas, Togoba and Atoifi; and I came to know names such as Pascoe, Ferris, Stewart, Barnard, Lee, Mitchell, Cobbin, Winch and Hawkes.

When I arrived in Papua New Guinea with this background, it was with a deep sense of honour that I discovered I was to have the privilege of serving with long-standing, deeply committed Australian missionaries and their families, such as Pastors Don Mitchell, Colin Winch and Lester Hawkes, the author of this book.

Although we arrived many years after they had commenced their ministry, I quickly gained an immense respect for the work that they and many others had done in the years that preceded our arrival. Living in isolation and far from family for years at a time, in places where there were no hospitals, no educational facilities for their children, no ready supply of building materials, let alone fresh fruit and vegetables, they gained a foothold and planted churches against incredible odds. I was blown away by the vision and motivation that compelled these Australian missionaries to go.

The vision of men and women like Lester and Freda Hawkes was—and still is—God's mission! They built schools, provided health care, trained nurses, and promoted health and hygiene. As medical missionaries, they went in response to the great commission of Jesus Himself. And when we go in the name of Jesus, failure is not an option.

I thank God for all those who have given their talent and time in mission. I hope the stories in this book will help refresh our collective memory and inspire a new generation of readers to expect adventure in God's service.

Dr Barry Oliver
President
South Pacific Division of Seventh-day Adventists

CONTENTS

Foreword v

God's Plan 1
The Call 4
Secret Joy 8
Voyage to Papua 11
Aroma Mission Station 15
Village Life 18
Papuan Canoes 22
The *Ambon* Arrives 25
The Dispensary 28
Snakebite 31
Freda's Confinement 34
Cause for Worship 38
Bush Patrols 41
River Adventure 45
"You Stink, Too!" 48
Unwelcome News 52
Kidnappings and Crocodiles 55
The Papuan Sabbath 59
The Move to Madana 62
God's Protecting Hand 66
Diphtheria 70
Tragedy Strikes 73
Making Do At Madana 76
The Devil Attacks 81
Babaguina 86
Evacuation to Australia 91
Bena Bena 95
Salt, Water and Tithe 98
Poisonous Mushrooms and Deadly Crossings 103
Church Dedication 111
Bill Paslow 115
F D Nichol 119
The First Camp Meeting 123

Symbols of Sorrow	127
Called To Yani	131
A Memorable Arrival	135
Amen!	138
Into Bomai	141
Learning the Culture at Yani	145
"Poppa Belong All"	151
A Hasty Departure	155
Leprosy Care	159
The Rebellious Mare	164
Wartime Reminders and Galip Nuts	169
Earthquake	173
Leaving Saidor	177
Bogia	181
Dealing With the Unexpected	184
House Fire	187
Omaura	190
Belly Spirit	196
Tears of Thanks	199
Amazing Escape	203
Snakes Alive!	208
Tambu!	213
Sowing Seeds in the Markham	217
"Now I Can Scratch, Too!"	220
Cannibal Country	224
Pitcairn Island	231
"P" for Pastor	237
The Unsinkable Fridge	242
Appendicitis	246
Lost at Sea	251
A Close Call	255
The *Bounty* Anchor	260
Rabaul	264
God Protects Again	267
When God Calls	271
Afterword	274

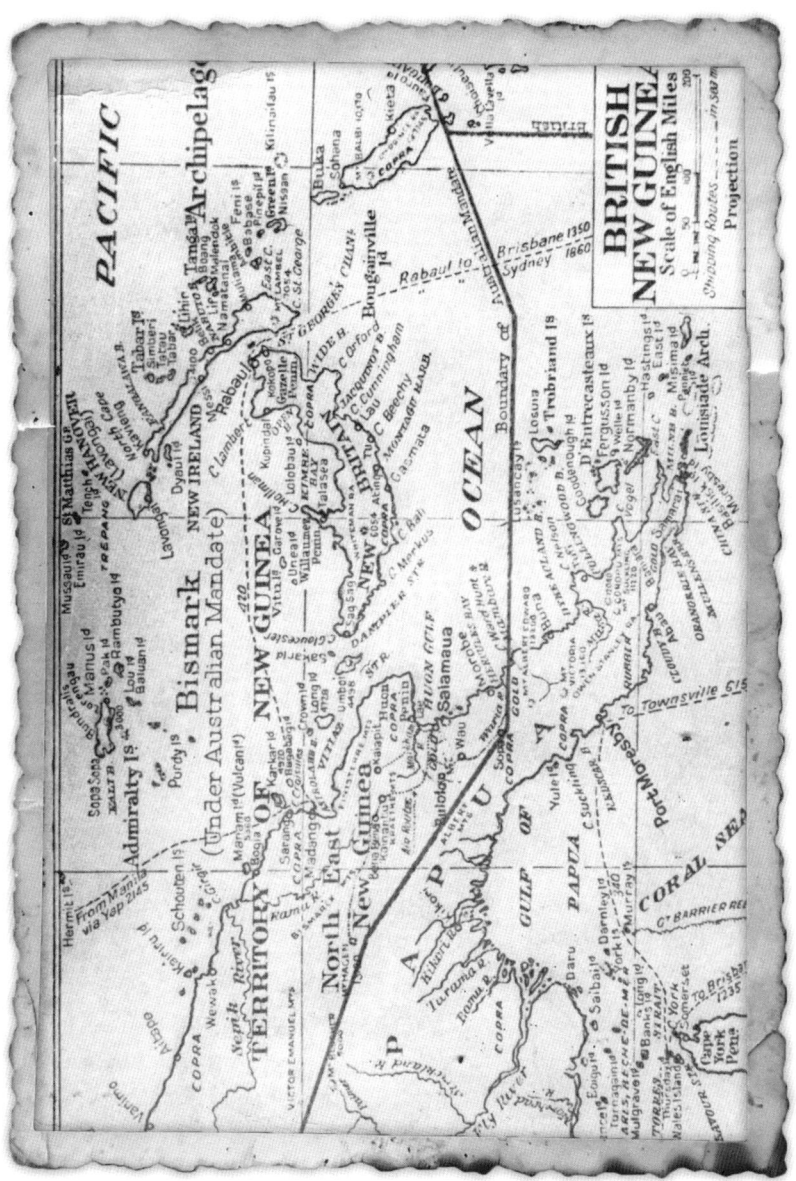

British Papua and the former colony of German New Guinea. From 1919 to 1975, both were administered by Australia.

Freda and Lester Hawkes ready to board their ship to Papua New Guinea at Sydney wharf on September 3, 1946.

GOD'S PLAN

"The Lord is trustworthy in all he promises and faithful in all he does. The Lord upholds all who fall and lifts up all who are bowed down" (Psalm 145:13, 14).

It was a warm, spring afternoon in the northern suburbs of Sydney, Australia, and I found myself struggling to keep up with the church administrator as we strode rapidly away from the Sydney Adventist Hospital toward the South Pacific Division office, headquarters of the Seventh-day Adventist Church in the region.

"Are you married?" Pastor Thrift asked.

"No, not yet," I replied.

"Well, you'd better be," he said abruptly. "We want you out there in January."

The words stopped me in my tracks. My thoughts raced as I watched him stride across the green manicured lawns and past the brilliant flower beds that have always been a feature of the hospital gardens.

It's so soon, I thought, mouth wide open. *We're engaged to be married, yes. But married and gone by January? I must tell Freda.*

It was 1945 and, according to this man, before long we would not only be man and wife, but living in the wilds of Papua, far from Australia and home.

I hurried to share the news with Freda, my mind spinning.

"Freda," I exclaimed, when I found her. "We have to get married!"

"Why?" she asked, eyes wide. "What's the rush?"

"They want us there as soon as possible!"

In those days, nursing students were not allowed to marry while they were in training. She stared at me, not quite comprehending the reason for such an outburst. So I explained, "They want us there in January, Freda! We must plan to marry before we sail! That's only a few months away!"

Freda and I had always made a practice of talking to God about our lives. But this information called for special prayer. Somehow, in just

When God Calls, Expect Adventure

a few short months, we would have to finish our studies, graduate, farewell our loved ones, get married and prepare for our departure.

As Freda and I discussed all the plans that would have to be made, I noticed she was calmer than I was. She saw the problems that had to be overcome and she set out to solve them in her own practical way. And—although there was much to be done—she was pleased.

I knew this was an answer to prayer. I felt the "call" so strongly in my heart. I had not the slightest doubt in the world that God had called me to serve Him as a medical missionary, and that I would not want to do this without Freda at my side.

But there was more. There was a story that had been handed down in my family, which was very important to me.

In 1861, my maternal grandmother—Mary—was born in a small, northern Victorian settlement. The region surrounding McCallum's Creek had lured many determined prospectors who had flocked to the southern Australian colony at the height of the gold rush. Mary was born at a time when gold fever still ran high and men continued to roam the colony of Victoria, inspired by stories of fabulous discoveries and dreams of unimaginable wealth.

Naturally, there were no services and drinking water had to be collected from what the family called a well. It was an old, disused mine shaft that had filled with water over the years and served as the family water supply.

Five years old at the time, Mary was asked to fetch a bucket of water for the kitchen. She ran to the well quite happily but as she neared the hole, she tripped and tumbled down the old mine shaft. Jagged rocks lined the walls and the dark, cold water seemed to rush up toward her as she fell, crying out with fear. But before she could splash into the inky water, she felt strong hands grasp her at her waist and neck. She was lifted up and placed gently face down on the lush grass beside the well.

Shocked and confused, Mary lay there for some time, feeling the place where the hands had pressed against her back, then looked for the stranger who had saved her. There was nobody to be seen.

Mary got up, left the bucket beside the well, and ran back to the kitchen where her mother was hard at work.

"You didn't fetch the water," said her mother. "What is wrong child?"

God's Plan

Mary told her mother what had happened at the well. She explained how she had fallen but had felt strong hands lift her up and place her safely on the grass above.

"Mother," she said, "I looked, but nobody was there."

Mary's mother paused. "Are you sure?" she asked.

"Yes. I looked, Mother, but I couldn't see anybody."

"Well," Mary's mother said, "it must have been an angel. He has a plan for you, Mary! Just you wait and see."

The Cameron family had faith in God, and as opportunity presented itself, they would attend church. Mary eventually grew into a young woman, but religious training had not formed a major part of her life. Years passed and although the memory of strong hands lifting her out of the well remained with her, she was able to comprehend only faintly what had happened. Occasionally she wondered why God would do something so outstanding for her.

Mary married Walter Dunlop and learned about Seventh-day Adventists through her husband's mother, who had been baptised in 1889. Mary's faith in God developed steadily but still she had found no answer as to why God had singled her out to be saved from the well.

Life was busy caring for a family of nine children. Then one day, late in her life, there was a family birthday party. Mary Dunlop was the matriarch of the group. Someone began to list all the descendants of hers who had taken up positions as church workers, missionaries, pastors, teachers or wives of such.

Amazingly, almost every one of Mary's nine children had members of their families who were serving as missionaries, church pastors or in some other posting in church service.

"Now, at last," said Grandma, "I know why God saved me from that well when I was a child. God saw the future. It was not for me that He did it. Rather, He saved me because He saw the ministers and gospel workers that would be among my family."

THE CALL

"The Lord will vindicate me; your love, Lord, endures forever" (Psalm 138:8).

I grew up confident that God had a plan for me. Even before I had heard my grandmother's story, I had decided to serve the Lord as a missionary.

I remember clearly one particular evening when a returned missionary showed some "Magic Lantern" pictures in the Mechanics Institute hall in Warburton, my home town when I was five years old. They were black-and-white pictures but I can still see in my mind the attractive faces of two young people he showed. They were from the Pacific—and they fascinated me.

Later, my father told me that as I was preparing for bed that evening I said in my small-boy voice, "Dad, I'm going to be a missionary when I grow up."

I never varied from that ambition and after my schooling was complete I began to consider the training I would need. Many friends, including my church pastor, were emphatic that to be a missionary I must first go to Avondale College to do the ministerial course. "Of course, you must go there," they said. "You must."

I could not agree. Although many years have passed, I still feel sure it was the Lord Himself who impressed on my mind that an intimate understanding of ancient biblical languages might be helpful, but hardly the most effective method for reaching those in lands where He was calling me to serve. I was convinced that a practical knowledge, such as how to treat disease, would open doors that even the best knowledge of ancient languages could never open.

Even though Ellen White founded Avondale College, it seemed to me she was wise when she said, "The Holy Spirit never has, and never will in the future, divorce the medical missionary work from the gospel ministry."* I am still impressed when I read the statement, "Some utterly fail to realise the importance of missionaries being also

The Call

medical missionaries. A gospel minister will be twice as successful in his work if he understands how to treat disease."**

As I contemplated my training, I decided that for me there would be a different method of ministry. I would meet the medical needs of people first, as Jesus often did. Then I would minister to the spiritual ones. I knew this was my calling.

Little did I know that God had another pleasant surprise for me. I did spend a short time in study at Avondale, but had I stayed there I would never have met the beautiful young lady who was to be such a support and partner to me through the years ahead. In January 1942, our class of would-be nurses entered the Sydney Sanitarium and Hospital—affectionately known to most people as "the San." Here, for the male students, a complete course in theology was taught alongside the full government-approved nursing course. This combined course of study made an excellent foundation for what God was calling me to do.

However, a serious problem soon arose. It was war time and the United States armed forces had informed church officials that they intended to take over the San for military purposes. The news was shocking because the San had been established for God's work. For

Even in 1949, the Sydney Adventist Hospital was fondly referred to as "the San."

When God Calls, Expect Adventure

weeks after that announcement, the whole staff spent much time in organised prayer gatherings pleading that God would overrule so that His work would not be seriously disrupted. It was also clear that there would be need for trained workers to move quickly into Pacific island mission posts vacated as a result of the war with Japan.

Just days before the American forces were to take over the San, I was passing through the hospital kitchen. I noticed Freda Tiller, a classmate who had caught my eye several times before. One of 10 females and four males in the class, she was also one of the quietest. She was dedicated to her training and to her Lord.

Trying to make small talk, I asked her, "Freda, if the Americans take over the San what do you plan to do?"

"I'm not quite sure what I'll do or where I'll go," she replied. "But I know one thing. I'm going to be a missionary nurse somewhere."

I saw a direct sign from God in that statement. Here was a young lady with a similar outlook to mine. Like me, she dreamed of being a medical missionary and I knew at that moment that I had to get to know her better. Fortunately for me, she didn't seem to mind at all! As work duties allowed, we would go for walks in the bush and gullies at the back of the hospital. Our salaries were only 75 cents per week, so there was no money to go where there were costs involved.

Graduation was due in December, 1945. For several years Freda and I had been seeking the Lord in prayer. We wanted to know what the future held for both of us. Where did God want us to serve Him?

Around August of that year, just as the war came to a close, church leaders had met to decide how to staff those island mission fields that had been so recently ravaged by the war. Then came the telegram, addressed to me: "You are called to work in the Papuan Mission."

If people were capable of jumping over the moon, I would have done so that day. I saw myself as one whom God had in mind when He saved Grandma Mary from certain death in that deep well. To me, the call was clear—it was a call from God Himself and He wanted me to be a medical missionary.

But the weeks went by with no further word. September was followed by October. Then came that day when I saw Pastor Thrift striding through the hospital lobby and gave chase. I almost had to run just to keep up with his huge steps. After months of waiting, his comment that we would have to be married soon had come as a shock.

Then there was another matter to be considered. Late in 1942, I had been required to spend some time in the army, which meant I was unable to finish at the same time as the rest of the nursing class. For me, my four years were not complete until January 13, 1946. And the hospital was firm in forbidding a student to marry until his or her time was fulfilled. I would have to remain as a student nurse until January 13, doing all the work a fourth-year student would normally do.

I decided to learn all the additional skills I could, and studied diagnosis and prescription, also spending as much time in the surgical theatre as possible. I knew that in the Pacific islands there would be few doctors. In the meantime, Freda would have to organise the wedding.

God answered our prayers. The American forces did not take over the San and the teaching program was not disrupted. It was a great relief to all of us. So many mission stations in the Pacific had stood empty during the terrible years of war and we were looking forward to resuming the church work as quickly as possible.

---

* Ellen White, *Health and Healing*, page 4.

** Ellen White, *Medical Ministry*, page 245.

SECRET JOY

"Lord, you alone are my portion and my cup; you make my lot secure. The boundary lines have fallen for me in pleasant places; surely I have a delightful inheritance" (Psalm 16:5, 6).

We set the wedding date for January 15 and Freda looked beautiful dressed in a lovely white wedding dress she had borrowed. It was a scorching hot summer's day. Before long the delicate curls of butter set beside each plate on the reception table were no more than pools of yellow oil. Not everything ran smoothly. Although she had ordered a small posy of flowers, the florist got mixed up and she had to carry a huge bunch of highly scented flowers that was almost too heavy for her. Sadly, because of wartime restrictions, my parents were not able to be present.

But we were married—and now we were ready and willing to answer God's call. Although we had only a small amount of money in our pockets, God had called and we were confident He would provide.

Yet we were learning that things seldom happen according to plan. We were ready to go. The war was over, Germany had been defeated, Japan had surrendered, the armies that had occupied the Pacific islands were gone. We had married quickly as advised and we expected to be on a boat any day soon.

"What is it?" Freda asked sometime later, noticing my dismay.

"There is a delay," I answered despondently.

"Why?"

"I've had a phone call, darling. There is no berth available on any ship. After telling us we must get married in such a hurry, it now seems that all passenger ships are fully booked. We can't depart yet."

"When then?"

"I don't know. It could be some time. We will just have to trust in God."

Clearly we would not be able to go to Papua—not yet at least. We contacted the Mission Appointees Committee who gave me a temporary job as "tent-master" for Pastor Merv Ball, who was conducting a tent mission in Orange, a town in mid-west New South Wales.

"That's fine by us," I replied, grateful for work while we waited. "But what does it mean to be a tent-master? What will I be expected to do?"

"It means that you will be responsible for the care and protection of the tent at all times, plus other duties as may be requested of you, such as giving Bible studies."

"Fine," I said. "I'm happy to do that. But what about housing? Where will Freda and I be living?"

"Oh," my new employer said, "I think you must have misunderstood. A tent-master sleeps behind the stage of the tent. That's where you will live. There's always the danger that vandals will want to damage the tent or its equipment and you must be there to protect it."

"OK," I said, still not understanding. "But what about my wife? Where will she stay?"

"Lester," came the pointed reply, "a tent-master's position is always for a single man. It wouldn't be safe or proper for her to sleep in the big tent. She will need to stay in Sydney—or wherever you choose for her to stay. Of course, we hope these arrangements will not be for too long. You really should not have married so soon!"

We had just had our honeymoon, been married for two weeks, had virtually no money in our pockets and now we were being asked to separate for who knows how long!

What was Freda to do? There seemed only one decision to make. She applied for and was accepted into a course in obstetrics at the Paddington Women's Hospital.

On the other hand, I was to take my 1924-model Norton motorbike and go to Orange. That was asking a lot of that old bike, which had a habit of breaking down about every 10 miles.

One evening, a day or so before I planned to start out for Orange, Freda mounted the pillion seat of the bike with her case of belongings between us. The night was wet and gloomy, a perfect reflection of my heart. We had no idea how long we were to be separated.

At the gate to the hospital nurse's quarters—beyond which men were forbidden to go—we said goodbye. As I held her hands in mine, the future appeared bleak. We would be separated by several hundred

When God Calls, Expect Adventure

miles! In just two days' time, I was to ride to Orange where I might remain for the rest of the year or until shipping could be found.

God, I said to myself. *I just can't see Your hand in all this. I can't.*

The next day a telegram arrived: "Lester. Vandals have burnt down the tent at Orange. Request you assist Pastor Grolimund at Parramatta."

I felt angry that the tent had been burnt—but I wanted to shout and leap with relief at the same time. I held a high regard for the things of God but there was secret joy in it for us, because now we would only be a short distance apart. Although we were both busy, I would be able to see Freda from time to time and I thanked God for that.

To my further delight, Pastor Grolimund was a great man to work with and I came to enjoy city evangelism. God saw that it was to my advantage to gain experience that would stand me in good stead later on.

While I was gaining valuable experience with evangelism, Freda was learning about women's health. We were able to meet from time to time, but not often.

I now know that we were a little like the apostle Peter. He had been with his Lord for several years and was eager to tell the world about the Messiah. Then came the day he was with Jesus on the Mount of Olives. When Peter heard the command "Go into all the world," he was sure he had all the preparation he required. How excited he must have been! But just as Peter was ready to answer that first command he heard another, "But tarry thou . . . till thou be endued with power."

Peter was not quite as ready as he had imagined. And neither, I know, were we!

VOYAGE TO PAPUA

"The earth is the Lord's, and everything in it, the world, and all who live in it; for he founded it on the seas and established it on the waters" (Psalm 24:1, 2).

It was late in August 1946, one year since the first telegram, when we received word from the Mission Board to say that shipping might soon become available. Freda and I packed all our belongings into a couple of old sea chests and two packing cases.

Again we were ready to move. Then, at about 4 pm on Tuesday, September 2, word came that a cabin was available for us on the *Montoro*. To our surprise, the vessel was to sail at 2.30 pm the very next day. What a rush! I had a motorbike to sell, last-minute packing to do, people to advise, friends to farewell and many other details to attend to—all within less than 24 hours!

At the wharf the next day were not only family but also many of our classmates to see us off. We met returning missionaries travelling on the same boat. There was Pastor and Mrs R H Tutty, and Pastor and Mrs Tom Judd from Victoria. Plus we met the Gibletts, who, like us, were going out for the first time. The ship's captain, Bill Wilding—better known and better described as "Wild Bill"—kept us in fits of laughter all the way to Port Moresby.

Each day Freda and I watched the ocean as it changed from the grey-blue of the colder climes to the Reckitt's Blue of tropical waters. During the day, our eyes moved regularly to the skyline ahead of the ship, looking for the first sighting of our new home.

On the third morning of our trip, we were on deck at sunrise. Looking ahead, we saw a small green island coming into view, standing guard outside the Port Moresby harbour. Inside the harbour we passed

When God Calls, Expect Adventure

the bombed remains of numerous ships sunk during the war. The most prominent was the *Macdhui* lying on its side, rusting away in the tropical heat. The ship had travelled often between Australia and Papua, and was remembered fondly by most Australians living there.

As we approached it, the wharf took on the appearance of a wartime scene. Only ex-army vehicles were to be seen. There were trucks and jeeps and motorbikes too, all left behind by various armies. But it was the native people who fascinated us most, with their colourful wrap-around "ramis" or loincloths, their huge black hairstyles, and in most cases, with red, betel-nut-stained teeth and lips. Among the bedlam—and wearing a David Livingstone-style pith helmet—was Pastor Charlie Mitchell, waiting to welcome the new Adventist missionary group.

This was a different land, heavy with the rich perfume of frangipani, and decorated with the colourful leaves of countless varieties of croton and bright hibiscus flowers festooning the dark green shrubbery.

I had been looking forward to this day for so many years. It had never occurred to me that I might succumb to culture shock. Before we had reached the mission house on Ela Beach, my semi-Victorian upbringing took a rude jolt when I saw mission boys race over to bargain for bananas and pineapples being sold by laughing girls dressed only in swirling grass skirts. The girls wore no upper garment and seemed not to be the slightest bit self-conscious. I had to bite my lip and stop myself from calling the boys back. Freda experienced similar shock, especially at the sight of men whose clothing consisted of no more than a string or a small covering.

I had many things to learn, and an equal number to unlearn. Many established concepts needed rapid re-adjustment and the process was beginning already. That afternoon, Pastor Eric Boehm drove down from the Bisiatabu Mission station in his ex-army truck carrying a load of ripe pineapples. Each person in the mission house was handed half a pineapple and a spoon. Never in my life had I been given more than one precious slice of pineapple—and it was so sweet!

Someone must have seen the look on my face when my half pineapple had been eaten, because I was invited to take another half. Of course, I did. To me it was a taste of heaven!

The next day we went back to the wharf to check on the boxes of personal goods we had brought with us on the *Montoro*, only to find that having been the last items to go on the ship in Sydney, they had been the first to be taken off and were now stored at the extreme end of the customs shed, with no hope of getting them out for days.

This raised a problem! Dr Tom Sherwin had arrived for a limited tour around Papua and was scheduled to travel with us on the mission ship *MV Diari* on its trip east. Dr Sherwin and Pastor Mitchell couldn't wait several days for our cargo to be released. Pastor Mitchell made arrangements with a local trading boat to collect our boxes a week later and bring them to us at Aroma, the mission station that was to be our home.

Encouraged to take some food items, Freda and I purchased a few items, such as potatoes and onions, and some house-cleaning supplies that we had not included in the boxes we had brought from Sydney. We would just have to go without our precious possessions and hope to be reunited with them soon.

I inspected the *Diari* as we boarded the following day. Vessels like

The *Diari* was a mission boat used in Papua. It is shown anchored on Dora Creek behind Cooranbong's Sanitarium Health Food factory and Avondale College.

When God Calls, Expect Adventure

these were essential in the islands. It was about 40 feet (about 12 metres) long, old but well kept, and only had about 32 inches (80 centimetres) of freeboard amidships. The sunken cabin had four bunks with one door leading out onto the small back deck and another to the wheelhouse. There was no toilet or cooking facilities.

The *Diari* had an ancient three-cylinder diesel engine, which did not start easily. It needed three huge blowlamps to heat the glow plug on each cylinder head until they were red hot and able to ignite the diesel. I felt sorry for the poor engineer who had to squeeze into that stifling hole called the engine room, then light and tend to those outsized blowlamps until the glow plugs on each cylinder head were cherry red, and finally, wind the engine over until it started. It must have been terribly hot!

Freda and I arrived at that season of the year known as the "Laurabada," the time of strong, constant south-easterly trade winds that blow off the water day and night for nearly half the year. East was the direction we had to go, which meant the wind howled into our faces throughout the trip. Against such a gale, we were forced to spend three miserable days cramped inside. It was almost impossible to sleep as the *Diari* smashed its way into the oncoming seas.

Dr Sherwin's stomach very quickly began to rebel. He lay on his bunk feeling as miserable as a man can be. Every time he made a move or opened his mouth to say something, no matter how trivial, one of the crew would rush to him with a bucket. Freda and I made do as best we could.

On the second night, we anchored in a reasonably sheltered cove, not far from a sandy beach. Dr Sherwin asked if he might be permitted to sleep on the beach, as some of the native passengers had done the previous night.

Pastor Mitchell's face showed worry as he asked, "But what about the crocodiles that prowl the beach at night?"

I watched the doctor's face change from questioning, fear, to uncertainty as he thought for a moment, but decided it was still worth the risk just to be on solid ground. He looked up just in time to catch the twinkle in Pastor Mitchell's eye. However, I did grin as I noticed that the doctor made his beach-bed with the Papuan people between him and the water.

AROMA MISSION STATION

"One thing I ask from the Lord, this only do I seek: that I may dwell in the house of the Lord all the days of my life, to gaze on the beauty of the Lord and to seek him in his temple" (Psalm 27:4).

The *Diari* finally dropped anchor in the lee of Paramana Point early in the afternoon of the third day. What a glorious scene it was! I only had eyes for the beauty of my surroundings. On the outer side of the submerged coral reef was pounding white surf but the calm blue water on the inside of the reef shelved off to a wide, almost-flat, dark-sand beach as easy to walk along as if it were paved, but so much nicer.

Thousands of small grey sand crabs had patterned the surface of the beach with a myriad of tiny sand balls. As we approached, each crab would lift its outsized nipper defiantly, threatening us bravely before scuttling madly into the safety of an incoming wavelet.

On the landward side of the lagoon, the sand was dry and blown up into sand hillocks. The dunes engulfed the first rows of tightly planted coconut palms, the trunks of which intertwined in a most fantastic fashion as each searched for the largest patch of light. That day, the south-easterly winds roared overhead, tugging at all the palm fronds so that they looked like long, streaming hair on a group of mad motorcyclists.

In the sky above the coconuts, mighty frigate birds faced directly into the wind and soared, almost motionless, their wings seemingly pinned to the blue backdrop of sky, their long forked tails opening and closing like a child playing with a pair of scissors. Now and again one of them would tip downward in a lazy glide, only to rise and resume once more the position it had held earlier. From that day on, I often looked up at them and marvelled at their elegance and gracefulness.

When God Calls, Expect Adventure

Beautiful as the scenery was, we had come to work with people. We disembarked in the safety of the lagoon and began our walk down a long stretch of beach toward Aroma mission station, which was still hidden from our sight.

While we were hiking, our small group was surrounded by scores of happy, naked children who laughed and screamed and raced in and out of the water. They were from the many villages we passed and were delighted to see us. We enjoyed their playfulness and curiosity. Every few steps, we passed another large dugout canoe hauled up on the beach.

Our anticipation grew as we approached the mission compound. Finally we arrived at our new home. Freda and I exchanged looks. Despite our excitement, this was not quite what we had imagined. We had known that the Aroma mission station had been set up as a small medical outpost to care for the needs of the thousands of inhabitants of this 6-mile (10-kilometre) beach. Aroma was one of only eight mission stations operated by the Adventist church in the whole of Papua New Guinea at that time. God had granted us the high privilege of caring for this station and our expectations had run high.

Standing outside the station, the reality of our situation struck home. The mission property fronted the dry sand of the beach and boasted a quaint, old-world picket fence with a gate. However, in places the fence was lost under the drifting sand, while at others it almost fell over where the wind had blown the sand away.

There was no lawn around the house, but there were a number of interweaving coconut palms and two large-leafed shrubs that never produced flowers. Even the small one-bedroom house, which had originally been built almost 6 feet (1.8 metres) above ground level, had times when the sand almost reached the floor level. At other times, one or two of the posts would be left waving in the wind because the sand had been blown away. The other buildings, including the small clinic, were made from heavily weathered cement sheet and a roof of rusty iron. There was no running water. Light would need to come from lanterns and candles.

To our surprise, there was nobody there to greet us and the station looked as if it had been abandoned. Of course, Pastor Mitchell knew

Aroma Mission Station

the station was not deserted. Mrs Alma Wiles had been camping in the house and caring for the station until we arrived. But she didn't show up when we got there, which seemed strange. When we finally entered the house, we found Alma sick with malaria, so sick she could hardly get out of bed and when she did get out she found it hard to stand. Despite this, she gathered her strength and cared for everyone most ably.

Alma usually worked at Korela, another mission station about 20 miles (30 kilometres) away. Alma was one of the early Australian missionaries and had pioneered the work in the New Hebrides with her husband until blackwater fever had claimed his life. She had buried him without anyone to assist her or provide comfort, and now she worked in Papua.

Most of Alma's goods were at Korela and she had brought nothing across for us, expecting we would have our own supplies and belongings. Unfortunately, we arrived with nothing except a few potatoes and onions, plus some cleaning supplies that this sand-scoured house hardly needed.

That night we made do with what we had. Freda was careful to make sure we always travelled with a pair of sheets and we used the double bed while Alma slept on a cane lounge.

The local trading vessel dropped anchor behind the reef the following day, so we hastened out in the large mission canoe to collect our goods. The captain's reply shook us. "Oh, your goods? I couldn't get them. They were at the back of the shed behind all the other cargo. It might take six weeks before I can get your boxes out here."

Disappointed, we returned to the station to survey what we had and learn more about the people around us. Freda and I had no choice but to settle in as best we could.

VILLAGE LIFE

"The Lord had said to Abram, 'Go from your country, your people and your father's household to the land I will show you'" (Genesis 12:1).

From a glassless window on one side of the house we looked down on Pelagai village, the nearest village house was about 30 yards (27 metres) away. Each building was about 10 yards (9 metres) long, standing tall on its stilts, end on to the beach and the wind. They had a rounded palm-leaf roof, shaped to look like a blanket on a horse's back. Like Abram, we found ourselves in a strange new land.

The entrances to the houses were met by a notched log that formed a simple ladder rising near the centre of the floor to meet a trap door that could be lowered over the ladder. At night, the man of the house always slept on that trapdoor so no-one could enter without waking him.

One of the most interesting features of these houses had to do with the floor timbers. Part of the bride-price a young man had to pay before he could marry the girl of the house was to supply the father with at least one floor timber. The plank he brought in was long enough to cover the full width of the house, up to 5 feet (1.5 metres) wide and about 4 inches (10 centimetres) thick. It was usually a lovely red timber, polished by the bare feet that walked on it. Being hand-prepared without steel tools it was not perfectly flat, but was usually close to it.

They had no separate walls—the leaf roof reached right down to floor level on both sides with window shutters strategically placed at each end of the house for cross-ventilation on hot days. A hole in the floor served as a toilet.

So close was our own house to the village that we could hear the inhabitants talking or coughing during the night when the wind subsided. As we studied the village closely, we remarked that we had never seen so many children—and not one child wore a strip of clothing.

Never had we seen so many pigs either. They lay in the cool shade

Village Life

under the village homes, snuffled around and tended to their squealing piglets. To Freda and I, pigs were unhygienic, unpleasant animals that caused disease. However, the pigs constituted the only sewerage and waste disposal system the villagers possessed. They cleaned up everything that dropped, except small amounts that fowls beat them to. Like most Melanesians, to these people, pigs were also a source of great pride and personal wealth. They were essential in bride-price ceremonies. The fact that they contributed to disease was something the people seemed oblivious to.

The village and its environment had been cleared of most vegetation, leaving only food trees, such as coconut or pawpaw, plus a number of ornamentals like hibiscus and crotons. We came to feel that God must have had a special interest in croton plants, their leaf-form and colours varied so widely. Only a God who loved beauty for beauty's sake could have dreamed up the varieties we learned to know and love. Leaf-forms went all the way from flat to tightly twisted corkscrews, from blacks through reds, yellows, greens and everything in between. Many were spotted, others were serrated, and almost any shape one could imagine was to be seen among them. Every one was beautiful.

Pelagi Village at the end of World War II. Villagers talk with Australian soldiers between tall, well-designed houses.

When God Calls, Expect Adventure

From our vantage point, we could see that the women's dress consisted of several layers of grass skirts, sometimes as many as six layers, one above the other, each new one being fitted over the previous skirts. In time, we were told, the inner one would simply fall away.

The traditional dress of our male neighbours could hardly have been more different to mine. Where I wore trousers and shirts, shoes and socks, many of the men wore nothing more than one string skilfully arranged to satisfy their standards of modesty and practicality. At the time of our arrival, their dress was already changing rapidly. About half of the men were wearing ramis, a calico cloth wrapped around the waist. Within a few years, the traditional strings had disappeared.

Like most young people from Australia, I had been brought up on Bible stories, including the story of David and his sling. According to the song we sang "the sling went round and round, and round and round, and round and round and round . . ." The Papuans often carried a sling with them. So I was interested to find out how they used them.

One day I asked a village man to show me. He bent down and picked up a small round stone and placed it in the sling's pouch. The stone from the Papuan sling was not swung "round and round, and round and round" as the song indicated. Just one sharp swing and the stone smashed with a sharp, loud "crack" into the coconut tree.

The sling consisted of a pouch with strings about 8 inches (20 centimetres) long from either side. The string from one end of the pouch was wound around and held by the middle finger, while the string on the other side was held between the thumb and forefinger. When the stone was to be thrown, there was just one short swing of the arm and that stone went with tremendous speed and accuracy.

The girls gloried in a head adorned with black, wavy hair. However, we discovered that this could only be so until she married. According to local culture, all married women must have their heads shaved with a broken shell or shard of broken bottle. It was explained to me that the reason for cutting the wife's hair was to make sure that she would not be attractive to any man other than her husband. Like the men's standards of dress, these customs were also changing.

Joining us at the window, Pastor Mitchell exclaimed, "Look at the head-hunters. Over there."

As Freda's eyes followed the direction he was pointing, a momentary look of concern crossed her face. Sitting beneath a house in the village was a woman with a clean-shaven head searching carefully through a girl's hair for nits. That was "head-hunting"—Papuan-style—and I was grateful to be told that although warriors had practiced real head-hunting in the past, this was the only "head-hunting" we could expect to see.

A little farther along in the village, a man was having a shave. He was lying down, his head resting on his wife's lap. She was using a recently emptied bivalve shell as a blunt pair of tweezers to pull the facial hairs out, one at a time. The man appeared to be peacefully sleeping through the process.

Everywhere we looked Freda and I were confronted with new sights and sounds. I was glad to have the company of experienced missionaries, but I was also impatient to get down to the business of medical missionary work.

The next day, the *Diari* left us, taking Pastor Mitchell and Dr Sherwin further along the coast. We had no beds, no bedding, no food or much of anything else. The wind was so constant and the sand so invasive that it didn't take long for us to learn that the first thing to do each morning was to wipe the blown sand from our faces before opening our eyes. Despite our best efforts, it came in through cracks in the floor and walls, and there was nothing we could do but get used to it.

Because our own supplies were delayed, Mrs Wiles, Freda and I set off in the mission canoe to Korela. Again it was a case of fighting blustery winds and choppy seas but this time we were using indigenous transport without the benefit of even an old diesel motor. To make any headway, the canoe had to tack constantly. The trip was slow and very wet but it was exciting, too.

PAPUAN CANOES

"When Jesus heard what had happened, he withdrew by boat privately to a solitary place. Hearing of this, the crowds followed him on foot from the towns. When Jesus landed and saw a large crowd, he had compassion on them and healed their sick" (Matthew 14:13).

Our trip to Korela Mission went smoothly and we were grateful to return with much-needed supplies. Although our trip was uncomfortable, I learned to love that mission canoe, both for what it was and for what it allowed us do.

Its largest log was 53 feet (16 metres) long and the secondary log some 48 feet (14.5 metres). Each had been hollowed out until it left a skin of no more than 4 to 6 inches (10 to 15 centimetres) thickness. Lashed between the two logs was a deck some 6 feet (1.8 metres) wide by 15 feet (4.5 metres) long. A great square canvas sail hung sideways from the one main mast lashed in the centre of the larger of the two logs. A huge steering oar slid into a special slot near the stern of the canoe. Stable and strong, the canoe was capable of carrying a dozen people.

On that first journey, I noticed that the manoeuvre of tacking was quite different from most ocean-going vessels. When the time came to change tack, the sail and its boom were swung to the opposite end of the canoe while the steersman carried the huge steering oar to that end and slid it into its slot. What had been the bow of the canoe now became the stern.

Having no keel under the canoe meant there was naturally a lot of sideslip. Being tied between the central mast and the stern, the sail exerted a greater tendency to sideslip at the stern. But the steering oar determined whether the greater amount of sideslip was at the bow or the stern. The two ends of both logs were decked over to be almost waterproof so that in heavy seas the canoe slid smoothly through the waves. These ocean-going canoes rode so well it was quite comfortable, regardless of the size of the seas.

We had returned from Korela only two days previously when Alma

Papuan Canoes

made a surprise suggestion involving another canoe adventure. Food for the students was running low and a short distance up the nearby Keagola River there was a mission garden cared for by a garden boy, who also cared for the local village church. She suggested that Freda and I take a river canoe she would borrow and go up there for a couple of days and take a few meetings while the students who came with us did some work in the garden. We would then bring back some food for the Aroma station.

The river canoes were much smaller. Like the ocean-going canoes, they were made of two hollowed-out logs of similar length with a small platform between, just wide enough to sit on. Freda and I took up our positions in the middle and enjoyed the first of what would be many river trips.

The scenery along that riverside was most interesting and very beautiful in a rich, tropical way, although tempered by the sight of mudslides used by the many river crocodiles. Some could grow so big that they could easily swamp a small canoe. A man without a weapon would be no match for their enormous jaws.

We had travelled some distance up the river before we actually saw

Alma Wiles loved to hold and care for children. Prior to serving in Papua she had worked in the New Hebrides (Vanuatu) where her husband tragically died of blackwater fever.

When God Calls, Expect Adventure

a crocodile. Generally they heard the paddles of the canoe and slid into the river before we rounded the bend. When at a shallow part of the river we had to get out to drag the canoe over a sandbar, we were very conscious of the fact that there were crocodiles not far away. All we could do was hope they were well fed and afraid of the splashing made by our noisy group.

At the Keagola village, we had a difficult time. Although I was eager to preach, we had no-one who could interpret adequately for us, so taking meetings that could be understood was near impossible. The students working the gardens were smart enough to seek our directions, knowing that we neither understood their type of gardening nor knew how to speak to them in a language they would comprehend. The food offered to us was so strange and new that it was hard to eat. It consisted of black maize, fire-baked sweet potato, plantain and fern leaf. We soon became hungry.

Fortunately we had taken a supply of medicines with us. Practically every child, and most adults, presented with a skin disease known locally as "grili." It is a fungal infection that spreads very readily. The skin becomes red and infected, afflicting sufferers with constant irritation and tenderness. Grili is not at all nice to look at, and requires a consistent and lengthy treatment, neither of which we were in a position to offer, considering the time available to us in the village. Later in our mission service, we came to accept it but being new it worried us no end.

That night Freda had a distressing dream in which a child covered from head to toe with this repulsive disease was trying to get into our clean, warm bed with her. She grabbed his hand and was endeavouring to push him out with all her strength, but he would not go. It worked her up so much that she woke, wide eyed in the half-darkness, only to find it was her own hand she was trying so desperately to push out of the bed! The medical conditions we saw and treated took a toll on us and we felt we had been given a heavy responsibility.

After our first trip, Freda and I wondered if we had accomplished much at all. Sharing the gospel was impossible without interpreters and the medical conditions we treated needed more time and medicine than we had to give. We did the best we could, loaded the canoe with garden produce and returned to the mission station to find Mrs Wiles in better health and the house made much more liveable.

THE AMBON ARRIVES

"Leaving the crowd behind, they took him along, just as he was, in the boat. . . . A furious squall came up, and the waves broke over the boat, so that it was nearly swamped" (Mark 4:36, 37).

Just two weeks after we arrived at Aroma, the *M V Ambon*—the new mission vessel—anchored at Paramana Point quite unexpectedly. Captain Jack Radley had on board a large group of new missionaries travelling from Australia, some en route to Rabaul and others to the Solomon Islands. Like us, they were taking up appointments in Pacific nations and resuming the work begun by the Seventh-day Adventist Church before the war.

Their trip had been far from smooth and some of the people were not at all well, particularly Edna Lock, wife of Pastor Lester Lock. A combination of severe seasickness and malaria had her to a point where she was vomiting blood and it had become clear to all on board that she needed time ashore to recover. Dr Cyril Evans, who was also a passenger on the boat, instructed Captain Radley to remain at least for the weekend while Mrs Lock recovered her health.

Unfortunately for our unexpected guests, our belongings were still in Port Moresby. Mrs Wiles had only brought across from Korela the barest of essentials for the three of us and there was only one double bed. Now, more than 20 people wanted nothing more than to sleep on steady land, and asked to come and sleep in our small one-bedroom house on the beach. Mrs Lock was given the double bed. Most of the others brought mattresses from the boat and Mrs Wiles managed to borrow a few basic beds from the mission teachers. Fortunately for us, food was available from the boat.

Having so many people in such a small house placed a strain on all of

When God Calls, Expect Adventure

us, especially Freda as she attempted to show the hospitality expected of a good hostess. It was hard to find blessings in this arrangement for us but we believed, as we are told in Scripture, that "all things work together for good." It certainly had in the past for us and this would be no exception.

For many years, another group of Christian missionaries had been operating in the Aroma district. Rather than work together to bring the gospel message to people who needed it so much, they had been intent on building an earthly kingdom and had been telling the people that Seventh-day Adventists were of no consequence and could boast "only two old women and a dog in Australia."

From time to time, the Australian missionary for that group would come and conduct the worship service in their church. When the service was over the minister had the habit of going to the door of the church with a small box filled with sticks of tobacco. As the members filed out, he handed each person a stick of "twist tobacco." Many of the members told me they never went to church other than at those times when they could get a free stick of tobacco.

But seeing the large new boat and the group of 27 Adventist missionaries walking through the village opened the eyes of many of the village people. Although we preferred to gain respect for the quality of our mission work, at least we gained some new respect during this visit. So this experience worked for good in our work.

Another positive was that the *Ambon* had brought the first mail we had received. Only those who have lived in isolated places will ever be able to understand what a letter can mean at such times. The bag of mail was eagerly upended on the kitchen floor and all personal letters read from beginning to end, following which Freda and Mrs Wiles spent the whole night cooking over the small wood stove so they could provide something for our guests to eat.

After the *Ambon* departed, Alma Wiles stayed with us, as our mentor, to help get us on our feet. We thanked God almost daily for the helpful instruction she gave us. Her real duties were at Korela, so finally she had to leave. After she departed, there were only two people on the station who could understand and speak some English. Pastor Tauku from the Solomon Islands spoke a smattering of English, and Lui Oli,

The Ambon Arrives

our school teacher, spoke some also. Lui would later become president of the Central Papuan Mission.

Remembering that God had given the "gift of tongues" to His people originally so people could hear and comprehend the Bible message in their own language (see Acts 2), I determined to get to know the language as quickly as God would grant me the ability. Amazingly, He did help me. Nine weeks after our arrival I preached my first sermon in Motuan without an interpreter. That ability was indeed a gift from God and He alone is to be honoured. Before long I began to do all my thinking, and even my dreaming, in the Motuan tongue but I still don't know what the local people thought of that first sermon.

One of the kindly expressions Alma Wiles passed on to us came from a slight misquotation of Isaiah 51:1. She would repeat to us, "Remember the pit from whence they were digged." If ever anyone tried to lift people from the pit it was Mrs Wiles. Another expression we must have heard from her almost every day was "we have nothing to fear for the future except as we forget the way the Lord has led us in the past."

Several times toward the close of each day, she would stop for a moment, then say, "I must not let a single day go by without having done some missionary work." And off she would go to talk about the Lord to someone.

I still thank God that I was given that kind of example at the beginning of our mission service. For me, mission service required meeting the needs of the people, understanding the circumstances from which they had come and sharing the gospel message.

THE DISPENSARY

"They will turn to the Lord, and he will respond to their pleas and heal them" (Isaiah 19:22).

The arrival of daylight each morning would reveal a group of village people waiting outside the dispensary for medical attention. We learned early that this was one of the best times to get close to the people and demonstrate the Christ-like spirit of service we so longed to show. Men and women would line up from the crack of dawn and wait for us to treat their complaints. Their conditions were many and varied including grili, scabies, malaria, even crocodile and pig bites.

We would offer medicine and advice, and take the opportunity to talk to the women who would usually melt away into their house or garden when we drew near. When caring for their medical treatment we were able to show sympathy, minister to their needs and win their confidence. As Ellen White suggested, "There is need of coming close to the people by personal effort. If less time were given to sermonising, and more time spent in personal ministry, greater results would be seen."* Freda and I learned this was true.

Sometimes through the day but more often during the night, we would be called to attend a medical emergency. About 3 o'clock one morning, we were called to Maopa village about half a mile (almost 1 kilometre) away where a newborn baby was in trouble.

Arriving at the house, we passed the old granny of the family and noticed a bundle in her arms wrapped in a blanket against the morning chill. Wondering if it might be the baby in trouble we had a look, only to find a small piglet, snug and warm, nursing from the old woman's breast. Such sights were not uncommon and reflected the status and wealth pigs brought to a family. So important were they that

The Dispensary

women would suckle them, when necessary, as they would a child.

Inside the house, we found the old woman's daughter in deep distress. The child had been born at least 24 hours earlier but because the afterbirth had not come away, the child lay naked and helpless on the cold floor, still attached to the mother by the now-useless umbilical cord. Local tradition demanded that no-one could cut that cord until the afterbirth had been expelled. It was a pitiful sight and Freda rushed to help, applying the obstetric knowledge she had learned in Sydney prior to our departure.

In a few minutes all had been corrected. The afterbirth had been delivered, the umbilical cord cut and the infant placed in the arms of a woman who had been watching. Without medical help, both mother and child would probably have remained there until one or both of them died. We received several smiles from a very thankful mother.

Then came a ritual we saw many times following childbirth. The mother who had just given birth turned onto her stomach to permit the other women present to take turns walking up and down her back. As they explained, it was "to get the baby-bag back into place and to stop bleeding." After this uncomfortable activity had ended, the new mother was reminded to go down to the ocean to collect a bucket of seawater with which she was to scrub the floor of the house. By their logic, she had soiled the house so she must clean it, while all the other women sat and watched her do it in her weakened state. Only then, with the rudimentary cleaning complete, was she given her baby to nurse.

On another occasion, five-year-old Orana came to us with a badly fractured elbow, an injury sustained when she had fallen from a house. She had landed on her elbow and the broken bones had penetrated through the skin, right into the ground. To treat her compound fracture, her father had chewed together tobacco and kerosene, which he then spat over the wound and the protruding bones.

After a week of such treatment, he decided things were not getting better, so they came to us for help. Freda and I cleaned the wound and set the bone back in place. It seemed miraculous that she had not succumbed to a major infection. We prayed for her and checked

When God Calls, Expect Adventure

the wound daily. Despite what must have been tremendous pain, little Orana remained positive and a few weeks later, to our joy, she went home, a smiling and happy girl.

Then there was the 10-year-old girl who presented with an enormously distended stomach and what at first seemed like a terminal heart problem, compounded by kidney failure. Her situation seemed bleak. We did not have any x-ray equipment nor the skills to perform complex surgery.

As it turned out neither of our first impressions were true. Proper treatment of her digestive tract produced literally hundreds of worms. The creatures had infested her digestive tract, causing the huge enlargement of her abdomen. At the same time they had robbed her of the nutrients in the food she was eating and were starving her. Never before had we seen a worse case!

Medical emergencies ranged all the way from minor cuts to attacks by pigs, or people mauled by crocodiles or bitten by poisonous snakes. Without expensive antivenom, snakebite treatment could be a hit-and-miss affair, as we were to soon discover.

* Ellen White, *The Ministry of Healing*, page 143.

SNAKEBITE

"But Paul shook the snake off into the fire and suffered no ill effects. The people expected him to swell up or suddenly fall dead; but after waiting a long time and seeing nothing unusual happen to him, they changed their minds" (Acts 28:5, 6).

A short distance along the coast lived Mr Piloti, an Italian trader. He had married Kila, a local village woman. To us, he was a perfect gentleman, always dressed in his starched whites when he visited. But life had not always been quite so smooth for him. His stiff right arm was the result of a knife fight he had once been in and his stiff left leg was the legacy of a gun battle.

Mr Piloti called in one day as Freda was sewing at her old treadle sewing machine. She remained seated as he removed his pith helmet, placing it on the table, and took a seat. They talked for a short while until Freda felt a strange sensation on her foot resting on the treadle of the sewing machine. Looking down, she saw a large snake slithering across it. Instinctively she jumped up, trying to get away from it.

"Be calm, Mrs Hawkes," Mr Piloti instructed. "Don't frighten it. Try to be still."

It was great advice, of course, and easy to give when the snake was on the other side of the room but just as he said that, the snake turned in Mr Piloti's direction and made straight for him. With his one good arm, he swung his walking stick at it—and missed.

Then with remarkable speed for a man with one good leg, he tried desperately to get away from it as fast as he could. With his stiff-arm and stiff-leg hindering him he leapt aside, panic etched on his face, and sighed with relief as the snake took refuge under our bed.

Some encounters with snakes were not so humorous. Mavo, a student at Korela who was about 15 years of age, was playing football one lunchtime when he chased the ball into thick grass. Unfortunately, Mavo stood on a large, red-bellied black snake, which bit him on the foot and slithered away.

When God Calls, Expect Adventure

The boy yelled with pain and ran back to his friends. Pastor Syd Stocken and Mrs Wiles were called immediately for they lived right on the station. They followed the standard first-aid treatment recommended at the time, which involved cutting the wound and extracting the blood and venom, then tying a tourniquet around the leg. Poor Mavo's eyes were wide with fear as they worked to save his life.

The snakebite had occurred during the "Quarter-end" when all the district village teachers regularly came to Korela for a few days of refresher training. These teachers were now summoned and asked to form a prayer circle. One was sent 12 miles (20 kilometres) to call me. In the meantime, Mavo was taken into one of the buildings where he was laid down and gradually began to succumb to the snake's powerful poison.

This particular snake's poison works to paralyse the lung muscles, at the same time thickening the mucus of the throat so as to choke the victim. Mrs Wiles applied hot foments to the throat as Mavo's condition worsened and Pastor Stocken administered artificial respiration. When I arrived, I used a long tube to suck the thickening mucus from Mavo's throat. The teachers were in constant prayer. By now, Mavo was unconscious and unaware of the small group gathered in a praying circle around him.

During the next two days, Mavo's heart stopped beating five times. Each time he "died," we renewed our prayers and redoubled our efforts, applying heart massage to revive him.

Finally, Mavo's condition appeared to stabilise and on the third evening we were so sure he was recovering that we left him alone with his relatives, sleeping in the dispensary. Just before daylight the next morning, I was woken by loud wailing, a sure sign of death. The death wails of the people of Papua New Guinea are the most soul-wrenching sound I have ever heard and on this occasion the noise made us all race to the room where Mavo lay.

The crying in the room was deafening. I looked at Mavo and, to my dismay, he appeared to be dead. His formerly strong young body was lifeless and still, his eyes closed, and there was something restful about his repose.

"We are too late," I began to say but at that moment I saw the slightest twitch in his throat.

Snakebite

Frantic, we bundled the relatives out in haste. Artificial respiration, foments and, above all, prayers were commenced immediately and the dispensary became a hive of activity. The teachers re-formed their prayer circle while we pled with God for mercy as we worked. About 20 minutes later, Mavo began breathing again. God had won! Mavo made a full recovery, having died five times and having survived the commencement of his family's mourning.

Later Mavo himself became one of God's faithful workers and spent many years of his life witnessing to his own people about the Saviour who had saved his life from the snake. Many years later, I met his son, Barnabas, who was a doctor working in the Penrith Public Hospital in Sydney.

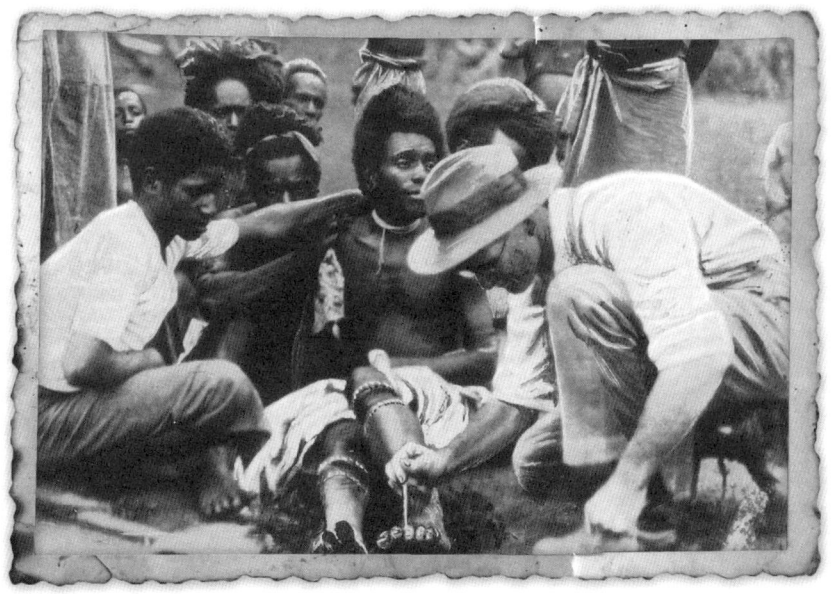

W N Locke seeking to save the life of a snake-bite victim. Snake bites were a common problem on the Papuan coast.

FREDA'S CONFINEMENT

"He will be a joy and delight to you, and many will rejoice because of his birth"(Luke 1:14).

We had come to Papua to heal and provide medical care but we had been there only a few weeks when Freda had to face a real problem. It was a Wednesday evening and we were in the mission church for prayer meeting with about 20 people. Freda knelt beside one of the crude wooden benches but, during the prayer, something bit her on the ankle.

It was a sharp bite and she rubbed it vigorously, but was unable to see any evidence of an insect or spider. The bite began to hurt almost immediately and rather than subsiding, it became very painful and inflamed. Within a few days, it had turned into a nasty ulcer right over the anklebone. The pain became so great that soon she was unable to walk and had to lie down most of the day.

Freda tried to do things around the house but walking had become a source of agony. Alone and cut off from the rest of the world, we tried every possible medication we could lay hands on but the ulcer only became larger and more painful. For weeks, Freda was a total cripple.

The stubborn ulcer refused to heal fully and she carried the injury with quiet suffering for many long months. As if to add to our worries during this time, we discovered Freda was expecting our first child. The ulcer did not heal after Freda gave birth.

The time finally came when Freda needed to go into Port Moresby for the birth. Mrs Mitchell, the wife of the mission president had suggested by letter that she bring a number of items with her when she came, as one could never be sure when one could get back home again. I made a portable food safe out of an old packing case, while she packed a few

Freda's Confinement

cooking utensils and clothes. Because shipping was so uncertain along that coast, we arranged with the *Doma* on its outward trip to collect Freda on the return trip, knowing it would still be about six weeks before the expected time of birth.

Mission policy of that time forbade the husband from accompanying his wife when she went in for what was called "confinement." The men were expected to remain at their post of duty, so Freda had to travel alone.

The *Doma* was a dirty 100-ton trading vessel with just two tiny cabins for those who requested such a luxury. Freda was relieved to find another woman on the boat, the celebrated anthropologist Margaret Mead. They were to share a cabin. Ms Mead did all she could for Freda's comfort but I am sure neither of them anticipated one form of help she furnished.

During the night, a large rat became entangled in Freda's hair and her cabin-mate helped untangle it. That must have been quite a sight. I can't help but smile when I think of a pregnant missionary and celebrated anthropologist doing battle in the middle of the night to free a struggling rat trapped in my wife's hair. If Freda had been further along in her pregnancy, she may well have given birth then and there!

Knowing there were still six weeks before our child was expected, I was not greatly perturbed when our ex-army radio ceased to function. For the next four weeks, I was busy doing all the things a missionary has to do, including rebuilding the war-damaged homes, overseeing a school, tending to school gardens, maintaining equipment, preparing meetings and training staff. This all needed to be done before I could depart for Port Moresby and time was running out.

It was a Thursday when Alma Wiles arrived at Aroma on a mission errand. After a few minutes, she looked at me quizzically and said so calmly, "And what do you think of your son and heir, Lester? What is his name to be?"

I spun around to face her. "What do you mean?"

She blinked with concern. "You heard the news, didn't you?"

"No," I replied, shocked. "I haven't heard anything since Freda went in to Port Moresby. Are you sure?"

"I am. Your son was born two weeks ago."

When God Calls, Expect Adventure

"But how did you hear? I have not heard anything!"

"It was announced over the ABC news bulletin. Didn't you listen?"

"No," I replied. "My radio is out of operation. You're not just joking are you? Because, I mean, the baby isn't due for another two weeks."

"No, Lester. I'm not joking at all. I heard it over the 7 pm news broadcast weeks ago. I was sure you would have heard it yourself. White women often have their babies early in the tropics, you know."

"What am I to do?" I asked, distressed at the thought of Freda having delivered our child alone and worried now for her health.

"Well, men are allowed to go in to bring their wives back home, you know."

I quickly located a native canoe that was sailing as far as Hula the next day, Friday, and would take me with them. That Sabbath was spent in the Irupara village with Pastor Tauku and his wife. On Sunday morning, I boarded another double-hull canoe that was heading for Port Moresby. We were sailing into the prevailing wind, so travel was painfully slow. We spent the first night anchored off the Kapakapa wharf in a vain effort to avoid a cloud of mosquitoes preying on us.

On Monday evening, the sun had set and the sky had a black, ominous look as we neared Port Moresby Harbour. In January, it is common for short but violent storms, known locally as a "guba," to hit. This guba fell on us suddenly. Forked lightning began to strike the water around us. The rain fell in sheets. The direction of the storm constantly changed, so the crew were constantly battling to change sails and make other adjustments in an effort to bring the canoe to the beach.

Several times we were blown right out of the harbour. Once the wind blew us back out the south entrance, the next time out the eastern entrance. One brilliant flash of lightning actually saved us. We were being driven furiously, without sail, before the howling wind when the lightning flash revealed that we were heading directly onto a small outcrop of rocks. Quick work and a long pole saved us. Finally—to my relief—the canoe hit Ela Beach directly opposite the mission house. The Papuan men who crewed that boat were master sailors!

Looking and feeling more like a drowned rat than a respectable missionary, I knocked on the door of the Mitchells's home. When it opened, I was shocked to find a group of the church leaders from

Freda's Confinement

Sydney seated in the room. They wished to speak with me so I "dripped in" to meet them, feeling very ill at ease. They had sailed up on a new 65-foot (20-metre) mission ship, the *Melenesia*. I was told that the *Melenesia* was leaving the next day, going past Aroma, and that it was expected that Freda and I, and our new son, would be able to travel on it.

Only then was I excused to go up, still dripping water, to meet Freda and our new son, Lyndon. The door opened and Freda led me over to the bed where she drew aside the mosquito net to show me my "son and heir." I stood there, studying my son and wife, proud as a man can be. It was a moment to be remembered for all time and I praised God!

Freda had another humorous story to tell me. Alma Wiles had kindly allowed her well-trained house-help, a man named Au Nama, to go with Freda to assist with laundry work and other domestic chores. Au was a great help because the hospital did none of that for their patients and Freda would have been lost without him.

At that time, little cotton dresses were commonly worn by all newborn boys and girls, so Freda had made a few to take with her when her labour pains began and she went into hospital. She handed the first two or three dresses to Au, asking him to wash and iron them and bring back the next day.

But not only did he wash them, he starched them as stiff as cardboard. Then he ironed them carefully and brought them to the hospital using small bamboo coat hangers he had fashioned just for the occasion. He brought them into the room proudly and placed the dresses on the bedside table. The starching was so well done that the dresses simply stood there.

The nurses were in fits of laughter as they came into the room to see dresses standing without need of support. Au Nama had done the best he knew, but babies and their needs were not exactly in his field of experience.

Back home at the village, people were mystified at our arrival. No-one had ever seen a baby with clothes on. "Are white babies made the same as 'ordinary' people?" some wondered. One of the women waited for her opportunity to investigate and had a quick peek under the strange garments to see for herself if our child was a "normal" boy.

CAUSE FOR WORSHIP

"Before they call I will answer; while they are still speaking I will hear" (Isaiah 65:24).

There were many dogs in the village. They were of a lean, long-eared variety and always hungry. A short while after sunrise, and a short time before sunset, they would often gather and form a circle. They sat down, heads facing inward. After a moment or two one would lift his muzzle to the sky and begin to howl, until the whole pack would join in.

The howling would go on for five minutes or more, rising and falling in volume. It almost seemed that they were following a conductor. Finally they would stop, the gathering would break up and each dog would go its own way. We watched it many times from our window and joked that the dogs were holding morning and evening worship. It was a daily event that rarely failed to bring a smile to our faces.

But many times we had real cause to lift our voices to the Lord and praise Him for His goodness. Shipping was so irregular that we could never be sure when—or whether—our orders would be delivered. Even when orders were delivered, other problems sometimes arose, like the time we asked for a case of dried peas and received instead a chest of tea.

Without fail, the reply that bothered us more frequently than any other was "Out of Stock" or "Back-ordered." At times, as much as three-quarters of an order was marked "Out of Stock." We found those words hard to digest!

People often let us down but God never did. There was the Sabbath morning when once again an order had failed to materialise, so we took stock of what we had. It amounted to a little less than half a four-gallon

Cause for Worship

tin of ex-army dried cabbage! There was nothing else—and our supplies were exhausted. At that time of the year, the village people lived on nothing beside fish and coconut, so there was nothing else available locally.

Before we went to church that morning, we laid our needs in the hands of our Lord, telling Him we were leaving the matter in His care.

Following the worship service, we spoke with some of the church members for a little time, then walked home. Just as we came to the bamboo fence, I remember saying to Freda, "So, what will we be having for lunch? Boiled cabbage and coconut?"

At that moment, we looked up toward the back door and caught sight of a white enamel basin on the top step. On investigation it proved to be full of tinned and packaged foods.

Freda and I looked at one another in blank amazement. No village person bought or used this kind of food. There, before our eyes, were rice, flour, butter and canned fruit, even a can of beetroot.

We inquired of everyone nearby, "Did you see who put this here?" No-one had seen it put there and no-one had seen a stranger in the area. No note was with the food, yet it contained just the kind of food we longed for, the kind of food no Papuan person would even have to give to us.

Freda and I took the food inside and gave thanks to God for this miracle. The right supplies were given to us at exactly the right time—and that basin of food lasted exactly long enough to tide us over until the next boat arrived with our order. Only God could be so precise.

Some weeks later, I found myself walking along the beach to a village I planned to visit. To do so I had to pass Mr Piloti's place, so I decided to call on him. For some years he had operated a small trade store adjacent to one of the villages. We talked for a time and I told him how God had supplied us at a time when we were in real need. I also mentioned that I was mystified as to the method God had used to perform this miracle. I was doing this to give him something to think about.

Mr Piloti looked thoughtful for a moment, as if recalling a distant memory, then called to his wife in the local language, "Kila, do you

When God Calls, Expect Adventure

remember some time ago I asked you to take a present to the mission?"

"Yes."

"Did you do so?"

"Yes."

"What did you take?"

"You didn't tell me what to take, so I just took some different foods from the store. Why? Was that wrong?"

"No, that's quite alright."

Mr Piloti had almost forgotten about his instruction to his wife. He had never previously sent us a gift and he never did so again. Clearly it was God who moved on his heart to supply the need of two of His children at a time when they had a need.

Another time the food for the students had depleted to the point where I was out in the bush searching for a certain root that, while normally poisonous, may be used as food after a lengthy process of preparation. In my search I had only found one root, not enough to make even one meal. Just as I began to feel discouraged, a student came running to me calling, "Taubada [Big Man], you come. There's plenty of food."

I raced home to find a pile of vegetables in the kitchen. The missionary at the bush village of Keagola had decided he urgently needed some school supplies. Being the only person to travel in the canoe, he decided to fill the canoe with the sweet potatoes and pumpkin that grew so well in his garden. His produce had arrived in the midst of the lean season when we were unable to buy from the village people. How grateful I was that God did not need to rely on me to find edible roots!

Incidents like this reminded me how much we can and should trust God! So many times God's promise proves true and He always finds a way to fulfil His work.

BUSH PATROLS

"But you will receive power when the Holy Spirit comes on you; and you will be my witnesses in Jerusalem, and in all Judea and Samaria, and to the ends of the earth" (Acts 1:8).

One of the joys of medical missionary work was visiting each of the churches in the area at least once every three months. Because many of the churches were situated in the mountains, this required long treks—or bush patrols, as we called them. There were no roads so the only form of access was a combination of canoe and arduous walks.

Many of the people were marvellous children of God. They knew little but they trusted much. Alma Wiles's version of Isaiah came to mind often as I conducted my visits, "Remember the pit from whence they were digged." It was good advice. We cannot expect people to become suddenly like Jesus wants them to be, we can only lead gently.

For a man to have a number of wives had always been normal in this region. Until a man had more than one wife, he had little or no standing in his village. I remember the day I entered the house of an important chief. It was a long house with six doors on its long side. Each door was the entrance to that portion of the house that belonged to one wife. There were no walls between sections. Each wife had a fire in the centre of her section on which she cooked the food for herself and her children. I was amazed at the lively banter that passed between the wives as they talked to one another.

This will help us understand the problem one believer faced. He had two wives at the time he decided to forsake his traditional ways and follow the Lord. His first wife was unwell, unable to do anything and needing constant care. The man himself had received no schooling and to complicate matters, he was totally blind. He knew no English, yet at the end of each quarter he could repeat, in English, every memory verse for the quarter, plus every doctrinal text.

The second wife carried out all necessary work for the three of them.

When God Calls, Expect Adventure

Every time I visited his village, he pleaded to be baptised before he died. My heart ached for him, but to uphold church policy at the time I could do nothing for him other than baptise his first wife. According to official church policy, he was living in a polygamous relationship and I was not permitted to baptise him or his second wife. To be baptised, he was required to divorce one of his wives!

I felt that the Catholic Church's stand on polygamy was more suitable and considerate. There was no-one to be pitied more than a wife who had been sent from her home, for whatever reason. The Catholic position was that a person joining the church may be accepted in the marital position as it stood at the time of acceptance, but he was not to add to his wives from that point on. This fine old Adventist man died without ever being baptised. I felt sorry for him. Few were more ready to be accepted into fellowship but he was denied it. I anticipate that heaven's books will be more flexible than some of the rules we followed here on earth.

When on patrol, we would often see huge piles of leaves alongside the bush track, which were the nests of bush hens. Some of these nests must have been almost 6 feet (1.8 metres) high by at least 10 feet (3 metres) across. At other times, cassowaries would cross the path ahead of us, or screeching cockatoos or parrots would dart over the treetops. The hornbill, with its outsized beak, seemed to have little fear of us.

On one such journey, we had battled flooded rivers to reach a certain village where we planned to stay the night. In the morning as I conducted worship, a large hornbill landed near the door of the church. The bird then began its head-nodding walk down the dusty aisle, as if agreeing with what I was saying, until it came to the platform where I stood. As I continued to speak, it began to peck at my boots. As you can imagine, the bird's actions were making it hard to concentrate on worship, for me and my wide-eyed audience. One of the men carried it to the door where he threw it into the air and it flew off to a nearby mountain.

Bush Patrols

One trip into the bush remains vividly in my mind. There were six or seven students with me on this trip and the smallest was Vagi Maraki, a name that meant "Vagi the Small."

The first river to cross was in flood and running swiftly. Vagi stayed close beside me on the downstream side, holding my left hand tightly. We hadn't gone far into the river before he was swept off his feet and floated like a leaf at the end of my extended arm. The water was so deep and swift that I could feel my feet also beginning to slip. In my right hand, I held a bucket in which I had my Sabbath shoes. To obtain more grip on the slippery rocks below, I dipped the bucket, filling it with water, and placed the heavy bucket on my shoulder. It was just enough to maintain my footing and bring both of us to the other shore, where we thanked God for His protection.

The next day we came to another river, which we crossed and re-crossed 28 times as we made our way to the next village. It was exhausting, hot work and at last, just before 3 pm, we began to climb a hill toward the village.

By this time, I was feeling faint from hunger. Part way up the hill, we came to a line of small huts, each with a fence around it. They appeared to be fowl pens from which the fowls had been allowed out for the day. I noticed that atop one post of each fence was a small shelf on which food had been placed, mostly sweet potato and sugarcane. I was certain this food was intended for the fowls and reassured myself that the village people would not mind if I took a little. I felt that I was in greater need of some of that sugarcane than any fowl was. So I took a short piece and began to eat.

"You have some," I said to the students. "I'll pay the village people when we get there."

The boys stepped back and stared at me with horror. So I handed a stick of sugarcane to Lui, a teacher, who shrank back with a look of fear. I was enjoying the cane too much to really think and no-one was saying a word, just staring. Finally one of the more mature men found voice and rebuked me.

"Taubada," he said. "That food is for the spirits. These are the graves of the dead and that food is for spirits only. People can't eat it. If you eat it, you will die. We don't want to die."

When God Calls, Expect Adventure

According to traditional beliefs, the spirit of a person passed out of the body at death yet remained, sometimes to protect family members and sometimes to harm them. Death and disease were often attributed to "spirits" and village people would take extra care to leave gifts for them.

Through my mistake, God granted me the basis for a great talk with the village people about God, explaining His power and love, and how Jesus has already overcome the power of the evil spirits. I explained how they have no need to fear Satan or any of his followers. The work of a medical missionary questioned traditional beliefs in the power of evil spirits. As our medicines healed, we taught the people that their conditions were treatable and preventable.

At last we reached the last village of this patrol, a long way up the river among the mountains. We had a blessed time as we conducted the Lord's Supper with the people there. Real victories were gained and it must have made quite an impact when we broke bread, drank a small amount and washed the villagers' feet as Jesus did with His disciples. At our request, the village people appointed one lad to return with us to be educated as a student at the mission. He would be the first from his district.

RIVER ADVENTURE

"He measured off another thousand, but now it was a river that I could not cross, because the water had risen and was deep enough to swim in—a river that no-one could cross. He asked me, 'Son of man, do you see this?'" (Ezekiel 47:5-6).

There had been constant rain throughout the whole trip, especially while we had been at this village. When it came time to leave, I found the village people had prepared a raft on which we could float down the river. The raft was made of wild banana trunks and boasted a raised platform in the centre on which the bedding and other valuables could be kept dry.

After a close inspection of the villager's handiwork I thought to myself, *This raft isn't big enough for all of us. How will they arrange things?*

When it came time to push off, four men, each carrying a long bamboo pole, boarded the raft with me. The others in our party had each collected a section of dry log on which they lay, somewhat like a surfer paddling a board. We waved goodbye to the village people and soon set off, singing and laughing together.

For the first half hour, it was a happy drift down a fast-flowing section of the river, the sides of which reminded me of a canyon walled with flowering creepers, lush green moss and vines. Every few minutes, a colourful or noisy bird would burst from one wall only to seemingly crash through the opposite wall of creepers. I am sure Eden must have had a section of tropical river just like this one.

Before long we swung into a narrow, twisty section of the river, where each person on his log had to work hard to prevent themselves being smashed into rocks. Time and time again I watched as they paddled madly away from what appeared to be certain disaster. The four

When God Calls, Expect Adventure

raftsmen strained and yelled, muscles bulging, as they used the sturdy poles to shove the raft away from dangerous rocks that threatened to dash it to pieces.

After passing through this dangerous section, I became sure the men out on the logs were having the most fun as they paddled madly to remain in the centre of the stream. Sitting on the raft did not feel like nearly the same fun, so I slipped off into the stream and took a section of tree for myself. The trip from then on was really exciting as I floated effortlessly, soaking in the beauty of my surroundings and enjoying the camaraderie of this remarkable experience.

An hour or so later we entered another quieter section of the river. Those of us on the logs floated some distance ahead of the raft. Having nothing much to do, the men on the raft were almost asleep, their legs dangling in the water. Suddenly one of them screamed, leapt up and began a mad dance. Lulled into a half sleep by the gentle river, he hadn't seen a snake swimming across the surface in his direction. The snake had seen an inviting hole just about water level and had stealthily swum into the man's gaping pair of shorts. Fortunately, the snake was as frightened as the man. It dropped back into the water and swam away.

By mid afternoon, we had gone as far as the river could take us and we had to strike off in a different direction. The raft was beached and unloaded, then pushed out into the stream again, while we followed a narrow bush trail to the next village. I realised that my back had received a heavy dose of sunburn while on that log, despite my shirt, but the usual afternoon rain helped to cool it a little.

As the rain closed in, we walked through the gloomy jungle. Lui Oli and one of the other men were carrying my bedding tied to a pole between them when Lui rolled his foot on a snake he hadn't seen. He yelled and jumped, only to land back down on the snake, rolling it again. He dropped everything as he jumped the second time and the snake went for its life. We thanked God for a second time that day that the snake hadn't bitten.

In the darkness of such rain, one often fails to see the long fine thread of thorns known as "Come Back Quick" or "Wait a Bit" thorns, the growing tips of the Lawyer cane found all through the jungle. They reminded me of a fishing line with hundreds of tiny hooks, positioned precisely to catch anything that passed by. True to their name when you run into one you most definitely do "Come Back Quick." To untangle oneself is not easy because each time you try to pull one set of hooks out another set grabs at your hand or fingers.

We plodded on through the rain. Unknown to me, we had broken into two separate groups and that portion of the team carrying my bedding and gear decided to go to a nearer village for the night. The small group I was with sloshed on to the village where we planned to stay. The local missionary welcomed us, a Papuan girl in her late teens who had sole charge of a school and its spiritual program.

My sunburnt back was getting very sore, and at the same time I began to feel the onset of malaria. I watched anxiously for the bedding and malaria tablets to arrive but nothing came, except swarms of mosquitoes.

The young missionary kindly offered me her bed, perhaps the only bed in the village. I was thankful, but when I looked at it I saw it was only about 5 feet (1.5 metres) long and very narrow. It certainly was not built to accommodate my 6-foot (1.8-metre) frame. It was constructed of small bush sticks laid lengthwise, none of which were straight, so the bed had many lumps.

I lay there all night trying to sleep. With wet clothes, clouds of mosquitoes attacking from above and below, malaria, a badly sunburned back and a short bed made of knobby wood, it was the most uncomfortable, miserable night I ever spent on patrol. Even so, I was humbled and thankful for the kind act of taking me in! The brave young missionary girl had little, yet she offered me all she had.

"YOU STINK, TOO!"

"Your lips drop sweetness as the honeycomb, my bride; milk and honey are under your tongue. The fragrance of your garments is like the fragrance of Lebanon. You are a garden locked up, my sister, my bride" (Song of Songs 4:11, 12).

Like many tribal groups, the village people had their own natural medicines and concoctions. They believed certain leaves acted as contraceptives. Others were used for a variety of ailments, some of which seemed effective, while others—I felt—had no beneficial effect at all. Yet other leaves were for cosmetic uses, some even used somewhat as we would use antiperspirants, to give a smell that overpowered the normal body odour or provided a delicious fragrance.

One deodorant leaf they used was quite remarkable. The young men would gather a few of these leaves and secure them under a woven "bangle" worn around the upper arm. So strong and repulsive was the odour that Freda and I could hardly stay in a room when it was present. However, this was not the effect intended for the girls. According to all the men I questioned, its smell was completely irresistible to the unmarried girls, who would go out to meet the men parading the smell along the beach. For them the leaves were aromatic, the smell as delectable and enticing as any fine perfume sold in cosmetic stores.

One day, a group of us were on a patrol. We were hot, so we had stopped to drink the cool, refreshing juice of a few green coconuts. Alma Wiles pointed to a leaf behind me and suggested I sample its scent. I took a few leaves and crushed them in my hands as I lifted them to my nose. It was the same vile leaves worn by the young men. My hand was saturated with the stench and I held it as far away from my face as I could, as if it were contaminated and dangerous. I couldn't bring the

"You Stink, Too!"

hand anywhere near my face or I'm sure I would have vomited.

Mrs Wiles almost fell over, she laughed so much. All the party were in hysterics as I decided that the best I could do was hold the offending hand behind my back as I attempted to compose myself.

"How can they put up with that smell?" I asked one of the men with me. "Their whole body stinks from it!"

"As far as we are concerned, you white men have bodies that stink, too!" he replied carefully.

The incident with the "perfume" reminded me that as much as I found many things strange, the local people must have found much about me strange, too. I know I was the source of a surprise on many occasions.

Several of the workers had accompanied me on a patrol to visit the bush churches in the hills behind Aroma. After morning worship at the final village on the trip, we requested that one of their young people come with us to attend school. A lad of about 14 was selected for the honour. We packed up and headed across the valley toward home.

About two hours later, we topped the last hill and looked down on a scene I always loved—the rich green coastline and the sparkling blue ocean and reef beyond. I glanced at our new recruit and saw him staring in amazement. I discovered he had never climbed these hills and didn't know anything about the ocean. Even many of his village elders had never come here, simply because it was not their village territory.

It is difficult for us to imagine that people could live within 10 miles (16 kilometres) of the ocean yet never have seen it. Surely the gospel was opening many facets in these people's lives.

But, while we came to provide medical services and to witness in Jesus' name, others came for different purposes.

One such man was an enterprising Australian who decided to try a new scheme. In Port Moresby, he bought a nice boat, about 30 feet (10 metres) in length, and fitted it out as a travelling trade store, stocking it with all the items he felt village people might purchase. The first we knew of him was when he came in through the reef at Paramana Point

When God Calls, Expect Adventure

and dropped anchor in the sheltered water. He then began to play out a long anchor rope allowing the heavy trade winds to blow his boat up against the sandbank that extended out from the beach. The plan was that the village people could wade out on the sandbank, then climb on board and do their buying.

It was a good idea—but his understanding of the ways of the sea was not so sound. The anchor he had dropped was a reef anchor intended to hold on rocks. It was small and had poor holding ability in sand. He had dropped back from the reef so far that his boat was now riding in waves that lifted it noticeably.

Each lift tugged on that small anchor, which dragged further through the sand. When I got to his boat, I was able to stand on the sand bank with my hand on the gunwale. This was dangerously close. The stern was already bumping on the sand, and the boat had begun to slew sideways.

I called him from his trading to warn him of the danger. "Watch out," I yelled.

He saw it immediately and tried to pull away from the sand using engine power. But it was too late. He was grounded. Gathering a large group of men, we pushed the bow away from the sandbank, but he turned too much in the other direction, so his whole port side now faced the howling wind.

This time the anchor dragged such a long way that it no longer held the boat. The rising tide did the rest and soon the boat was well up on the sandbank. To stop further movement, he fastened a chain to the sandbank warning beacon, preventing the boat from dragging further toward the beach. I found myself singing the old hymn—

"We have an anchor that keeps the soul,
Steadfast and sure while the billows roll."

Several times over the next two weeks at high tide, our mission teachers, who were excellent boatmen, tried to help him get the boat off the sandbank. When it seemed they were making progress, the chain tying the boat to the beacon snapped a link, allowing the boat to drag almost to the beach.

"You Stink, Too!"

But it was nearing the time for the king tides, which were to be at their highest at about 2 or 3 o'clock one dark, moonless night.

"If I don't get the boat off tonight, you can have it," the boat owner told me.

There was nothing I could have desired more at that time for the work of the mission than a boat. It was a real temptation to not give all the help required but—praise God—we did our best.

The night was pitch-black but we managed to free the boat from the sandy shore. Only by reading the compass could we tell which way the boat was headed. The wind and seas were heavy, but we finally managed to get it out into deeper water and anchor for the rest of the night.

The next day I watched as the boat headed out into the heavy seas, thinking all the time of what might have been.

UNWELCOME NEWS

"Praise the Lord. How good it is to sing praises to our God, how pleasant and fitting to praise him! He heals the broken-hearted and binds up their wounds" (Psalm 147:1, 3).

August 6, 1947, dawned like all others for the previous few months. The wind was blowing, reshaping and repositioning the sand dunes along the beach as the crabs scurried about, rolling small balls of sand out of their holes. The frigate birds hung in the sky and heavy seas crashed on the outer side of the reef. On this morning, however, the *Doma* lurched in through the break in the reef to find refuge while unloading its cargo. I went out by canoe to collect anything that might be for us and, as soon as I stepped aboard the *Doma*, the ship's purser called me into his room.

"I have a message for you," he said. "It came by radio from your mission HQ."

The purser handed me a message sheet: "Please inform Mrs Hawkes that her sister telegraphed from Sydney to say that her father took a heart attack and died on the 4th of August. He will be buried on the 7th. The family express their sorrow."

All the way home, I tried to think of a gentle way to break the news. Nothing came to mind. I climbed the steps and entered the kitchen. My face must have shown that something was wrong.

"What's the matter?" Freda asked.

"I was given this message for you while on the boat," I replied, heart breaking with the heavy news I was about to deliver.

Without taking the telegram, Freda asked intuitively, "Is it Dad?"

"Yes," was all I was able to answer. Her father was only 53 years old—far too young to die from a heart condition.

Unwelcome News

Freda sank onto the box that served as the kitchen chair, put her head in her hands and sobbed. The Papuan girl who had been helping couldn't understand and just stood there feeling sorry. I tried to comfort Freda—but what can one do in a situation like that?

Freda was a vibrant young woman who loved her family so much, but she was isolated in such a forbidding place and any contact with her family was impossible. She had learned that her father was to be buried the next day. Tomorrow. She could not so much as send a message to her grief-stricken mother. With all her bursting heart she wanted to be there to comfort her mother and siblings. But there was nothing she could do. She could not even let her mother know she had received the message the family had sent.

I watched as the tears fell, sadness mixed with acid frustration, because she was blocked, whichever way she turned, from doing what her whole being cried out to do. The Lord tells us that it is at times such as these, when our family are unable to support us, "the Lord will take thee up." And thanks be to His name, He did just that. In the difficult days that followed, when her heart ached to be with her family, Freda and I felt the Lord come close to us and comfort us.

———••———

In choosing to work at Aroma, Freda and I had made a conscious decision to bring physical and spiritual healing to the local people. For them, the two went hand-in-hand.

We had been working at Aroma about nine months, when church leaders in Port Moresby decided it was time to hold a baptism for the district. Because many of the baptismal candidates were from the Korela School and district, the baptism service was to be conducted on the banks of the Paili River. A group of church leaders travelled to Aroma for the occasion. I was asked to present the address by the river bank.

I chose to base my sermon on Romans 6. Sufficient advance warning had been given to enable us to call in those who were prepared for baptism from the villages, a group of about 20 people. A flat bank served as an ideal gathering area, while before us was a wide, placid river. The group were transported there in canoes and a couple of dinghies.

About 3 o'clock on that lovely Sabbath afternoon, I found myself

When God Calls, Expect Adventure

thrilled at the beauty and serenity of the scene. If ever there was a place where the harmony of heaven reached down to earth, it must have been that spot, that day. My heart swelled with gratitude to God that I could have a part in such a sacred service in such worshipful surroundings. In the hour that followed men and women would take a stand for Christ as their Saviour. They would be immersed beneath the water, as Jesus himself had been almost 2000 years earlier, and they would be symbolically washed of their sins. They would be reborn.

A song service of simple, beautifully sung choruses rang out over those waters to welcome the angels to the scene. Then came time for the prayer. I felt uneasy as I heard the dinghies being moved during the prayer. As soon as I opened my eyes, I noticed that a couple of the visitors had boarded each of the dinghies and were making their way out onto the water.

OK, I thought. *If that's what they want to do during prayer, there must be a good reason.* Trouble is they seemed to forget that voices carry well over quiet water. Jesus preached to the multitude on the shores of Galilee for that very reason.

I turned my back to the water and began to deliver—in Motuan—the sermon I had carefully prepared. But I was unable to gain the attention of the people. They were too interested in the activities of the foreign men and their boats.

I tried to keep preaching but next I heard the men in the boats calling to one another. "There's a good angle over here," one said.

"Right," came the reply. "We'll be over in a minute."

"Hey, it's even better from here."

"Great, the light is just right."

"What's your light reading?" another photographer queried. "My meter seems to be reading wrong."

And so it went, right through the sermon. All eyes were watching the antics in the boats and the many local people were commenting on what was happening. I finally cut the talk short because no-one was listening.

The baptism went ahead. But I felt the sanctity of the occasion had been compromised. I'm glad that many took a stand that day for their Lord but I did wish the missionaries could have shown more respect.

KIDNAPPINGS AND CROCODILES

"The Lord God said, 'It is not good for the man to be alone. I will make a helper suitable for him'" (Genesis 2:18).

Early in our stay it came to our notice that most of our native teachers and missionaries were unmarried men. For example, there was the teacher for the Aroma station, Lui Oli, whose wife had died a few years earlier. And there was Kila Kai, Kila Galama and Au Nama, plus a number of the others who would dearly love to be married and who had unsuccessfully tried to marry the girls who had been promised to them.

The difficulty was with the parents back in the village. They were fearful they might miss out on the coveted bride-price—commonly pigs—if the girls were to marry Seventh-day Adventist mission workers. Our staff did not keep pigs and the Adventist Church taught that the meat from these animals was unclean.

The parents were happy to have their sons educated. An educated son could bring money to the family. But to educate the girls raised a completely new problem. An education meant she would be less under the control of her parents. It might even mean they would lose her without gaining bride-price. Combined with a culture where girls were expected to remain in the village, the result was that few girls ever came to school, and it seemed that none of the intended wives of our workers were to have the opportunity to gain an education.

When God Calls, Expect Adventure

I had talked in the village with Pala, whose name was later changed to Esther. Pala had been promised to Lui Oli. She told me she would love to go to school and marry Lui, but her parents would hear none of it.

In my experience, the effectiveness of a male teacher or missionary is dependent to a surprising extent on his wife. A girl with no more training than afforded by village life can negate the mission work of the best of husbands. Our mission workers knew this, but were powerless to do anything about it. The families of the girls they sought to marry simply would not let their daughters go.

In my youthful zeal, I said to the unmarried teachers one night, "Well, why don't you simply go to the village, take the girls and bring them here to the mission? They want to come."

The men patiently explained how a Papuan marriage takes place and how such a course of action would be impossible. But it seems the thought took root. Only a few days later a group of them came to discuss the whole idea again—and we formulated a plan.

A few nights later when there would be no moon, a team of six men took the mission canoe and sailed some 20 miles (about 30 kilometres) down the coast to a beach just short of the Irupara village, where the girls lived. They beached the canoe around the corner, out of sight of the village, and walked along a dark bush track. I never learned how they managed it, but four of the girls slipped quietly out of the village and followed them to the canoe. Before daylight, the canoe was back at Aroma.

It is unlikely any such thing had ever occurred before in Papua. Everyone on the mission station expected the village men to arrive within a few hours to demand the girls' return. The threat of retribution was real and custom demanded that the families be recompensed for their loss. So the canoe—with the girls aboard—was sent on to the Korela station, a further 12 miles (20 kilometres) east. At Korela, Alma Wiles was operating a girls' home—a training school, in conjunction with formal education.

To our surprise, the village people never came. I later learned that the village people did want the girls to be educated but no-one wanted to be first to break with village tradition. What we had done was a face-saver for them. Surely the hand of God was there but we had failed to see it at the time.

Kidnappings and Crocodiles

Those young ladies later married and most of their husbands became pastors. Having wives who could read and write and understand more of what the husband was attempting, made the husband's work so much more effective.

I stayed in the home of Esther on many occasions. She made a wonderful missionary's wife. Later, when Pastor Lui had been appointed president of the Papuan Mission, Esther became a gracious hostess and a loving co-worker for her Lord. To paraphrase the Bible's description of Queen Esther, "Who knoweth whether you were kidnapped to the mission for such a time as this?"

Around the time of this "kidnapping," another man by the name Kila, one of the village church members, brought his friend Geno to see me. Geno stripped off his shirt to show me his back. Ugly, deep scars ran across his shoulders and buttocks. Both men were keen to tell me the story.

These two had gone hunting crocodiles in the swamps behind the Aroma coast. They each had a homemade spear gun consisting of a wooden body with a simple trigger mechanism, four lengths of tyre-tube rubber, and an iron rod about 4 feet (1.3 metres) long, which had a sharpened point.

The two had failed to catch even one small crocodile but Geno was wading out of the water when a large crocodile attacked from behind. In most cases, a crocodile will grab sideways, then twist their prey over, tipping them off their feet. But, as the scars showed, this crocodile had its upper jaw on the victim's shoulders and the lower jaw on his buttocks.

Geno tried with all his strength to get back to shore. In return, the crocodile tried to pull him into the deeper water where it could drown him. Neither could make any headway.

Geno screamed for Kila, who ran to assist. But Kila stopped at the water's edge.

Kila paused, considering the motives of the crocodile. "Geno, you must have sinned," he concluded. "Confess your sin and you'll be alright."

"I haven't sinned" Geno cried, struggled to get free as the crocodile began to drag him away. "Help me!"

"This would never have happened if you hadn't sinned," Kila

When God Calls, Expect Adventure

continued firmly. "You must have done something wrong. Confess."

"No, I tell you, I have not sinned!" Geno disappeared under the surface of the water for a moment, then reappeared. "Help me! Help!"

"Geno, this kind of thing only happens to sinners. Think hard. What was it? Tell me and I'll pray for you."

Almost exhausted but refusing to give in to the beast that was so determined to eat him, Geno suddenly thought of something. "I said something bad to my father. Forgive me."

"That must be it," Kila cried triumphantly. "Father, Geno has confessed his sin. You must free him."

Then Kila entered the water. He took both spear guns and, using them as levers, forced the jaws apart, enabling Geno to run for the bank. This left Kila in the precarious position of standing with the two spear guns in the crocodile's mouth. He pulled one out and rammed it down the crocodile's throat before running for the bank.

I used this story to explain the false picture they had of God. They had the impression that God hands out punishment for the slightest deviation and will only grant His help when we have bowed in confession before Him. This is a caricature of our loving God, whose only interest is in our best good.

Ward and Ora Nolan with a small girl who was rescued from a crocodile attack in 1938 at Daru, Papua.

THE PAPUAN SABBATH

"But the seventh day is a Sabbath to the Lord your God. On it you shall not do any work, neither you, nor your son or daughter, nor your male or female servant, nor your animals, nor any foreigner residing in your towns" (Exodus 20:10).

Several months after we arrived in Papua, a group of us—including Lui Oli and Pastor Tauku—planned some outreach activities. We decided to announce the Sabbath activities in the Motuan language.

"How will we use the word Sabbath?" I asked.

"No problem," one of the men said. "'Laga-ani dinana' means 'Rest-day-the.' It is back-to-front in English but they will know."

I raised what I saw as a problem, "OK, we understand that 'laga-ani dinana' means the Sabbath day of rest. But the village people won't because they now have their day of worship on Sunday. They will think we are coming on Sunday, not the true Sabbath."

"You don't seem to understand," said Lui. "They'll know alright because we're talking in the Motuan language. Each day of the week has a name, and the name for the white man's Saturday is 'Laga-ani Dinana.'"

"Are you sure?" I asked doubtfully. "What about the local people around Aroma station?"

"It's in our language, too. We have always had a weekly calendar, and on the last weekday we had a day of rest, too. Here in Aroma we call it 'Mara Vakula' but it means the same thing. You'll find this is true of all the different tribes all along the Papuan coast."

I was staggered to find this. So I asked, "If your people kept 'Mara Vakula' in the past, why do so many of them now worship on Sunday?"

They tried to tell me the story but it was so amazing I found it hard

When God Calls, Expect Adventure

to accept, so they suggested I go to see Kualua, an older church member living in a village further along the beach.

After my arrival I sat in an open, leaf-roofed house, with no walls to hinder the sea breezes and there I listened to an intriguing tale.

The old man patiently explained how in the days before the coming of the missionaries or any other white men, the people had their "Mara Vakula." At the end of each week, the men sat in village conference to discuss their issues. When the London Missionary Society came, they commended the people, saying, "This is great. The only trouble is you are holding the meetings one day too soon. Hold your village meetings on the next day—Sunday—and we will teach you about God."

At the next village gathering, the village elders decided to do that. Such a change would make no real difference. Kualua went on to tell me how he went home that day and thought about it quite a lot.

"What did you decide?" I asked.

"During the night, a man in bright white clothes came and stood just there, right beside where you are sitting." Kualua pointed to a spot only a couple of feet away from where I stood. "I woke up frightened. But the man in white told me, 'The things you heard today, you and your family are not to follow. You and your family are to continue to keep Mara Vakula. One day, before too long, another missionary will come who will also keep Mara Vakula. You and your family are to listen to him.'"

"So we didn't change to Sunday when the rest of the village people changed. Then Pastor Ross James came to Aroma. The day he came to our village, I talked with him and asked him what day he kept as a day of rest. When we found that he kept Mara Vakula, we decided this was the missionary that 'the man in white' had told me about. So we followed the teachings of Pastor James. That was why the work of the SDA Mission became strong so quickly on the Aroma Coast."

As I walked back down the beach, I wondered about the man in white. God had been at work here before we had arrived, and even before Pastor James began his work in 1931. I began asking questions among other language groups along the coast and found that in all instances where I could get hold of the older men, they confirmed the fact that in pre-mission days their village also followed the weekly cycle with the seventh day as their "Day of Rest" or their "Day to Stop Nothing."

The Papuan Sabbath

In the Hula language, the traditional name for the seventh day was "Puka Omana." Among the Bakaka people who lived behind Hula, the word was "Koe Pogina." In numerous other languages it meant exactly the same. The name always referred to "Day of Rest," "Day to Stop Nothing" or something similar.

Because these names pre-dated the coming of explorers, missionaries and traders, the week could not have been introduced by any Western influence. It might even date back to the time of the dispersion of languages at Babel! To find the Sabbath set aside in the so-called "primitive" lands was not expected.

Many years later, I spoke to the then 90-year-old Ross James and asked him if he remembered the day he talked with Kualua about Sabbath-keeping. His face lit up as he declared, "Certainly I remember that day. I remember it very well indeed. I remember Kualua and his family, and I remember how the work in the Aroma district opened up so quickly when they discovered that I worshipped on the day that had traditionally been their day of rest."

Baptisms were always an exciting time for missionaries and frequently occurred in rivers in the sea.

THE MOVE TO MADANA

"For in Him we live, and move, and have our being" (Acts 17:28).

Maintaining the Aroma station was not easy. There was no land for gardens, nor trees nearby from which to gather building supplies. The property had been purchased originally as a small medical outpost only. But to consolidate the church work it was essential that there be educated people in each village.

A school was essential, but it could not be built at Aroma. When a nearby copra plantation was offered to the mission, the church leaders felt this could be no less than the leading of the Lord. At that time, coconut (copra) was still one of the world's most important oil crops.

Madana plantation was purchased from the Miller family. It had been a small copra plantation, not big enough to be a moneymaker in the usual sense but suitable for a school. The income from the copra would assist in school finances.

There were no removalist vans to call in. We would have to transport everything on our trusty canoe. Two 1000-gallon (about 4500 litres) water tanks, the fridge, several boxes of other gear all went on the initial canoe load. The first couple of kilometres of travel was smooth going behind the reef, but from then on it was the open sea for about 6 miles (10 kilometres), then into a lagoon to land on a beach. From there, it was a further 6 miles up a track on the old army truck that came with the plantation.

We saw the canoe off, then mounted our bicycles. I had fixed a box on the handlebars of my bike in which six-month-old Lyn was sitting. He loved it and laughed all the way as we first rode along the 3-mile (5-kilometre) beach, then crossed a river by canoe. After another beach, we set off inland toward Madana. Soon we had to carry everything

The Move to Madana

through a waist-deep mud swamp about 85 yards (80 metres) wide. I helped Freda and Lyn through, then returned to carry the bikes. The next part of the track was hard, and twisted and turned as it dodged beneath hundreds of coconut trees.

Wham! A heavy, ripe coconut dropped with a frightening thud just an inch behind Freda's rear wheel. How we thanked the Lord she was not a split second later, or me a split second earlier.

A further few metres along the track, without the least warning Lyn and I found ourselves on the ground. The front forks of the bike had snapped off, throwing us unceremoniously onto well-worn path. Like any mother, Freda grabbed Lyn in her arms, thankful to find him unharmed.

The move had already been difficult for Freda. Together we agreed that Freda would have to carry Lyn, while I shouldered the bikes. There was only one more river to cross, then a short walk. The river we had to cross was not wide, but it was dark and deep, and a favourite hideout for crocodiles. The canoe we used to cross over was a small dugout log, necessitating several wobbly trips to get everything across.

We arrived at our new, two-storey house. The lower floor consisted of a kitchen in one corner, bathroom in the opposite, and all the rest was a combination of dining and living room with mostly lattice for walls. The upper floor held just two small bedrooms, divided by a short hallway connecting the front and back verandas.

And millions of mosquitoes. As I walked along the plantation paths, the back of my shirt would become almost black with the myriad of mosquitoes that settled there. There were all kinds of mosquitoes, including the Anopheles, the dreaded malaria-carrying mosquito. We soon learned to recognise the different types of mosquito by the sting we felt. At the meal table, we developed a practice that took years to reverse. We always sat sideways so we could kill the insects as they landed on our legs. This was despite often having a full mosquito net hung over the table and chairs.

We also had a large curtain type of mosquito net that hung from the ceiling and draped over the bed to the floor. The procedure for getting into bed was to jump and shake ourselves, while shaking the net, to dislodge the mosquitoes resting on ourselves or the net. We would then

When God Calls, Expect Adventure

open the net quickly and duck inside, before using a torch to locate those that had managed to get in with us.

Sometimes while in bed we would place an arm against the net. Instantly clouds of mosquitoes would land and begin to attack. We would wait a moment before beginning to draw the arm inward. As we did so, the whole net would be drawn until the drag forced the mosquitoes to let go. It was amazing how far the net could be drawn across the bed.

The second-most numerous wildlife on the plantation was snakes. These, too, came in all different kinds, from harmless tree snakes climbing the coconut trees in search of frogs to red-bellied blacks and taipans, not to mention huge carpet snakes, a kind of python. I sometimes boasted that a visitor could stop me at any moment and, without taking one step, I would be able to point out a snake. Every time I was tested, I was able to do so.

One evening, Freda and I walked down the track, she holding the umbrella, while I held the hissing pressure lamp. She walked on the narrow track, while I walked in the wet grass beside her.

"You should be more careful," she warned. "There could be a snake in the grass."

"Snakes don't come out at night," I replied in a foolhardy manner. "I'll be fine."

Without that warning, my next step would have landed me on a 7-foot (2-metre) Papua Black Snake, one of the world's deadliest. God must have been watching. And He must have continued to watch over me as I put the lamp down and picked up fallen coconuts to try to pound the snake. Freda implored me to leave it alone but I wouldn't. Then I knocked the lamp over. It should have gone out, but didn't. Again God must have intervened. When I had immobilised the snake, we went back to the house, where I collected my old army rifle and returned to finish the job.

Another time, Freda needed some vegetables from the garden. On the way, she passed the fowl house so decided to check on the nests to see if there were any eggs she could pick up on her return. In a nesting box at about eye level, she noted three eggs. I'll get them on the way back, she thought. As she was returning from the garden about 20 minutes later, she put her hand in to collect the eggs—without looking. Instead of feeling eggs, she felt a snake's body and her hand came out much quicker than it went in!

When the snake was captured and killed, Freda noticed three bulges along its length. For interest she cut the reptile at each bulge. The egg first swallowed was now only a small amount of yolk. The second egg was more recognisable and the last one to be swallowed was almost complete. We marvelled at the speed with which digestion had occurred.

There was a special grin on Freda's face one lunchtime when I walked in. She took me outside to see the morning's activities. On a stump near the house lay the bodies of three large snakes. Our baby Lyn had been crawling out on the grass near the front door of the house. Freda saw a movement a few feet in front of him. It was a large black snake. Freda called the Papuan girl helping in the house to bring a bush knife. With that knife Freda chopped the snake up, then, feeling proud of her victory, laid it over the stump. Still carrying the knife, she looked around the house to make sure Lyn was safe. She saw another large black snake sliding through the grass and with the confidence of a previous victory she soon had it laid beside the first one.

A short time later, she went to the small outdoor toilet, situated over a deep pit perhaps 30 yards (almost 30 metres) from the house. Pushing the door open, she moved in, only to have something large fall on her shoulder, then slide off onto the floor where it lay in a coil. It was a non-poisonous snake—a green python—about as long as she was tall, but she didn't stop to check it out. Quickly collecting the knife, she chopped it into many pieces.

Such were regular encounters during our time at Madana.

GOD'S PROTECTING HAND

"The Lord is my light and my salvation—whom shall I fear? The Lord is the stronghold of my life—of whom shall I be afraid? (Psalm 27:1).

Time and again we saw how God protected us in times of real fear or danger. For example, there was the time an urgent call came from one of the villages. A mother was in trouble giving birth to her child. It was several miles to the village, so Lui volunteered to show Freda the way.

On the station were two horses that no-one could separate. They were named David and Goliath. David was a small hack that invariably led the way—so Lui rode him. Goliath was a huge, lumbering but friendly draught horse. Freda mounted the saddle on his broad back and off they went.

At the village, large fresh banana leaves served as sterile sheets and, using a few other simple procedures, the baby was soon delivered safely. On the return trip, part of the track led down a steep shale hillside. David's sharp hooves were able to dig into the shale but Goliath's huge feet tended to slide until he lost grip and stumbled, throwing Freda right over his head.

Freda landed on her back with her head uphill. From that position she watched with horror as those huge feet came down, one on each side of her head—and stopped! How he could stop just like that is something ordinary logic could never explain. Normally it would be impossible for

God's Protecting Hand

a stumbling horse to halt as he did on such a steep, loose surface.

We are convinced God had a hand in restraining the momentum of that huge body. Goliath just lowered his head and looked into Freda's face, nostrils flared and his breath hot on her cheeks.

She thanked the Lord for His protection.

———•———

One experience illustrated graphically the extreme need for the gospel of Jesus to change hearts. A man from West Papua had come to work as a village teacher. One night he brought his wife in. She was in labour, expecting the birth of her child, and they sensed possible complications. We took them to an unoccupied house, which was being used as a delivery room.

I was heating some water when Freda called urgently, "Here, take the baby, quick. It's twins."

Hardly had I begun to clean the child, when Freda called again, "Hurry, I think it's triplets. Be ready."

Within five minutes, the third child had arrived. Each child so far as we could see was in excellent health, though certainly underweight, as is common in a case of triplets.

Because the infants were underweight, Freda decided to care for them herself for a few days, supervising their feeding and general care. We were surprised how readily the mother agreed to Freda caring for her new infants. A couple of days later, Freda proudly returned them to the mother. We were mystified when the woman seemed surprisingly reluctant to take them. The only explanation we could come up with was the fact that three would be a handful for anyone. However, they took them and returned to their home.

About three weeks later, a visitor asked us, "Did you hear that all three children are dead?"

"What? Surely not! They were healthy. What happened?"

"You see. That mother had never been to a mission school. She still held to the village belief that having more than one child will always bring bad luck."

"But what happened to the children?" we asked. "What caused their deaths?"

When God Calls, Expect Adventure

"They died because she didn't feed them," the visitor explained, "We could hear them crying and crying from our house. Their cries got weaker and weaker until finally they just died from hunger."

If only that mother had been given the opportunity to imbibe more fully of the love of God, what a difference that would have made. It was a tragedy that superstition should result in the death of three perfect babies.

There was so much ignorance all around us. Of course there was desperate ignorance of God and His love for humanity, but there was also much simple medical ignorance. We were so thankful that God had equipped us and directed us to combat both at the same time.

In the various villages were native missionary families who were doing their best. The mission had placed them there. In each case the men went under the title of "Teacher," but their level of education was minimal. A few had reached to the level of Grade 3—but not many.

One man had been doing his best in a remote village. One day he was bitten on the foot by a large black snake. Following traditional medical practice, he tied a tourniquet just above the bite. Because there are two bones in the lower leg, the supply of blood is not stopped or even significantly slowed by a tourniquet placed below the knee.

A runner dashed to the nearest station, which was the Korela School, while the teacher and his helpers followed as fast as they could. About halfway to Korela, he began to experience a severe headache. He reasoned that the poison had left his leg and had gone to his head. So he removed the tourniquet and tied it tightly around his head! By this time he needed help even to stay upright.

Down at Korela, Syd Stocken had heard of his problem and had set out by canoe across the lagoon to give help. The two groups met part way up the Paili River. The teacher was still alive but in great distress. Syd placed him in the canoe and, as the others paddled, gave all the help he could. But the teacher died just as they reached the river's mouth. A simple understanding of how a snakebite operates may have prevented that man's death.

God's Protecting Hand

As in all new stations, one of the first tasks to be tackled is to make sure there is sufficient food for the staff. I joined the group of men as they set out to dig a new garden on the Madana property.

Each man hefted a pair of "digging sticks." These were sharpened hardwood sticks about 7 feet (2 metres) long and thick enough to grip comfortably, maybe 2 inches (5 centimetres) diameter. We were about 8 or 10 men who stood shoulder to shoulder in a line holding one digging stick in each hand.

At the command from one person, we began to pound those sticks into the ground until they had penetrated about 8 inches (20 centimetres). At the next command all sticks were leaned backward, lifting a whole slab of turf. Another command and all right-hand sticks were pushed well under the turf and held there while the left stick was also pushed under. Another command and all sticks were lifted so as to lift a huge slab of turf and turn it over. Another command and the line of men moved a step back and repeated the process. Huge slabs of turf were turned over every 30 seconds or so. It was amazing how quickly a garden was prepared.

The women followed, quickly planting sweet potato runners, which would grow and produce a crop in three months. They planted other crops as were suitable.

Later we located an old single-furrow mole-board plough and tried to hitch Goliath to it, but failed because we had no proper harness. We also tried to prepare new gardens using the old truck to pull the plough, but that was too expensive to use other than those times when manpower was short.

DIPHTHERIA

"'On the day when I act,' says the Lord Almighty, 'they will be my treasured possession. I will spare them, just as a father has compassion and spares his son who serves him'" (Malachi 3:17).

Many times while walking those lovely, twisty trails along the coast I wished I had a small boat. I was certain I could have done so much more for the village people, and even more for the teachers who lived in some out-of-the-way places. I spent time in prayer telling God of the need. I even selected and planned the place beside the slow, black-watered river with its graceful biri-palm banks where I felt I might be able to build a boat.

Then exciting news came to us from the Korela mission. The mission headquarters in Port Moresby had supplied them with a boat. The principal of the school Stan Gillis, and his wife Ivy, were ecstatic. They sent an invitation for us to spend a weekend with them so we could join with them on the boat's maiden voyage.

After arriving at Korela, we discussed how to make the maiden boat trip worthwhile. The boat was a 13-foot (4-metre) aluminium shell with a single-cylinder Simplex engine but we were all so proud one would have thought it was a prestigious yacht. Not one of us so much as thought of simply making it a pleasure trip. We decided it would be good to return to Aroma and pick up some goods that we could use.

As we headed out into the open ocean, the spray began to drench us, but it was exciting and the weather was fine. Graham, the Gillis's young boy, and Lyn, our son, sat at the front laughing at the rise and fall of the boat, while we adults at the back talked as we hid from the sun and the salt spray.

The seas were lovely all the way to Aroma but the weather had changed by the time we were ready to return.

When the boat emerged from the shelter of the reef, we faced big seas against which our boat butted almost ineffectually. The little engine was almost drowned by some of the waves as they broke over the sides.

Diphtheria

The two Papuan men with us were bailing almost constantly. Then a wave swamped and killed the engine. We managed to get it to start again, but obviously we would never make it as conditions continued to deteriorate. We headed for the beach where the two women and the children jumped off to walk. They were more comfortable and both they and the boat could now make better headway.

Stan and both the Papuan men were soon seasick. I am sure the Lord blessed, because, unusually, I was not seasick at all. Every time a wave killed the engine, Stan would put his hand across the intake while I pulled the rope. We had to do this many times that afternoon.

By late afternoon, we had only reached the dark waters at the mouth of the Madana River. The women and children re-boarded and we puttered up to Madana to stay the night. What a relief it was to be back on land.

Being such great friends, Lyn and Graham shared the same large cot for the night, draped in mosquito nets, as we adults talked about our adventures and challenges. Next morning, Monday, we left the women at Madana while Stan and I took the boat around to Marshall Lagoon. At the river's mouth, the tide was so low that the boat bumped against the bottom often. Finally it became necessary for us to drag the boat across the bar.

Reaching the deeper water, we pulled the starting rope. The engine started but the propeller refused to turn. Somewhere we had hit something that had caused the metal key between the shaft and the propeller to shear. Fortunately, Stan had brought a bag of tools in which we found a rusty bolt and an old, almost-as-rusty file. Using a sand-bogged tree as a workbench and fingers for a vice, we filed four sides on that old bolt until it fitted as a replacement key. In time we reached the lagoon. We then took the truck to Madana to collect our wives and children.

Upon arrival, it was clear Graham was not well. When Stan asked his son what was wrong, he replied, "Daddy, I've got a headache in my throat."

Nothing appeared wrong in his throat, so we took them down to the lagoon where they set off for home a short distance up the lagoon.

On Wednesday morning, Ivy sent an urgent message for either Freda or I to go have a look at Graham, who—said the message—was very sick.

"This doesn't sound too good," I said. "I'll go right away."

When God Calls, Expect Adventure

"Here, take this medical book with you," called Freda.

Ivy was at the door as I arrived. She looked worried. Graham was in his cot, so we sat him up and I looked down his throat using a torch. Ivy also looked and we saw a large, ugly grey patch at the back of his throat.

"Diphtheria," she cried as her hands rose to her face.

"It certainly looks very much like it," I commented. "But first let's rule out all other possibilities."

The book told us nothing more than we already knew. For treatment it simply read, "Treat with antibiotics."

We had no antibiotics, for the simple reason that antibiotics were not issued to any mission stations anywhere in Papua at the time. Nor was there anything else in our medicine cupboards that would be helpful. There can be few situations more frustrating than to know what to do, but have nothing to fight with. I looked at Ivy as she held Graham close to her. Her face almost shouted her feelings of love mingled with fear.

Stan dashed off an urgent note to the nearest radio-transmitting station, asking them to request urgent medical assistance. The letter was given to a team of Papuan men who were sent off by canoe. Stan did his best to impress on them the need to make all haste. Now there was nothing to do but wait!

Stan and Ivy Gillis with beautiful Graham.

TRAGEDY STRIKES

"This is what the Lord says: 'Restrain your voice from weeping and your eyes from tears, for your work will be rewarded'" (Jeremiah 31:16).

The canoe trip should have taken less than a day. But the idea of haste completely escaped the men entrusted with the urgent message. We later learned that it took them four days to reach the radio station because they had welcomed the opportunity to visit friends along the way.

The fourth day since they left was a grey, wet, windy day. How we were praying that the message would get through quickly! We also prayed that maybe God could send help from some other source—and that it might arrive soon. While we prayed, we fought the diphtheria with the only weapons we had. Feeble though they were, we administered foments and gargles and steam inhalations. It was all we could do.

We were certain our prayers had been answered when we saw a boat coming up the lagoon. Sure, it was small—only about 35 feet (10 metres) long—but at least it was a boat capable of travel to Port Moresby. Stan and I grabbed a canoe and paddled furiously to meet it. Before we reached it, the boat turned up a side river. We followed until we caught up just as it tied up at the Paili Plantation wharf.

We hastened to talk with the owner of the boat, a well-known plantation owner from further down the coast. He gave us a moment to state our request, then simply stood there, his .303 rifle on his arm as he said, "No-one will be taking my boat out into seas like this."

"But this child is going to die if we can't get medical help," I implored. "It's most important that he be taken to medical help as soon as possible!"

When God Calls, Expect Adventure

"Well, there's nothing I can do about it, mate," came the callous response. "The boat is not going out—and that's that."

With those final words, he walked away. There was no use talking further, his heart was hard as stone. I felt so desperately angry. For their part, Stan and Ivy were devastated. Their hopes had been raised, then cruelly dashed.

On the Wednesday, Freda came to care for Graham while I went back to care for the station. In any case, Freda is a better bedside nurse than I am.

The following day, I heard a new sound. It was a Sunderland Flying Boat heading in the direction of Korela. Grabbing the truck, I drove to the lagoon where the Sunderland had now landed and was anchored out on the water. Taking a canoe, I went out to the plane where I met Dr May, the second-ranking medical officer in the Papuan government. He had come to take charge of the case personally, this being the first reported case of diphtheria in Papua New Guinea's history.

Freda later told me that the Sunderland had circled Korela station, then dropped a note reading, "If this is the station with the sick child, put out a white sheet."

The tears were pouring down Ivy's face. She was crying with relief and apprehension. She ran inside and almost emptied the linen-press of white sheets, which she had spread all over the yard and lawn. Graham and his cot were placed in a canoe and paddled as fast as possible down the lagoon to where the flying boat was anchored.

On the way down, Ivy remarked to Freda, "I think Graham is a little better, don't you?"

Freda agreed. He did seem brighter.

Dr May stepped smartly onto the canoe as it drew alongside, made a quick check to confirm the diagnosis, then immediately administered an injection of penicillin. Within minutes, the whole Gillis family were bundled aboard the flying boat and the engines roared. Soon, they were heading for Port Moresby and the hospital.

Freda was about done. She had given her all, hardly sleeping at all while caring for Graham. But to add to her worries, she remembered that Lyn and Graham had slept together just the night before Graham complained of the "headache" in his throat. That meant they had spent a

Tragedy Strikes

whole night together during the most contagious period in the progress of the disease.

An ambulance was waiting in Port Moresby when the Sunderland landed and raced the family to the hospital, where the staff were preparing to receive the case. The kindly sister in charge said to Stan and Ivy, "We'll care for him now. You go and get yourselves settled, then return and you can sit with him."

They had no car, of course, so it took Stan and Ivy about half an hour to walk to the mission headquarters, where a phone message from the hospital was awaiting them.

The message told them that Graham had died about 10 minutes after they left the hospital. It was such a tragedy! All of us were heartbroken. "Why Lord?" we pleaded. "Why would you allow this to happen to an innocent child?"

When the time came, Freda and I went down to meet the small coastal trader on which Stan and Ivy returned to their duties at the school. Never had Freda and I felt as upset as we did that day. To see Stan and Ivy come bravely back to their isolated outpost was difficult as the very isolation of that post had been the cause of Graham's death. My heart was just bursting with the desire to call out, "Here, take our son, Lyn, to fill that empty place." It was a foolish thought, I know, but our hearts ached to do something for those grieving friends of ours.

Only God can do something to fill emptiness such as our friends experienced. Thank the Lord He did do so for that brave young couple. From that day on, I had a new and better concept of the terrible loss my heavenly Father must have felt when He permitted His only Son, Jesus, to come to this earth to die. What made His case so much more severe was knowing in advance all that Jesus was going to endure. Surely He does understand when we suffer the loss of a loved one or friend.

There was one small good to come from that terrible experience. After Graham's death, both government and mission medical posts were granted antibiotics to administer where appropriate. Many lives were undoubtedly saved as a consequence of this.

MAKING DO AT MADANA

"See, I will bring them from the land of the north and gather them from the ends of the earth. Among them will be the blind and the lame, expectant mothers and women in labour; a great throng will return. They will come with weeping; they will pray as I bring them back. I will lead them beside streams of water on a level path where they will not stumble, because I am Israel's father" (Jeremiah 31:8, 9).

We had been in Madana for several months and we had tried our best to make the station a success. In an effort to make transport less expensive, we had resurrected an old Morris truck from its rusting place in the grass. The engine had long gone, but we stripped all other unessentials from it, retaining the chassis and steering system, including the lovely wooden steering wheel. Then we built a tray on its back where we could load the bags of copra, and fitted it up so the draught horse, Goliath, could draw it.

Or so we reasoned.

The day it was completed all the staff and students clambered onto the tray and Goliath was hitched up using makeshift draglines. Someone sat at the steering wheel and off we went. But not too far. In the absence of tubes, we had stuffed the tyres with grass, but they soon went flat. In any case, the old frame was too heavy for poor Goliath. And the draglines were not strong enough either.

We had no choice but to abandon that idea. Our "glorious experiment" was taken back to where it came from and still rusts there in the long grass, as far as we know.

There was a great spirit on the station despite the snakes, mosquitoes and isolation. Everyone did their best to see that things succeeded. One evidence of this was the fact that the teachers and students came earlier and earlier each morning to begin the day with worship.

I was determined that they would never catch me sleeping in, so I rose each morning well before they arrived. And they didn't want me to think they were slacking, so they came earlier, too. And so it went in a circle, resulting in morning worships held in the dark. There was no good reason except our desire to outdo each other!

The ex-army Ford truck that came with the station was having problems. There came the time when we had two important visitors from church headquarters in Australia arrive to see the work in our district. Pastor Andrew Dawson and Pastor T C Lawson were collected from their boat, and brought through the swamp to the station. But, when it came time to return them to the boat, the truck engine would not start.

The fuel pump was no longer working. Its diaphragm had ruptured, which meant no fuel was getting to the engine. Not wishing to worry our visitors, I gathered a few items from the dispensary with which I made some substitute arrangements. An enamelled enema can held the fuel, with a length of rubber hose leading to the carburettor. A lad sat on the cabin roof holding the enema can and in that way we gravity-fed the fuel down to the motor instead of through the regular fuel pump.

Pastor Lawson took one look and almost rolled on the ground with laughter. When he got his breath, he roared, "Fancy giving an enema to a truck!"

Pastor Dawson was considerably more cautious. "Are you sure it will get us to the beach?" he asked doubtfully, perhaps fearful of the long walk back.

To our relief, we got our guests to the lagoon. But Pastor Lawson kept breaking out in giggles at the sight of the enema can and tube going down into the bowels of the V8 engine.

Not long after, I noticed another problem developing in the engine. A crack had developed in one of the cylinder heads allowing water into one cylinder. I sent to Port Moresby for a replacement head, which arrived several weeks later. The old truck limped down to the lagoon to collect the part. After collecting the replacement head, I started the engine for the return journey. There was a mighty bang and a circular section of the head blew completely out, exposing the problem cylinder.

When God Calls, Expect Adventure

A small portion of metal from the cracked head had finally broken loose and dropped into the cylinder. As the piston came to the top, there was not sufficient clearance, so it simply rammed that part of the head completely out. To get home we had to have a man standing on the bumper bar slowly pouring water into the radiator to compensate for the water that was being blown out the now-open cylinder head. We made it home and soon had the engine repaired.

About this time, the government had asked the mission to administer and operate two leprosy colonies, which at that time were called "Hansenide colonies." One day, in the mail we received a note from mission headquarters stating that they had voted that we take responsibility for one of these medical institutions. The plan was for us to take an early furlough, do a little study on leprosy, then return. It was hoped that the Hansenide colonies would be ready to commence by that time.

In our place, Pastor Eric Boehm and family had been asked to take over the care of the Madana mission. This provided a challenge because we wanted to have the station operating as well as possible when the Boehms were to arrive. So we put added energy into our partially-completed project of new staff and student houses, each made from local materials.

A team had been up the Marshall Lagoon and had cut a pile of mangrove trees that now had to be transported from the beach to Madana by truck. When loaded on the truck, the forward ends of the timbers reached high up above the cabin. Collecting and loading had taken time and it was 9 pm when we were ready to go home.

Everyone piled on board, including some women with their babies. The truck was not normally used at night, so no-one knew the battery had begun to lose its ability to hold a charge. We had travelled only a short way when the lights dimmed then went out, leaving us to find our way in the dark. We had not so much as a match and it was an extremely dark night. I would just have to say a prayer and remember enough of the twisty road to go home slowly despite the dark.

We hadn't gone more than about 100 yards (about 100 metres) when

Making Do At Madana

we ran into a coconut tree. The impact bent the heavy bumper bar right into the tyre, thereby locking the wheel. We tied the bumper bar to the tree and backed away, straightening the bar. Obviously it was foolish to go further without a light of some sort. Someone was able to borrow a small hurricane lamp from a local village man. It was small and weak, but with someone sitting up on the cabin roof holding the lamp we had just enough light to make out trees and the faint outline of the track in front of us.

Even though slow, it seemed we were doing well. Maybe I was too much like Peter when he walked on the water, a little too confident. We had travelled about 3 miles (5 kilometres) when there was a crash and the truck came to a sudden stop. Women were screaming. The man with the lamp fell off the front of the truck, dousing the flame in the lamp.

I jumped out to find out what had happened. All I could hear was crying. It was frustrating because I couldn't see and no-one would answer me.

When things settled down, I discovered that the long timbers that reached above the cabin had been higher than a particular coconut tree leaning across the track. The timbers had slid up over the coconut tree, then snapped in half as they were bent back. We unloaded the timber and left it by the road for the night.

Now we had no light at all. We crept homeward even more slowly. The track across the swamp was narrow and winding. Part-way across, we failed to turn early enough and the truck's front wheels sank into the mud. There was only one thing left to do, leave the truck where it was for the night and walk the remaining distance home. It had been a miserable night!

But more was to come. The nearer we came to the plantation, the more we were wondering why the sky was lit up ahead of us. Little by little, the sky became red—the colour of fire. We ran, only to find the mission copra processing and storage shed on fire. Inside that shed had been stored all the copra we had dried and bagged ready for shipment. Its value represented about a year's budget for the district and now the whole drying shed was burning.

We had no water with which to fight the fire. All we could do was

When God Calls, Expect Adventure

watch it burn, the flames shooting triumphantly above the treetops. The tears of frustration I shed that night would have done some good in extinguishing the flames, if only I could have managed to get near enough to the flames. At times like this, one wondered if God had forsaken us altogether.

Not all returns were as sad and depressing as that one. Returning home one day, Freda and I could hardly believe our eyes. There, in the lounge room, were our two horses—David and Goliath—just standing there enjoying themselves amid our furniture. In fact, they made it clear they liked it there and had no desire to move.

Gwen Howell with children Barry and Glen at Aroma with David, the mission horse.

THE DEVIL ATTACKS

"Keep me safe, O God, for in you I take refuge" (Psalm 16:1).

On many occasions we witnessed the direct intervention of the Lord. One incident could have been disastrous. I was working not far from the house when suddenly I heard cries for help. I saw Geno and his wife running for all they were worth toward our home, terror etched on their faces, with Uvau in hot pursuit. Uvau held aloft a huge machete with which it was clear he wished to cut Geno and his wife down. His face was contorted with fury!

With a prayer for help, I raced out and jumped between the fleeing couple and the angry man. The married couple raced into our house, while I prevented Uvau from following. I blocked his way and tried to talk with him, but something was wrong. I could not get rational answers and he was clearly not himself. I tried to wrestle the knife from him, but such was his strength and fury that I had no hope of doing so.

"Help me, Lord!" I cried.

I tried again to take the knife, using every ounce of strength I had at my disposal but it was hopeless. It seemed Uvau was powered by a malevolent force. Suddenly I stepped back and strange as it might sound, I suggested we kneel and pray. He refused. Instead, he swung the knife about in a vicious, random manner, slashing backwards and forwards as if aiming at unseen foes.

Trusting in the Lord's strength and protection, I dared to kneel on the track with him standing over me, bush knife in hand. I prayed aloud that Jesus would take control. "Lord," I prayed. "Help me, Father."

I stood again and tried to take the knife. Again Uvau resisted. Instead of handing it over, he sunk it into the trunk of the coconut tree beside us and stood glaring at me. I knelt again and, closing my eyes, I prayed

When God Calls, Expect Adventure

for the Lord to take over and defeat the devil. I prayed for a minute or so, then stood.

To my surprise, Uvau had begun to weep. I led him back to his room where we talked for a time. I told him to sleep and he did not wake for almost 24 hours.

I returned to remove the knife from the coconut tree. It was so deeply embedded it took quite a time and a lot of strength to extract it. It was more than Uvau's strength that had driven the bush knife in so deeply. I am convinced that a superhuman force came upon him that night.

When Uvau woke, we talked together again. The story he told was frightening. He had been resting when a being such as he had never seen before came to him and demanded that he take the knife beside him and kill someone. Uvau felt he was "under orders," which he was powerless to disobey. He got up, grabbed the knife, and set out to get someone.

One of the students had seen the crazed look in Uvau's eyes and raised the alarm. A few folk escaped by climbing trees. Others fled into the bush, while Geno and wife raced to us for protection. Uvau told me he was convinced the devil came to him and gave the order. I agreed.

Years later, I again met Uvau who had become a missionary for the Lord and was doing good work.

When the Boehm family arrived, it was time for us to leave. After showing them around the station and giving as much information as we were able, the hour had come for us to go down to the beach to meet the ship on which we were to leave. Eric suggested I drive the truck for the last time. Half way across the swamp, there was a loud bang and the truck stopped. I wasn't sure what had happened but Eric recognised it as a broken back axle. We put the truck into four-wheel drive in order to engage the front wheels, but still we could not move.

Eric crawled underneath and banged the front-wheel drive into connection, using a piece of metal for a hammer. At the beach, he asked me to turn the truck around ready for the return trip. To do so on such a narrow beach meant backing away from the water into the dry sand before turning. As I backed up into the sand, there was another crack.

The Devil Attacks

The front axle had also broken! The truck now had no power to move at all.

Freda and I had to board the waiting boat. I had no opportunity to help Eric further. We left them there, stranded on the beach, miles from their new home. I still shudder with embarrassment as I remember the way I felt leaving them there, as I had to do that day.

The mission headquarters had made the changes required in order to cooperate with the government in staffing the two proposed leprosy colonies. But the government was not yet ready to go ahead, so we were left with no station to care for and nothing specific to do. It was not a nice feeling.

While waiting for the government, Freda and I were asked to care for Babaguina, a new station located behind the government outpost of Abau, some distance further east along the Papuan coast. We made a quick trip to Port Moresby and were returning on a small coastal trading vessel. Lyn was now at the stage of learning to walk and wanted to use his new-found ability to investigate so many interesting things around him.

The deck of this small trader was not designed for children. The only protection from going over the side was a cable about 3 feet (1 metre) high tied to the infrequent stanchions. The safety barrier was alright for adults, but no barrier whatever to a small boy wanting to crawl or walk everywhere. We tied a rope to his waist and had to restrain him on a makeshift leash.

It was quite a relief when we arrived at Marshall Lagoon where the boat would stay for a few hours while they loaded copra. This allowed us opportunity to get ashore for a while. Leaving our goods in the cabin, we went to Korela where we again met the Gillises, as well as the Boehms and Alma Wiles.

"Come and see this sewing machine a friend sent to us," called Alma. We all went inside to have a look at a hand-operated Wertheim sewing machine. It was second-hand but a real treasure. We were all so interested in working out how to operate the machine that the children were forgotten.

When God Calls, Expect Adventure

Suddenly there was a shout in the Motuan language from Ope, a local Papuan missionary, "The master's boy has fallen down the hole!"

Eric Boehm thought of his son as he raced to the pit toilet. I thought of Lyn and raced to the cement underground water tank, the entrance to which was just a little above ground level. I saw instantly that the lid was not in its correct position. Throwing the lid aside, I looked down. There was Lyn on his back, floating just below the surface of the water. There was no time to think. I dropped feet-first into the tank and grabbed him.

Lyn was as limp as a wet rag, with no suggestion of life in his body. Lifting him above the surface, I tried to squeeze the water out of his lungs but with no success. I looked up to see Freda's anxious face. By this time Eric had joined her. He reached down while I reached up as far as I could. We had to make several attempts before I was able to lift one of Lyn's arms high enough for Eric to grasp his hand and pull him out. The water in the well was just deep enough to cover my nose when my toes touched the base of the tank.

They laid Lyn on his chest across the sloping pathway with his head downward while they administered the old Holger-Neilsen method of artificial respiration. At that time this was the method practised by all first aiders. I don't know how long they worked on him—but it seemed a long time.

Freda recognised the need to warm Lyn, so she raced inside and stirred up the fire in the wood stove, placed blankets in the oven until they were warm enough and brought them out to wrap Lyn in. She did this two or three times. Several folk took turns pumping his chest.

The first few strokes forced water from his chest, which formed a small pool at the far edge of the path where he was lying. Understandably, everyone forgot me down the well in their concern for Lyn. At last, Eric came and was able to reach down and pull me out. I was asked to take my turn at resuscitation. Through our combined efforts, Lyn began to show signs of life and he began breathing without assistance. Some of the women, including Freda, unashamedly cried for joy.

But we were not out of trouble yet. We took him in, laid him down and changed his clothes, wrapping him tightly until he was snug and warm. Late in the afternoon, Lyn woke a little and watched Don pushing

The Devil Attacks

a toy car while making the sound of an engine. "Burrrrrr," Don said.

Lyn copied with a short "Burrrrr," then closed his eyes and went to sleep again. He woke at about 8 pm, almost as though nothing had happened. Miraculously, he appeared to have suffered no ill-effects!

It was a thankful missionary group who met that night to pray and give thanks. The Lord had been kind to us. We saw the hand of our Lord in sending Ope to the well at precisely the correct time. However, it was difficult too! Why had our son been saved, yet Graham's life been lost to diphtheria? Why would a loving God help one and seemingly not help the other? We will not know those answers until we are in heaven. All we could do was offer thanks and trust in Him.

While Lyn slept, Stan and I went down to the boat to advise the captain that our family would not be resuming the trip with them. It was disappointing to find that someone had seen their opportunity while we were at Korela and had stolen all of our clothes!

BABAGUINA

"But I trust in you, Lord; I say, 'You are my God. My times are in your hands; deliver me from the hands of my enemies, from those who pursue me. Let your face shine on your servant; save me in your unfailing love. Let me not be put to shame, Lord, for I have cried out to you" (Psalm 31:14–17).

Babaguina—sometimes called Wagiadai—was an interesting station, situated a few miles up the river from Abau. The mission station that was to be our next home was located on a small knoll, which stood out into the river. The water's edge of the main river marked one boundary, while a quiet little creek formed a second boundary. Behind it was virgin forest.

Syd Stocken had built the house from native materials, and it boasted a grass roof and plaited bamboo for walls and floors. The view down the river was beautiful, always interesting and always changing. At high tide, the water flooded up until the mangrove leaves dipped in the quiet stream. But as the tide flowed seaward, the looping roots and unique diminishing base of the mangrove trees became exposed. At times, the roots looked like looping necks of cranes, birds feeding in the mud.

The mud itself was a source of interest with its thousands of mud crabs. They were small crabs, less active than those at Aroma, but these boasted the brightest colours. One might have a body of bright yellow with an outsized brilliant-blue nipper, while another might have a body of fire-engine red with a yellow nipper. These nippers were larger than the rest of the crab and it made us laugh as we watched their antics. The only explanation I could offer for these bright colours is that it was another example of the extravagant love of God for this world, and His desire that even the drab mangrove mud should be brightened with colourful crabs waving outrageously big nippers.

Just for fun, I sometimes pointed a stick at a crab. It would rear up and thrust out its outsized nipper. The laws of gravity seemed to demand that the small creature topple over. It was great to watch them as they chased one another over the mud, under the roots, and in and out of the water. They seemed to be having such fun.

There were also climbing fish to watch. Only about 2 inches (5 centimetres) long, they jumped out of the water and scuttled across the mud to climb an aerial root of a mangrove or maybe to climb over a fallen branch. They seemed to have glorious fun as they chased one another around, over and under logs and anything else. Every few minutes, they stopped and stood up using their two flippers as props, much as a seal does, their two bulging eyes staring unblinkingly. Then off they would go on another frolic. Crossing shallow water, they could move like lightning.

We would also watch the village people from further up the river paddling their canoes past. Or the students having fun in the water, despite the common and often large crocodiles. One huge crocodile had his favourite mud slide directly across the river from our house. We would see him resting there much of the time. The students had special respect for him. When they were down by the river they would watch carefully. If he was resting on the bank, they would swim and have a hilarious time. But the moment he slid into the water, all the students would decide they were clean enough and beat a hasty retreat.

One day, I made a trip by small canoe down the river to Abau. We passed at least 11 crocodiles just resting on the banks. Shortly after our time at Babaguina, a team of professional crocodile shooters came and bagged 300 crocodiles in just four weeks. I was told that some crocodiles were caught at night foraging for dogs under the village houses.

Kila Galama and his wife were on the station with us. During this time, in 1948, the mission began taking delivery of a new fleet of mission ships, built at the Halvorson yards on the Parramatta River in Ryde, a suburb of Sydney. A Captain Reece was employed to see to the delivery of the boats, but it was decided to use capable island men for crew. Kila was a capable man at sea, so he was chosen to be one of the crew to go to Sydney.

Only a few Papua New Guineans had ever been to Australia, so on the day Kila returned to Babaguina, people from all over the district crowded onto the station to hear his story. He came to us first and I tried to ask him questions, like, "Were there many people you saw?"

The answer was short and overly respectful. "Yes, many people," he replied softly.

"Did you see plenty of cars?"

"Yes, many."

It was obvious we were not going to get much from him, so we suggested he speak to the others as the students wanted to hear what he had to say. They were waiting eagerly just outside the house.

Fortunately, the plaited bamboo walls meant we were able to hear all he said to them. He spoke in the Motuan language and we could clearly hear him speaking to his own people with great animation. In reply to their questions, he made remarks like these:

"Yes, there were huge crowds of people, more than you could ever imagine."

"What houses did they have?" a student asked.

"The houses were not like our houses at all. Many of them are built on top of another. There were many standing up in a big pile that went way up into the sky!"

"How do they get to the top houses?" another listener asked. "Do they have a big ladder on the outside?"

"No," Kila replied knowledgeably. "These houses were big houses and they had a small house inside. The door of this small house would open and we would go into it, then its door would close. Next we would get a very funny feeling in our legs and stomach, and the door would open and we would be at another house higher up."

Then he spoke about the traffic. Most of these students had never seen a car, all they had seen were one or two trucks, so he spoke of all traffic as trucks. "You could never imagine how many trucks there were on their roads," he exclaimed. "Some were big and some were small. And they went very fast. I was frightened. But I must tell you about some very big trucks I saw. These trucks carried about a hundred people at one time, and they had iron wheels that ran along two iron roads."

Someone stopped him with the question, "But if they had two iron roads, what happened when one road went one way and the other road went another way?"

"But the two iron roads always went the same way," Kila explained.

"Then, why did it need two roads?"

Somehow that question never did get settled—but Kila went on, "These big trucks always had two men in them. One was a driver, and the other man carried a bag and people gave him money to put in that bag."

This caused a few "oh's" and "ah's" as Kila carried on. "These trucks had a wire rope up above them and a long arm that reached up to grab hold of that rope. Twice I saw that rope spit fire at the arm. And once I saw the arm come off the iron rope. The big truck just stopped. It couldn't move. So the man with the money bag got out and pulled the arm down until he made it grab hold of the iron rope again. Then the big truck could go again, up the hills and round the corners, and carry so many people. The truck got its power from the fire-spitting rope."

He stopped for a moment, then added words I have never forgotten. "You know, that truck and its arm made me think of prayer. As long as our arm reaches up to God, we have power to go any place we need to go. We have power when we trust in God. But when our hand lets go of God, we can't go anywhere."

They were words of wisdom and I was overjoyed to hear him talking about God so powerfully. Having said that, the group moved off to the students' quarters, where they talked until all hours of the night. We wished we could have heard more of that conversation, but we thanked God for that which we did hear and for the understanding of God it demonstrated.

———•———

Another worker who went to Australia was Pastor Mave, who travelled in company with Pastor Eric Boehm. He came back deeply impressed with the glass doors, which he told us could "smell."

Talking to a group of students one day, he said, "I was following Pastor Boehm when we came to glass doors that were closed tight. But when Pastor Boehm came near the doors they must have smelled him because they opened. No-one touched them."

The students stared at Pastor Mave, intrigued with the idea of doors that could smell and open of their own will.

When God Calls, Expect Adventure

"I stopped to look. I was scared," Pastor Mave continued. "How did that door open without anyone touching it? Just then the doors closed behind Pastor Boehm, leaving me outside. I could see him getting further away, so I went up to see if I could open the door. But the doors must have smelled me too, because they opened before I touched them. I jumped back in fear and they closed again. By now Pastor Boehm was a long way off. So I ran up to the door, and it smelled me and opened again. This time I rushed through before it could bite me. As soon as it couldn't smell me, it closed behind. Was I scared when I discovered that even doors can smell people."

The Boehm family took over at Madana in the early 1950s. Pictured from left are Ken, Robert (baby), with Grace, Don, Ray (with tie) and Eric.

EVACUATION TO AUSTRALIA

"I removed the burden from their shoulders; their hands were set free from the basket. In your distress you called and I rescued you" (Psalm 81:6, 7).

Babaguina land must have been a rich land—if one is to measure richness by the size of the rats that enjoyed romping around our house at night. The internal walls were only just high enough so one could not look over into the next room. But at night, the tops of those walls made a race track for the biggest rats we had ever seen. They were almost as big as cats and totally unafraid of humans.

At first, I thought those rats played a role in the events that were to unfold. Our time at Babaguina was only a matter of a few weeks. It was intended that we stay longer but a medical problem arose which changed plans. Freda began experiencing severe abdominal pains, the worst kind she had ever felt. For a little time, we could not pinpoint the problem. We even sent to Abau to ask the medical man there to come and have a look. He was not a doctor, but had spent some time as a wardsman at a large Sydney hospital, which at that time was sufficient training to hold the post of District Medical Officer. This entitled him to carry the title "Doctor" in that out-of-the-way station.

The medical officer examined Freda and declared it was a case of hepatic abscess. We were sure he was wrong in his diagnosis, but we were thankful he left us with a few ampoules of morphine. Shortly after he left, when the excruciating pain returned, I noticed Freda's skin had turned yellow. This convinced me she had a case of gallstones, which was the cause of the intermittent and savage pains.

The senior officer at the government station invited us to stay with him, while he sent through to Port Moresby with a request for transport

When God Calls, Expect Adventure

for Freda to the Port Moresby hospital without delay. The next day, an ex-wartime torpedo boat roared into the Abau anchorage. We were placed aboard and sent on our way to Port Moresby.

As so frequently happens with gallstones, when the stone causing the pain moves its position or passes through the bile tube, the pain ceases. It was night when we arrived at the Port Moresby wharf. Freda had no pain by now and felt like she was the biggest fraud ever to enter the harbour. Waiting for us on the wharf was an ambulance and its crew, a doctor and a nurse, plus the mission officers and quite a crowd of interested onlookers who had come down to see what was bad enough for a boat to make a mercy dash to Abau.

The stretcher-bearers raced to the boat, looking for their patient, but Freda walked out with a face as red as a tomato. The doctor talked to us for a few minutes and everyone was kind enough to understand that gallstones often act in this manner. They drove us directly to the hospital where tests confirmed a gall bladder problem. They also advised that we should fly to Sydney for medical attention. We travelled in an old DC3 that seemed to drop down at every town on the Australian east coast until we finally reached Sydney.

It was Friday night when we arrived. Bill Zeunert had been sent to meet us. For two years, all our travelling had been by canoe or the old Madana truck. Speed and traffic were matters we had almost forgotten. Bill was well known as a modern Jehu—the Bible character known as a fast and furious chariot driver—and had just taken delivery of a new Holden of which he was so proud. To make matters worse, our plane was a little late and Bill had an appointment he had to meet.

As we raced through the streets of Sydney, I was convinced Bill only knew two positions—flat out or screeching halt. It would be an understatement to say I was extremely relieved when we reached our destination, although Bill was a good driver. And we continued in good hands. As always, Dr Tullock did a superb job of removing the gall bladder, after which Freda had no further problems.

While Freda convalesced, I spent some time at the University of Sydney doing special studies on leprosy. But by the time furlough was over, the Papuan governing authority had only made arrangements for one of the leprosy colonies. The second one was to commence soon.

Evacuation to Australia

Having had previous experience with leprosy, Len Barnard was asked to head the first station. Early in 1949, I returned alone by ship to Lae, on the north coast of Papua New Guinea.

In Lae, I joined a group of missionaries camped in ex-army Quonset huts on the outskirts of the town. We formed a happy family. Making up the group were Laurie and Gwen Howell, also Ward and Ora Nolan, plus others who came and went. One of the best memories was of the interesting worship times we held together each day.

The mission had purchased several incomplete army jeeps. Our group were in the process of making these usable. I joined in enthusiastically. To restore them required numerous replacement parts, which we obtained by going to the ex-army "vehicle parks" where hundreds of vehicles of all kinds sat in military lines rusting in the bush.

While in Lae, I began using pidgin English. For days, I had been asking Ward to translate for me when I needed to give a message to one of the New Guinean men who assisted us. One day I asked Ward to tell Pirinavi—a native from the Bena district—something. Ward said, "Go on, Lester, you've been here a fortnight. That's long enough for anybody to learn pidgin. Tell him yourself." And he was right. I should have been trying earlier.

A few weeks later, I boarded the *Malaita* en route to Madang, taking with me one of the completed jeeps. The *Malaita* docked late at night. I watched the mission's jeep as it was swung off onto the wharf. A couple of the mission boys had been asked to meet and guide me to headquarters. After waiting for a few minutes, we climbed into the jeep and drove away. The night was dark and it seemed spooky driving between banks of long grass, in unfamiliar territory, not having any idea where I was going.

Pastor and Mrs Gander allocated me a bed in the nearby house of a friendly plantation owner and during the night a most spectacular storm swept over Madang. The most tremendous flash of lightning woke me. It had struck and split a tree right outside the house in the most dramatic brilliance and display of power I have experienced. As the first faint light of morning began to appear, I looked out the window

When God Calls, Expect Adventure

and all I could see was water everywhere. I was sure I had been floodbound. But the house I had slept in had been built beside one of the beautiful waterways of Madang.

Pastor H M S Richards—of Voice of Prophecy fame—arrived for a visit during the time I was there. He remarked as he stepped from the plane, "This must surely be the Venice of the Pacific." The mission station was right on the banks of one of these arms of water and the more opportunity I had to see Madang, the more I fell in love with it.

The next few weeks were spent happily visiting the local villages and taking meetings in the churches. I also assisted Pastor Gander who was reclaiming engines and other useful items from barges sunk during the war in the water beside the mission.

Bena Bena mission shown from the air. From left to right can be seen the dispensary, workshop, expatriate missionary homes, "native" staff homes and gardens.

BENA BENA

"I waited patiently for the Lord; he turned to me and heard my cry. He lifted me out of the slimy pit, out of the mud and mire; he set my feet on a rock and gave me a firm place to stand. He put a new song in my mouth, a hymn of praise to our God" (Psalm 40:1–3).

The exciting day came when Freda and Lyn arrived from Australia. Because the opening of a second leprosy hospital was still some time away, we were invited to go to Bena Bena to care for the medical work on that station. We flew up with Bill Paslow in his Dragon Rapide, a small two-engine biplane capable of carrying a 1200-pound (550-kilogram) load.

Bena is in the Eastern Highlands of Papua New Guinea. Gold prospectors had discovered more than one million inhabitants in the isolated Highland valleys in the 1930s and missionaries had followed with permission of the government authorities. The first foreigners had passed through Bena in 1935 and now here we were, little more than a decade later!

We landed on a small grass airstrip at about 5000 feet (about 1500 metres) above sea level. The moment we emerged from the plane we were surrounded by staring men and women dressed in traditional bark dress with shell and bead ornamentation, their bodies liberally covered with rancid pig grease. These people were shorter and more muscular than the Papuans we had known and had had much less contact with foreigners. The many tribal groups in the Highlands each had their own languages and territory that would be defended at all costs in the frequent fighting that broke out.

Across each man's forehead was a band of brilliant, iridescent-green Christmas-beetle wings. Some of the men had colourful feathers in their hair and almost every one carried his bow and arrows at the ready. They were not pointed at us but were strung anyway, ready for instant use. Others held stone axes made with a short handle and the blade fixed in it crossways, something like an adze. A length of cane coiled across each

When God Calls, Expect Adventure

man's chest intrigued me. It was only later I learned its significance.

I thought I would have been immune to the chill of fear. But I failed that day for a few minutes. These men were fierce warriors and everything in their demeanour bore testimony to centuries of tribal warfare.

Each woman had a string bag slung from her forehead. None had ever washed, I guessed from the pungent, overwhelming smell. Cleansing, I learned later, was for them a fresh application of pig's grease. This gave a desirable shine to the skin, and also protected against the cold. The women wore thick grass skirts, covering them from waist to calf muscles. Beyond that they had no covering at all. Many carried digging sticks for the strenuous task of sweet potato cultivation, important both as food for humans and the many pigs found in each village. The string billum bags were dirty because they were workbags, designed to carry heavy loads of sweet potato on the woman's back, with the "handle" extended across the woman's forehead.

Laurie and Gwen Howell were building a new mission station, which we had come to visit. It had been decided to shift from the site located high on the Sigoiya hilltop, where Stan Gander had lived before the war. This new station, known as Hogisopa, was much closer to the airstrip, had better garden land and, more importantly, water could be channelled around from a mountain stream some 2 miles (3 kilometres) away. Bena Bena was shaping up as a neat station. Laurie was always a competent planner and builder. Being at such altitude, it had a pleasant climate, rarely hotter than 30 degrees Celsius (85 degrees Fahrenheit).

We were assigned a little plaited bamboo house, comprised of two very small bedrooms and a small "lounge room." The kitchen was a separate building, just off the back veranda, while the toilet was located over a deep hole a short distance from the house. Adjacent to the toilet, we had a shower room. It, too, was very simple. A 4-gallon (about 15-litre) drum was opened at the top and given a handle, while a tap with a shower head was fitted into the base of the drum. A bucket of warm water was pulled up by rope, then the tap turned on to allow the water to flow. A few timbers on the ground allowed us to keep our feet clean as we showered.

It was simple—but we were quite happy. We had no furniture so the small rooms were no problem. What we did have was one of the grandest views one could imagine. We looked across the Bena River valley to the mighty Mt Michael standing proudly to our south. An American visitor once said, "This is a million-dollar view." He was right.

Laurie had been a qualified engineer before becoming a missionary, so I enjoyed working with him and learning a lot. When we arrived the water race for the hydro-electric system was nearing completion, and Laurie was in the process of assembling the pelton wheel and installing the lengths of 6-inch (15-centimetre) pipe, which were to make the pressure pipe. I worked on installing the electric wiring for the mission station. Laurie and I had a great working relationship. At the same time Freda and Gwen also worked well together. Only a matter of weeks later, Bena Bena became the first Highland station to be blessed with 24-hour electric lighting.

No church building had yet been erected, so all services were conducted under a large clump of bamboo near the boys' dormitory. The speaker stood under the bamboo, while people crowded around. The women with their babies sitting on the ground, while the men sat or stood in the outer circle. Apart from the students, they all wore traditional clothing. They were remarkable worship services to participate in.

SALT, WATER AND TITHE

"'Bring the whole tithe into the storehouse, that there may be food in my house. Test me in this,' says the Lord Almighty, 'and see if I will not throw open the floodgates of heaven and pour out so much blessing that there will not be room enough to store it.'" (Malachi 3:10).

Not long after arriving in Bena Bena, Freda and I planned to spend a weekend with the members of the church at Kafagamari village. To get there required a long walk on the Thursday. At the village the following day, we set up camp in the "Haus Kiap" or Patrol Officer's Rest House. These were usually one-room grass houses with a dirt floor used by the government patrol officers, whose job it was to begin enforcing Western laws in the Highlands.

Next we went to visit the village people in their houses. Like all houses in the Highlands at the time, each house was a small round building with an opening so small we had to almost crawl on hands and knees to get in. There was no other opening, and the small fire in the centre never intentionally went out. In many parts of the Highlands, husbands and wives lived in separate houses, and the boys stayed with their mothers until they were recognised as men. Indeed, men often feared women, viewing them as potentially dangerous and a threat to their masculine "forces."

It was lovely to meet with the people, and they did their best to make us welcome and as comfortable as they were able. We had some great meetings with them on Friday and Sabbath morning.

On Friday afternoon, we went out to see one of the interests in this area: making salt. Not far away was a small spring of water that bubbled to the surface. The water was warm and bitter, brackish to the taste. The village people took dried strips from the trunk of a banana tree and rubbed this into the saturated ground surrounding the spring, the idea being to collect as much as possible of the saltiness into the banana tree strips. When each strip of banana was saturated, it was taken home and left to dry in the sun. When all were dry, they were burnt.

Water was then drained through the ashes to leach out the salt. This water was evaporated over a slow fire until a cake of impure salt remained. That cake of salt was so valuable it was decorated and paraded for weeks around the district to demonstrate the wealth of the owner. Only after everyone was suitably impressed was it in order to taste the salt. Here, far away from the sea, salt was incredibly rare and the people went to great lengths to acquire the precious substance.

Is it any wonder that the Bible texts such as "Ye are the salt of the earth" came to mind?

By Sabbath morning, Lyn had diarrhoea. Freda checked Lyn's food and anything else that might be "off" but all seemed OK. I wanted to know more about the water that was brought for our use.

"Is the water coming from a clean place?" I asked.

"Oh, yes," I was assured. "We have built a fence all around the place for getting water so that pigs and children can't get into it. It's good water."

But something was causing our problems, so I went to have a look at the "place for getting water."

Proudly the village men took me to see. They pointed to the shallow hole scooped in the ground around which they had built a new pitpit fence that even reached over the hole. The hole was maybe 2 feet (60 centimetres) wide by about 6 inches (15 centimetres) deep. They were quite right, the pigs and children could not get directly at the water.

However, one glance showed that the hole was located at the lower end of a marshy slope, where water oozed out and seeped or dribbled across the ground toward the "place for getting water." Pigs were rooting and people roaming all over the marshy land above, and it was from that area that the water was collected.

Because there was no other source for drinking water, we were forced to go home that Sabbath afternoon. The experience taught us to be careful where water was coming from.

When God Calls, Expect Adventure

Early in 1950, the Howells went home on six months' furlough. By the time they left, we understood the running of the station. One of the questions I asked Laurie had to do with tithe. In the smaller stations where we had served up until this time, we had always personally purchased one-tenth of the garden produce. We would either use the food ourselves or distribute it in some welfare work. In that way, the "tithe" from the gardens was turned into money that could be reported.

I asked Laurie what arrangements applied for the tithe of the Bena station. He looked at me with some surprise as he commented. "But the whole garden is the Lord's. One only pays tithe on personal increase, not on that which is the Lord's anyway." He stopped for a moment before adding, "You could never do it here. If you tried to pay tithe on the Bena mission gardens it would cost you more than the whole year's budget. Where would you get money then to buy the soap and salt and clothes for the students? How would you get fuel for the jeep? How could you pay for the station maintenance?"

I had no answer, other than to say, "Well, it is your station. We're only relieving you, so I guess I'll do things your way while you're on furlough."

At that time, the gardens were producing well. I remember weighing a couple of the largest sweet potatoes to come from the Bena mission gardens. One of them weighed 28 pounds (13 kilograms), while the other weighed 32 pounds (almost 15 kilograms). I had never seen sweet potato as large as these. And they were quite sweet, despite their large size.

Within a few weeks, it was obvious we had entered a time of drought. With no rain, the gardens were not producing at all, which meant the food for the students dried up. Soon we were forced to send most of the male students home. The girls were not sent back to the village because, had we sent the girls, it is unlikely they would have been permitted to return. To obtain sufficient food for the staff and for the few essential students, we asked Pastor Masive to take a couple of boys with him each day and try to buy food from the village people. Some days he managed well, other days not so well. The village people were suffering from the drought as greatly as was the mission.

Salt, Water and Tithe

Then one day Masive returned with a wheat bag full of *kaukau* (sweet potato).

"Where did you get that from?" I shouted.

"Wait, there is another one to get. Then I'll tell you."

An hour or two later he returned with a second bag just as full, as I anxiously waited for the news.

"We went down to the village between the airstrip and the small river and asked if they had any food for sale," Pastor Masive explained. "Most of the people had problems themselves. But they told me to see a man named Solo. They said he had plenty. In fact, they were buying their kaukau from him, too."

"I found Solo in his garden and he agreed to sell some kaukau to us. While he was digging I noticed sticks standing at the end of some rows in his garden, so I asked him, 'What are those sticks for?'"

"He replied, 'I don't really know. You see, one day I went to church up at the mission and the Pastor Howell talked about the *ten-ten* [tithe]. He said that the 'ten-ten' wasn't ours, that we couldn't eat it. It belonged to God. So I came home and marked every 10th row with a stick.'"

On patrol with a group of native porters going from Bena Bena to Katagamari village.

When God Calls, Expect Adventure

Pastor Masive continued with his story. "So I asked Solo, 'Well, what will you do with the food in those rows?' He shrugged his shoulders. He said, 'I don't know. The speaker said I was not to eat it. Do you know what I can do with it?'"

I certainly did! For many weeks, the mission was fed by the only man in the district who practised tithing—and he didn't even understand fully what he was doing. That was a lesson I will never forget.

POISONOUS MUSHROOMS AND DEADLY CROSSINGS

"I call on you, O God, for you will answer me; turn your ear to me and hear my prayer. Show me the wonders of your great love, you who save by your right hand those who take refuge in you from their foes" (Psalm 17:6, 7).

No timber yards existed anywhere and we had a complete station to build—houses for students and staff, a workshop, a church, a school, dispensary, mission house and more. We employed several teams of men from Chimbu to obtain timber. Their task was to pit-saw pine trees purchased from the village people, turning the pine trees into various sizes of sawn timber. The pit-sawing was done out in the areas where the trees had been growing. First they were felled, then milled by hand. The large slabs of freshly cut timber would then be carried back to the mission.

One day there was a heavy storm. It was midafternoon when we saw a man from the saw-milling team come running madly back to the mission station, waving his arms and shouting urgently. It was clear from the way he was acting that he was the bearer of important news.

While catching his breath, he told how most of the other men on the saw-milling team were desperately ill. He explained that the cook

When God Calls, Expect Adventure

for the day had been searching for greens to add to their meal when he saw a lovely stand of mushrooms growing among the trees. Delighted with his find, the cook had picked them and added the tasty-looking mushrooms to the soup. The messenger had tasted a little and refused to eat more. Even that taste had made him feel unwell.

This was worrying news and we could see that our informant was showing signs of serious food poisoning. His body was shivering, his muscles twitched uncontrollably. He was becoming delirious and needed immediate treatment. The station's medical man, Oma, and a few of the older students were sent immediately to bring the sick men back to us.

Soon we saw the whole group of men running madly back from the bush to the mission. They were yelling and hollering as they came. The sickest men were being carried on the backs of Oma and the students. It was soon established that the mushrooms were of a variety well known to the local village people as being so poisonous they could kill. It was a cruel death, too, and now these men were succumbing to the effects of the deadly brew.

"Lord, we need Your help this time," I whispered.

"Line the men up in the workshop," I ordered. "Quickly."

Each of the men was given a shot of atropine and Freda quickly prepared a bucketful of an emetic solution. I raced off to the dispensary to collect the stomach pump, a long rubber hose with a smooth rounded tip at one end and a funnel at the other end.

The men squatted in a row in the workshop as we worked quickly. As I pushed the smooth end of the tube down the throat of one man, Freda would pour about a litre of emetic solution out of the bucket and into the funnel. Then I would withdraw the tube and we would move to the next man.

We had to move as quickly as possible and on down the line we went. Following right behind was Oma, our station medico, who would tickle the throat. The men would then vomit up the mixture of emetic solution and poisonous mushroom, gagging and coughing as they did so.

We worked three or four times down the line, repeating the process until we were certain we had removed all the poisonous material in each person's stomach. Many staggered out of the shed or were helped out

Poisonous Mushrooms and Deadly Crossings

by others to their beds, and some were ill for days, but thank the Lord, none died. One of the men was so affected that he was tearing down walls and threatening the lives of his friends. He had to be tied up so he would not harm himself. After a week, they were able to return to work.

It was enjoyably embarrassing to have the sick ones come up and hug our legs as an expression of gratitude when they knew they would live. That was the kind of reward we received from time to time, which made mission service so gratifying. It also afforded an ideal opportunity to point them to God who was to be thanked in this case.

Freda wrote a letter to her mother soon after and this is what she said:

In the morning when Lester went down they were alright—not well enough to get about, but OK. One told Lester how in the night he had had a dream. He went up to heaven but when he got there, they wouldn't take him in. They said he had been eating the wrong things, so he was sent back to another place. People were trying to put his head in a fire all the time. The other men in the room said he was asking for a drink of water all the night. Lester, of course, took the opportunity to talk to them. They were not mission men, just men who had come to work for pay. They seldom bother to come to worship. Well they all turned up on Sabbath. I don't know if it will have any lasting effect or not, but they were most profuse in their thanks.

There was a lesson in such events, too. There are many things we may choose in life that taste or feel good initially—but they are toxic. With prayer and help, they can be removed with difficulty. How wonderful it will be to hug the Saviour's legs and thank Him for saving us. We feel deep gratitude to the Lord that none died, which some certainly would have without treatment.

It had been quite some time since a mission patrol had visited the villages south of the Kauma River, so we arranged for Pastor Taula to lead a small group of students in visiting the villages and churches in that district. The group left Bena Bena on Thursday, planning to spend the Sabbath with missionary Loris in the Kauma village. But to get to the village they first had to cross the Kauma River.

When God Calls, Expect Adventure

On Friday evening we, back at Bena Bena, were meeting in the church to open Sabbath when a number of the students stood up to get a better look down the road. We saw Taula and the students running. They burst in and related a terrible story.

They told how they were crossing the Kauma River. Like many of the Highland rivers, it flowed fast and dangerously. Determined to carry on, some had managed to make it to the other side, with the help of the two coastal men who were accustomed to water. Then, one of our most godly students tried to cross using the same route as the coastal men. Apaiva's feet were washed from under him by the rushing torrent and he was swept into the vortex of a whirlpool.

Apaiva thrashed his way to the top once and waved frantically. Then the swirling vortex took him down again and he was sucked beneath the surface of the river. Apaiva disappeared from sight for the last time. The distressed students and mission staff searched downstream for hours, hoping he had somehow resurfaced safely, out of sight. Their efforts were futile. The young man could not be found.

We were shocked and heartbroken. *Why would the Lord allow this to happen?* I asked myself. *Why Apaiva?* We worshipped God, cried out to Him, and consoled ourselves with the observation that of all the students on the station Apaiva was perhaps the one most ready to meet his Lord. No-one had been more faithful than he. All we could do that evening was to trust his case to our Lord, who keeps accurate records and will reward His servants according to their faithfulness.

I believe Apaiva was living as close to the Lord as one with his level of knowledge could live and I expect to meet him again in God's kingdom. All of us must meet our Maker, Apaiva had just gone sooner.

We still had to make that patrol and I felt it my duty to go with them the next time, though I did not relish the thought of crossing that river. I'm sure none of the others did either.

When at last I stood on the bank of the Kauma, I watched as others crossed. The Highland students who could not swim crossed upstream where the shallower water still raged over river stones as a frightening rapid. Each student was taken in hand by either Taula or Loris, both of whom could swim. They entered the water and ran with the current, making their way toward the farther side. Next I watched Loris hoist

Poisonous Mushrooms and Deadly Crossings

our small generating plant onto his shoulder and run with it through the rushing chest-high water until he made it to the far side. I fail to understand how he kept his balance on those slippery rocks.

Because I could swim, I chose to swim across where the water was not so rough, just above the whirlpools. I entered that water with a cold fear gripping my heart. About two-thirds of the way across, one of the whirlpools began to draw me toward its gaping mouth. I began to panic. Thank God one of the students was near. He broke off a long length of pitpit—a wild cane similar to sugarcane—and pushed it out to me. I just managed to grasp it as the vortex was pulling me sideways. How I praise God for that deliverance!

Hardly had I scrambled to the safety of the bank, when I heard panic-filled voices and shouting. Looking back, I saw two of our students with absolute terror etched into their faces. They were being swept toward us by the river current. They grabbed at a jutting bank but were unable to hold on, the current being so powerful it tore their hands away. The last possible safe point was just below me, where their hands just managed to get a hold of the bank. Quickly our hands grasped theirs and we pulled them ashore.

Thank the Lord—we were at the exact place at the exact time and able to reach them.

During that patrol, we crossed many more rivers, most of them were far too wild to be forded in that manner. Instead, the village people had erected ingenious Lawyer-cane swing bridges, some spanning cliffs more than 50 feet (15 metres) above the water. Those flimsy bridges swayed frighteningly. Each bridge had been designed for one person to cross at a time and to me it felt that they might break, sending me crashing below at any moment.

The people of these villages had never seen pictures on a screen. We brought the small generator with us because we planned to show pictures. The problem was the generating plant was a small 12-volt generator, carried on a pole between the shoulders of two students. This meant that two people and the engine had to cross each bridge together.

Our hearts were in our mouths many times as we watched our students carefully place one foot after the other on the Lawyer cane that had to carry all that weight. One broken cane and they would drop to

When God Calls, Expect Adventure

certain death—but every bridge held!

We trekked as far as the slopes of Mt Michael, a mighty mountain that towers to a height of 13,000 feet (about 4000 metres). Sarif, the local missionary to the Mt Michael people, took me to see the men's house. This is the house in which all the men slept, including the married men. No woman was to set foot inside!

The house was protected by a stout, 5-foot (1.5-metre) high fence of sharply pointed stakes intended as protection against enemy raids. The building was long, its grass roof blackened inside by years of smoky fires. Each man slept in his own little section, his wooden fighting shield served as his bed, his bow and arrows laid carefully beside him. He used a small block of wood for a pillow.

Maybe half a dozen small fires were lined up and down the centre of the room. Tucked into the ceiling here and there were each man's valuables. There were shells to be worn on his chest, dried bodies of colourful Birds of Paradise and other items of ceremonial dress. Many of these special items were wrapped in bark to keep them untainted by the constant smoke that pervaded the room at all times.

I had noticed that many of the men of the Bena Bena district carried a length of curled cane across their chests. One day, back in Bena I was talking to a young man who wore this interesting piece of cane. He offered to show me how it was used.

I had known that only a young man who had reached manhood and had demonstrated the ability to swallow the cane was permitted to wear it, so I was interested to see how the swallowing was performed. But more amazing was that he would allow Freda to witness the swallowing. We were told that until this time no woman in Bena Bena had ever been allowed to see how it was done.

To make sure no other woman could inadvertently witness the ceremony, he led us a long way off into the tall grass where he found just the right spot. The grass was taller than our heads, and no hill or tree was within sight from which someone might be able to see. Our privacy was absolute.

First the young man drank some water—to lubricate his throat, I

Poisonous Mushrooms and Deadly Crossings

guessed. Next he carefully inspected the length of cane to make sure there were no rough points that might tear inside his throat.

The cane itself was a length of natural Lawyer cane about the width of a thick pencil and several feet long. It had been bent in the middle in a u-shape, perhaps using heat, so both sections lay parallel and close together. The cut ends of the cane had been curled into two circles.

Then the young man tilted his chin upwards, lifted the cane and slowly forced the smooth, bent u-section into his mouth. He pushed it down his throat carefully until only the curled ends protruded out of the corners of his mouth. They looked like huge down-turned fangs or tusks. He held this pose for maybe a minute or so, then withdrew the cane and spat into the grass beside him.

Bena Bena district man in the act of swallowing cane. This was a rite of passage to manhood and secret men's business.

When God Calls, Expect Adventure

So we had seen it done. But this much is certain: I had no desire to demonstrate my manhood by doing as he had done. It looked like risky business and uncomfortable indeed!

CHURCH DEDICATION

"I do not hide your righteousness in my heart; I speak of your faithfulness and your saving help. I do not conceal your love and your faithfulness from the great assembly" (Psalm 40:10).

A new church had been built in the Korafeigu village and its members invited me to go out on a certain Sabbath to dedicate it. It was only a small church, maybe only about 25 feet (8 metres) in length, by less than 13 feet (4 metres) wide. It had strong, plaited pitpit walls and a thick grass roof. Right behind the speaker, it had a single window, so small only a small child could have crawled through it. The seats were split logs set on low stumps on the dirt floor.

A church dedication constituted an auspicious day. Visitors came from far and near. Only one or two villagers had ever had the privilege of attending a dedication and such an important ceremony required one's best attire. Because there were only very few who claimed to be Christian among the crowd, most of the faces were painted in the brightest colours they could lay hands on.

Others wore either the feathers or the bodies of the gorgeous Bird of Paradise in their hair, or they sported rows of the beautiful green Christmas beetle wings across their foreheads. Each man—and many of the women—wore the best available to them. Each lathered his or her body with pig grease until it ran in small rivulets down their bodies. The same grease dripped from hair that had never been washed. All this was to honour the occasion and indirectly to honour the chief speaker—me.

As many people as could possibly do so crushed into the small church building. Then the local missionary and I tried to force our way through them to the pulpit at the far end of the church. A further group

When God Calls, Expect Adventure

of dignitaries followed us in. I never believed so many people could cram into such a small space.

It was a hot day, but still people tried to squeeze in tighter so they could see what was happening. There was not even space between the pulpit and the front row of people, who were the most important men loaded with the most rancid grease. They sat there with a look of importance and dignity for they were the "Big Men"—the great warriors, village leaders and orators of their area.

The doorway was completely blocked by people trying to look in, allowing no fresh air to circulate. As the air became thicker and the body heat rose, the smell of pig grease and unwashed bodies became more and more volatile until finally my stomach began to heave menacingly. There was no way I could reach the door, and there was nowhere I could turn if my stomach contents decided to leave me.

I knew it had to happen soon, so I pushed my head out the small window and took in several long breaths of fresh air. I was so thankful it was big enough for my head to get through. That revived me long enough to say one or two sentences. After another breath of fresh air from the window, I could manage another sentence—maybe two—before pushing my head out again for another desperate lungful of sweet air.

I must have looked ridiculous. My stomach was heaving, my head out the widow every minute or so, sucking in huge breaths of fresh air and popping back in for the next statement. Fortunately, I had an interpreter, so I breathed while he spoke. In that manner, we completed the worship service.

The sermon was possibly shorter than others I have taken in other places, but I feel sure the Lord understood and accepted that I had done the best I could under the circumstances. I hardly dare to think what the local people thought, but I hope they were not offended.

Many schemes were introduced to the Bena mission students in an effort to lift their understanding and improve their health. Traditionally, running noses were cleaned by removing the dribble with the fingers and wiping it down the leg. So Gwen Howell and Freda introduced

Church Dedication

handkerchief drill in morning line-up. It must seem odd that students would be asked to line up each day, show their handkerchiefs and be made to practise using them, but we thought this was a good thing to teach. Respiratory infections are common in the moist Highlands and many children perished due to conditions like pneumonia.

Freda and Gwen taught girls simple dressmaking techniques and even some fancy work to make the dresses more attractive. For a girl to wear Western dress was a source of great pride. We were interested in setting new standards of modesty and the girls were eager to learn these new skills. This was 1949, but when we returned in 1990 one of those "girls" came to meet us proudly wearing one of the dresses she had made 40 years earlier and only worn on very special occasions.

Clothing for the boys was not so easy to make. But the mission offered small payments for tasks performed and that money slowly collected until the student was able to purchase clothing.

I have often wondered if we missionaries served the people well when encouraging them to dress as we did, according to our notions of modesty and proper behaviour. It must have been difficult for our students as they navigated two worlds: their tribal culture and values, and the Western values and culture we were teaching.

We certainly encouraged prudent spending and honesty. Many of the students at the time were really men, some even married men, including a man by the name of Apaia. He had accumulated a small amount of money, and he came to me asking if he could buy an axe and a bush knife. I knew his wife needed clothing and that he also had some needs.

Apaia already had a knife and an axe, and I felt the money would be better spent on clothes. He insisted that he wanted to buy an axe and a knife. I sensed that there was some hidden reason he had not given me. So I told him he had to explain why he wanted to spend his money on items he didn't need. Finally, he explained.

During the war, he had been drafted to work for the government in Goroka, the main town in the Eastern Highlands Province. The group of draftees would be sent out to do certain tasks and would be issued with the appropriate tools, which were to be returned at the close of work each day. He noticed that some of the men would "lose" their axe or

When God Calls, Expect Adventure

spade during the day. In the evening they would get a dressing down for being so careless, but when allowed to go home they suddenly "found' the tool and took it home with them.

Apaia tried the same scheme and had managed to take an axe and a bush knife home. He then explained that since he had come to the mission, he could understand that what he had done was stealing, so he wanted to make things right with the government. I felt proud of him as he told me this. Clearly the Holy Spirit was moving on his heart. He purchased his axe and knife, and took with him a note I had written to the District Officer explaining the reason Apaia was returning the tools.

I proudly awaited his return, keen to know what had happened. But the District Officer looked at the note, then simply said, "OK, put them down there"—and turned to other business.

There was no thanks for Apaia or any commendation. Not even recognition that Apaia had done something the government wished to see developed in the local people. Nothing! I felt the officer had failed miserably.

People like him, I concluded, should remain home. His kind are not likely to assist in the development of a new nation.

BILL PASLOW

"Do not withhold good from those to whom it is due, when it is in your power to act. Do not say to your neighbour, 'Come back tomorrow and I'll give it to you'—when you already have it with you" (Proverbs 3:27, 28).

Bill Paslow was not only an excellent pilot, he was quite a friend to us and helped us often, even at great personal risk and inconvenience. As the boss of his own air-charter company, he established a small round of stations that he serviced in his Dragon Rapide.

Even for the best pilots, the Highlands are notoriously tricky, with high mountain passes, fickle winds and weather that can change almost instantly. Some of the steep high-altitude airstrips are the stuff of aviation legend and a single mistake can be fatal. And planes as small as Bill's did not carry radios or any safety gear.

Every Wednesday, Bill buzzed us to announce his arrival and we would hasten down to meet him at the airstrip. There we collected butter and a few other items we had requested he bring. Because our Highland gardens were able to grow items not available on the coast, we usually had a box of garden produce ready—vegetables, passionfruit, lettuce and delicious red strawberries, when available. Before the church operated its own mission planes, his service was a vital link to the outside world.

The time came when Freda needed to go to Madang for the birth of our second child. We arranged with Bill to collect her on a certain day. Freda took with her one of the students, a Highland girl. The plane had been airborne only a few minutes when Bill shouted, "There will be a bit of cloud about, but don't worry. We'll be right."

The normal route to Madang was to climb as fast as possible as you crossed the Bena Valley toward the range of mountains that bordered the valley on the Madang side and a narrow gap known as the Bena Gap. This was a twisty, double gash in the range with a prominent peak in its centre. Most small planes used the gap, avoiding the need

When God Calls, Expect Adventure

to climb above the range, which was difficult flying even on the best of days.

As Bill headed toward the gap that day, he saw it was stuffed tight with cloud. This presented no problem to an experienced pilot like Bill, who simply took his bearings and noted his exact time. He knew the compass readings and the times for each shift in direction. Clouds meant no more to him than that he would be able to see nothing of the hills either side of the plane. After various twists, they emerged from the gap only to discover the whole north side of the range also under a total blanket of cloud. They could not go back because the entrance to the gap was no longer visible. He could only go on in the direction of Madang.

Bill continued to fly by compass bearing. By keeping time and comparing it to his speed, he calculated he had passed over Madang and was flying in open sky, somewhere above the coast. Still, there was no break in the cloud. He continued farther out to sea until he knew there were no mountains to watch for and slowly spiralled down to sea level, where finally he broke free of cloud.

The Highland girl who had accompanied Freda had never seen the ocean, so she stared at it for a time, wide-eyed, then shouted above the din, "That must have been a big fire to burn that much ground!"

Bill had turned toward the land. Skimming along the coast, he recognised some plantations and headed over the trees to land nonchalantly at Madang airport. For him, it was just another day of flying. For us, it was the act of a brave and generous man who was often prepared to risk his life.

Freda wrote and posted a number of letters to me while she was in Madang, but the only letter I received was the one she handed personally to Bill. He came roaring in with his hand out the window to show me the letter. The plane was so low that there was just enough time for me see what he was holding before I felt like I had to duck the plane's wheels. Without landing he swung round again, this time dropping the letter. After returning a third time to be sure I had received the letter safely, Bill roared off down the valley.

A month later I was in Madang. By this time, the Department of Civil Aviation (DCA) had been introduced to Papua New Guinea and were

Bill Paslow

trying to establish their authority. In doing so, they introduced rules associated with flying and the operation of aircraft, similar to those in more developed parts of the world.

Bill flew in late one evening. He was accosted by a DCA official who demanded, "What's the idea of coming in after dark?"

Bill simply brushed past the official with the comment, "What do you expect me to do? Stay up there all night?"

Sadly, Bill did lose his life on another occasion while he was trying to help the Adventist church. He had reluctantly accepted extra cargo, beyond the recommended limit. While trying to gain altitude at the head of the valley near Togoba, he crashed into the mountainside. The passengers survived, although Pastor Stan Gander almost lost his arm. Some said that Bill took the brunt of the crash.

While flying was—and still is—the quickest method of negotiating the Highlands of Papua New Guinea, driving was necessary, too. In 1949, there were no graded roads, few bridges and few vehicles capable

Clearing a landslide from the Highland Highway (1953) with Syd Stocken. Note the Willis jeeps in the background.

When God Calls, Expect Adventure

of handling the rugged terrain. Only World War II Willis Jeeps could really cope and we relied heavily on these.

Driving was a challenge! Independent studies showed that a jeep, even with its low range of gears, required a driver to make an average of 160 gear changes every hour. Much of the time it was essential to have mud chains on all four wheels otherwise it was impossible to navigate the heavy, cloying mud that instantly clogged up the tread. Because of the rocky, unmade roads we had to negotiate, chains frequently broke, ripping out the hydraulic brake lines on roads where a single slip would send the vehicle careering off a mountainside to certain destruction. We discovered that it was safer not to have brakes because when we knew we had none we drove cautiously, using the engine as a brake.

F D NICHOL

"The lookout reported, 'He has reached them, but he isn't coming back either. The driving is like that Jehu son of Nimshi—he drives like a maniac'" (2 Kings 9:20).

Word came through that we were to receive some important visitors toward the end of 1949. Certain Australian church officers were bringing Pastor F D Nichol from the General Conference of Seventh-day Adventists in the United States. Our part of his itinerary was small. All we had to do was collect him from one of Bill Paslow's biplanes at about 3 pm on a given day and put him on another plane at 6.30 the next morning.

We waited and waited. About 4.30 pm, a plane landed on the mission's airstrip but had brought no passengers.

"I arrived at Kainantu late," the pilot informed us with a shrug of his shoulders. "But my passengers weren't there."

"What happened to them?" I asked.

"They must have gotten impatient. They're coming by jeep!"

"Jeep," I exclaimed incredulously. "Do they have any idea how bad that track is?"

"Probably not," the pilot replied. "I found them a few miles up the track, headed in this direction and buzzed them. I reckon they're in for a hard time. That track hasn't been used since the war."

The pilot was right. There had been no vehicles on that track for years, most of the bridges were down and the road was considered by most of us to be impassable. Why such a high-ranking church official on a tight itinerary would want to even try it was a mystery to me. I had been along several miles of it from our end and, if the other end was anything like this end, it was plain they had a hard time ahead of them.

As the pilot lifted off and continued on his way, I filled a couple of drums with fuel, put a spare battery in the jeep and set out with Pirinavi to meet them. I was worried for the men in the jeeps.

It was almost dark when we reached an area known as Dirty Water.

When God Calls, Expect Adventure

Calling several of the village men over, we asked them, "Has any message come through of a couple of jeeps coming through from Kainantu?"

"No," they answered. "We haven't heard any such message."

"Friend, would you find out for us please."

One of the men ran to the top of a small hill nearby and, with hands cupped around his mouth, called out with all his volume, almost in a yodel. Each short phrase ended with a long "O-o-o-o-o-o" sound. Someone a mile or more distant repeating the message followed his call. All over the hills we heard others shouting in a similar manner, until the message became fainter and fainter. About five minutes had passed when a message returned, relayed by several Highland men over many miles. This was the bush telegraph at its best and it was amazing how fast a message could carry by this method.

One of the men beside us listened intently to the reply, then turned and said, "They have not reached Hengenofi yet."

"Hengenofi," I exclaimed. "That is at least 15 miles [almost 25 kilometres] away."

Pirinavi and I decided not to go any further. If the visitors had not reached Hengenofi, they had probably been forced to turn back. We also turned back toward home, but each time we came to a deep washout across the road, Pirinavi would jump out and plant a branch from a tree in the washout as a warning to any vehicle following.

Eventually we reached home and gratefully went to sleep. It was about midnight when we heard a jeep horn outside our house. Much to our surprise, the first jeep had arrived and aboard were just two men, Orm Speck and Herb White.

Pastor White called out, "The other jeep has broken down a few miles back, so we came to see if you could go and give them help."

A few minutes later, blinking tiredly, I was on the way. Near the airstrip, I passed several of the visitors walking up the hill in the darkness. I told them I'd collect them on my return. Finally I came to the last man. It was Lou Grieve still tidying up the disabled jeep. Its battery had failed so I passed over the spare I had brought, and left him to install it and follow when ready.

Turning for home, I first picked up our special guest, a weary Pastor Nichol. In the beams of our headlights we picked out Willie Pascoe, who at the time was the treasurer for the church in Australia. Later he became a treasurer at the General Conference, but at this moment he was wearing a dark suit with his trousers rolled up above his knees.

It was a dark night and the glare from the headlights highlighted Willie Pascoe's thin, white legs as he strode with determination up the hill. They stood out like fluorescent matchsticks. Pastor Nichol grabbed my shoulder in sham panic, "Brother," he said with delight. "I never realised the Australasian finances were on such unstable foundations. It frightens me!"

One by one we picked the men up, including Pastor Fred Mote and his son. We arrived soon after at the station and Lou rolled in on the repaired jeep a little later. Despite the lateness of the hour, it was time to hear their story.

Fearing the plane might not be coming, the adventurous group had departed in two jeeps for Bena Bena. All had gone well until they came to the innocent-looking Avani Creek. Because of the rain all passengers had piled into the jeep that had a hood, hoping to keep dry, while all the baggage had been piled in the back of the other jeep and covered with canvas. The jeep with the passengers made it across Avani Creek, but as Lou Grieve nosed his jeep into the creek he hit a deep spot and the engine stalled. Immediately the current began washing the gravel and sand from under the front wheels, causing the jeep to slowly sink further.

Pastor Nichol saw the case containing all his precious notes slowly heading into the water and exclaimed, "There goes all my brains." A crowd of village people who came to look soon plunged in, and dragged the jeep and its luggage out of the creek to the far side.

Pastor Nichol studied the dripping jeep and said, "They'll never get that engine going again tonight." Then he watched in amazement as the men drained the sump to let the water out and took much of the electric wiring out to dry over a fire before replacing it.

"I take my hat off to those missionaries," Pastor Nichols said to me. "That engine started the moment they swung it over!"

An hour or so further along the road, the brakes on one of the jeeps failed. When they came to the top of the next steep descent, both drivers stopped to plan a strategy. The jeep with the brakes and

When God Calls, Expect Adventure

passengers would lead the way, while the jeep without brakes would nudge up to its rear bumper. Both would rely on the brakes of the one in front!

The plan unravelled when the two jeeps began to bend in the middle. One headed for the cliff edge, the other for a deep gutter. There was no alternative but for the first jeep to let its brakes go and try to keep out of the way of the brakeless jeep coming behind them.

It was a crazy race as both vehicles careered to the bottom! No wonder the men were quite happy to walk when their jeep could go no further. Pastor Nichols described the road as being "made of black Vaseline." He said he wouldn't have missed it for $50, but he wouldn't have done it again for $500!

The two jeeps carried on into the night. Orm Speck was driving the first of the two jeeps, the one in which the visitors were seated. He had learned by the same bush telegraph we used that we had come out to assist them, so when he saw the first bit of bush standing up in the road he guessed it was a danger marker and that there must be a doubtful bridge ahead.

Not knowing that we were warning him of a deep washout, he decided the most certain method of getting across a questionable bridge was to do so with sufficient speed to make sure the bridge would not collapse before he was across.

They hit that washout at all the speed they could muster. The jeep jumped into the air like a frog that had received an electric shock and crashed down. When the jeep landed again, they stopped and inspected it for broken parts. Amazingly, nothing was broken.

It had taken them about 15 hours to make a 50-mile (80-kilometre) trip! It was 3 am before they got into bed, and they had to be up by 6 am to catch the plane. It was the shortest visit ever from such a senior church leader.

THE FIRST CAMP MEETING

"Not giving up meeting together, as some are in the habit of doing, but encouraging one another—and all the more as you see the day approaching" (Hebrews 10:25).

For quite some time it had been Laurie Howell's plan to build a church using permanent materials on the Bena Bena mission station. However, before he had time to put this plan into action the officers at mission headquarters sent word of a plan to hold a Papua New Guinea-wide camp meeting at Bena Bena for all who were able to attend. Camp was to be held in June 1950. This left insufficient time to saw timber and erect a permanent building. We had to work hard even to erect a temporary structure in the time available.

Most of the national people who came to camp were from local areas, of course. But the European missionaries from a much wider area were able to get together. Among these were some who had spent so much of their time in isolation that gathering at a camp meeting was a rare privilege and a real joy.

Camp meetings were by necessity short, especially as there were 24 local camps each year. People did not have enough money to buy food, or strength to carry vegetables, sweet potatoes or yams, plus children and personal possessions, sometimes through enemy territory. For some of them, coming to a camp meeting was the first time they had ever left their tribal territory. A huge highlight for the local people, most camp meetings were a long weekend and would be attended by 400 people at most. Shelter had to be built for all attendees.

During the Bena Bena camp, an infant dedication was conducted by Pastor J D Anderson. He had spent many years in the Solomon Islands as a missionary and at this time Robert Boehm, Gordon Stafford,

When God Calls, Expect Adventure

Leanne French, Kaye Barnard and our son Kenneth were all dedicated to the Lord. The children were publicly prayed over and as parents we solemnly promised to bring them up knowing the Lord.

It is interesting to look back and see that all those young people were later active in the service of the Lord. As one example, years later Ken and Kaye were married and returned as missionaries to New Guinea for more than 10 years.

The people in the Bena area also enjoyed gatherings and ceremonies. However, cultural beliefs demanded very different practices. Traditionally the parents always arranged marriages in Bena Bena. It was the normal practice for the girl's parents to select a suitable young man, but according to them he must come from a village that was potentially an enemy, or at least was not closely blood-tied to themselves.

Once the arrangements had been concluded and bride price negotiated, the girl was not permitted to so much as look toward the village of the young man. If the two villages were close to one another, she could not go to the side of her village that faced his. And the same applied to the young man, though the rules were not quite as tight for the man who by now was busy asking his relatives for assistance in acquiring enough pigs and shell money to compensate the family of the girl for the bride-price.

Should the girl be found going in the direction of the village of her intended, any man was obligated to shoot her in the thigh using a four-pronged arrow that every man carried at all times. There was no intention to kill her or even to maim her permanently. It was simply a punishment, a warning. Premarital sex for a girl was absolutely illegal. However, no-one ever told me of any punishment meted out to a young man for a similar offence!

The marriage ceremony consisted of a village feast and dance held in honour of the union. The marriage union was considered complete when the groom publicly ate food the bride had prepared. Later came a part of the ceremony we found hard to accept. The bride would sit on the ground with a group of her friends, her grass skirt parted to expose the outer side of one of her thighs. Her new husband took his bow,

The First Camp Meeting

loaded it with one of the four-pronged arrows and shot the arrow into her flesh. She was expected to accept this without objection, thereby showing she accepted him as the final authority in their union as man and wife.

Childbirth had many taboos connected with it. Men would have nothing to do with such occasions. Every time I asked a man why they were so afraid they gave a simple answer. They didn't want to get the "women's sickness," although no-one could ever describe to me what such a sickness was. Like other men in the Highlands, men were terribly wary of women's blood, especially menstrual blood, which, they thought, could even take the life of a man or inhibit the development of a boy into a strong young man.

As a consequence, one or more of the other village women assisted the woman giving birth, which had to take place outside the village. In most cases a small "nest" was created in long grass and there the birth of the child took place. Maybe this had its origins in recognition that there were fewer medical complications when the birth was away from areas made "dirty" by human actions.

From what we could learn, there were times when the woman had no-one to assist her. Such times must have been very frightening for the woman concerned. Childbirth occurred while the mother was in a squatting position, not the prone position mostly used in our culture at that time.

Sadly, many people who had a European Christian background seemed automatically to hold the belief that everything "heathen" was inherently evil or backward, while anything that originated in a "civilised" country was good and acceptable.

In many situations, the introduction of a so-called civilised practice tended to destroy something traditional that had fine elements in it. This raises the age-old question as to whether it is a missionary's duty to civilise. Or is it his or her duty to simply Christianise?

There is a greater difference here than many comprehend. I have seen many persons come to work as missionaries who spend almost all their time trying unconsciously to "Westernise" their students. Probably every mission board has had to face some newly appointed missionary and explain why certain ideas and practices are not acceptable, for the simple reason that his actions were based on the faulty notion that everything he has done since childhood is naturally the correct, proper and only way to do it.

Maybe we should take more time to see what it is the "heathen" people are doing and why they are doing it. Only after doing so should we speak up or make suggestions for alteration.

I regret the wrong we inflicted on people when we forbade them to dance when they only wanted to express joy that their gardens had produced so bountifully or to celebrate that the fishing had been especially good. Certain missionaries carried in their minds an aversion to "dance" as practiced in their home areas. For these missionaries, anything to which the name "dance" was attached received judgment as immoral. Sometimes this may have been true—but many times it was not.

Some attempts to "civilise" did have merit—at least for me. I am thinking of something Laurie Howell did at Bena Bena. He set up large loudspeakers directed toward the students' quarters and played classical music through them. Sometimes for hours at a time, the strains of *The Nutcracker Suite* floated loudly over the station in an attempt to elevate their appreciation of music. It elevated my mind, but I had a different background. Perhaps some missionaries assumed that "native music" left something to be desired! I certainly felt that way when I first heard it.

At that time, most foreigners held the opinion that the Highlanders had no appreciation whatsoever for music and, for their part, the Highlanders initially found it almost impossible to sing our songs. The kind of singing we would hear from them at a "Sing-Sing" was not at all harmonious to Western ears. As I understand it, their scale was really the ancient five-note scale that has not been heard in Western countries for hundreds of years. Today the Highland people can sing Western hymns as well as anyone, and their ability to harmonise is nothing short of amazing. I often wonder if Laurie Howell's loud speakers had anything to do with that change.

SYMBOLS OF SORROW

"Then young women will dance and be glad, young men and old as well. I will turn their mourning into gladness; I will give them comfort and joy instead of sorrow" (Jeremiah 31:13).

We were at first puzzled to notice that many people had joints of fingers missing. Almost all women had at least some joints missing and a small number had most joints gone. There were even a few who had not one joint of a finger left on either hand. Some younger girls also had several joints missing. The same was to be seen among the men, but I never saw a man with more than three or four joints missing. We discovered it was the sign used to signify grief at the death of some member of the often-extended family and the person could usually list who was represented by each amputation.

One day a man brought his child in for medical attention. Unfortunately, he had waited until the child was at the point of death before deciding to bring the boy in for help. It was too late to do anything to save the child and he died within a few minutes. The father shouted that he was going to cut off his finger. Freda tried to talk him out of it, but he would not listen. Within half an hour, he was back to show that he had cut off a joint of the finger—and Freda bandaged it for him.

To numb the pain, a grieving relative would give the elbow's "funny bone" a sharp whack with a stick, numbing the nerves of that hand. Then the blade of a bush knife was laid across the joint to be amputated. Someone would bring down a heavy stick on the back of the knife and the amputation would be complete.

Perhaps the depth of the sorrow came from the belief that the family member had left them to enter a terrifying spirit world. How much they

When God Calls, Expect Adventure

needed the message of the Bible! How much they needed to know that the Lord could provide comfort and bring joy to their lives.

Other practices disturbed us, too. In the western part of the New Guinea Highlands, we noticed a number of women wearing a leaf on their faces, almost like they had designed a small umbrella or covering for the nose.

We discovered that if a husband believed his wife had been unfaithful to him, he would self-righteously bite her nose completely off! Many of the women who had "lost" their noses denied the charge of

In some parts of the Highlands, a joint of the fingers was cut off to show sorrow for the death of a family member.

unfaithfulness—but that made no difference. If her husband believed the story, he felt it his duty to make an example of her.

Another practice that concerned us involved dental hygiene. Our observation was that in the Highlands, apart from the Kainantu-Omaura districts, people had clean mouths and teeth. This was a most welcome change because they did not chew betel nut. Betel nut has a mild narcotic effect, but for the juice of the nut to be chemically activated, one must chew it with lime. The result is stained lips, mouth cancers and prolific spitting of red-stained saliva.

The only people in the greater part of the Highlands with betel nut-stained mouths were teachers and pastors of another church's missions. These people had come from coastal villages where betel nut was used, so when they had finished their training and were appointed to the Highlands, they wanted their betel nut. In order to be helpful, their mission arranged for a constant supply of betel nut to be flown in for these men. These missionaries were easy to pick. They always wore a coat, had a walking stick, and boasted stained teeth. Some missionaries also introduced alcohol and cigarettes, as did traders and government officials. However, the Adventist Church took a strong stance against all of these harmful substances.

Prior to the coming of the white man, stealing was a rarity in the Highlands. The people lived under a system of communal ownership. Goods were not owned exclusively by the individual who used them. This meant that if one individual needed a certain item, he could simply take it or it would be given to him as needed. He was not "taking" it from someone else, for the simple reason that he owned it as much as the other person did.

In any case, if a man did take something that someone else felt strongly belonged to him in some special sense, there would be no way to hide the stolen item. Everyone knew everyone else's business too well to hide anything in a small community. The result was that there was little possibility of stealing, as we understand the term.

On the other hand, to take something from an enemy or from an enemy's village was not considered stealing. To a Highland warrior taking from the enemy was carrying out a duty every time he had the opportunity. In the frequent tribal wars, men raided and counter raided. Taking the enemy's possessions was desirable and expected, not something to be frowned on.

Most males had methods of demonstrating their good fortune. In parts of the Western Highlands, a man demonstrated his family's wealth by wearing on his chest a series of small bamboo sticks tied together in a kind of closed ladder pattern. He might have a chain of some dozen or more small sticks laced together, each representing eight units of wealth. It might be eight pigs, eight kina shells or eight wives—each of which was considered about the same monetary value. A dozen units would be impressive and few men could have "owned" that by himself. Importantly, what one man wore represented the combined wealth of his family unit, so his brother or uncle could wear an identical chain of sticks.

The first female students to come to the early schools also displayed communal wealth. They came with a left arm adorned with "bangles" made from some portion of a pig. Every time the man of the house slaughtered a pig, one part of the animal was placed as a greasy "bangle" around the daughter's left arm. This demonstrated the wealth of the father, displaying for all to see that he could afford to kill so many highly prized pigs. On her arrival at our school, she might have been wearing up to a dozen of these smelly pig parts. When a girl wanted to become a student, one of the first tasks we performed was to cut these off her arm.

CALLED TO YANI

"Then I said to you, 'You have reached the hill country of the Amorites, which the Lord our God is giving us. See, the Lord your God has given you the land. Go up and take possession of it as the Lord, the God of your ancestors, told you. Do not be afraid, do not be discouraged'" (Deuteronomy 1:20, 21).

Shortly after the Bena Bena camp meeting, we were asked to relieve Laurence Gilmore at Yani while he and June went on furlough. I chartered a small plane—an Auster—from Gibbs Airways to go visit the station before the Gilmores left. Austers are very small planes, with one passenger seat beside the pilot and another seat behind him. But with the wing above and windows all around, they are great for getting a view of the country.

But Austers didn't prove practical for New Guinea because they could carry so little and could not operate above 8500 feet (2500 metres). With valley floors at about 5000 feet (1500 metres) and mountains rising to as high as 15,000 feet (4500 metres), these small planes were forever ducking around narrow valleys, which could quickly fill with cloud. About 14 of these planes were left as tragic wrecks on hillsides before they were withdrawn from use in Papua New Guinea.

On this trip to Yani, there was just the pilot and myself in the plane, plus a few boxes of our goods. We took off from Bena Bena and headed for the Daola range of hills that separate the Goroka and Chimbu valleys. It was early morning and the Auster was doing its best to make sufficient altitude. A dip in the range—a "saddle"—was ahead at the end of a short valley. But the saddle was still considerably higher than we had yet managed to climb. The pilot asked me to look out for rising smoke from the native houses below. With the sun behind us striking the walls of that valley the smoke should rise indicating the wind speed up the wall of the valley and over the saddle. We saw many houses and people waving to us, even flashes of light reflecting off the kina shells they wore on their chests—but no smoke.

When God Calls, Expect Adventure

Time was running out. We still had more than 100 feet (30 metres) to rise before we could clear the saddle looming in front of us and it seemed we were already in a corner so tight the plane could never hope to turn around. I glanced at the pilot beside me who was now tense with concentration.

"With the sun heating that wall ahead the wind must be rising," the pilot exclaimed above the din of the motor. "We'll be right."

The windscreen filled with the saddle hurtling toward us. Just as it seemed we must crash into the mountain ahead, we felt a powerful lift under us and the plane rose at least 50 feet (15 metres) above the saddle on an unseen current of air. We were over and into the Chimbu valley. The pilot turned to me and said just one word triumphantly, "See!"

The saying "flying by the seat of your pants" came to life for me in the Highlands, although I prefer to think the Lord must have had His hand over the trip I took that day. The next day the same pilot—this time with a government doctor aboard—tried the same trick. There was insufficient rising wind that day to lift them over. They crashed into the mountain, wrecking the plane, and Dr Jamieson suffered injuries including a broken ankle.

After two weeks with the Gilmores, learning about their operation, it was time to go back to collect Freda and my two sons. I walked as far as the nearby Catholic mission station, where I discovered Father Labor—the local priest—was also about to walk in the same direction. He was a friendly man and we walked together all day. That evening he invited me to stay with him in another Catholic mission station.

The following morning the priest of that station offered me a horse for my onward journey. I had thought I knew about handling horses, but once mounted I could not stop him until he had run the full length of the small mountainside airstrip. He went like mad. Not even a plane, it seemed, could have travelled faster than he did.

That afternoon I arrived at the Kumul SDA Mission where Calvin Stafford lived. Calvin was pleased to see me, because he had had a problem with a decayed eye-tooth. He had already been to see the local government doctor who had tried to remove the tooth, only to succeed in breaking it off at gum level. The pain was still intense, so Calvin asked me to extract it.

"OK, where are the forceps and the anaesthetic?" I asked.

"There is some dental gear in this room," he replied, in obvious pain. "But don't worry about anaesthetic. I don't want that."

I looked at him, expecting to see a grin on his face. But he was serious. He really did not want anaesthetic to numb the intense pain that was sure to follow.

"But I'm going to need to use elevators—and they are excruciatingly painful," I countered.

"Yes, I know. But the last injection I had caused more pain than the extraction. I'd rather do without, thanks."

I still do not understand how he stood it as I used that dental equipment. The tooth was strongly embedded and required a lot of work before the stubborn root came out. His tolerance of the pain I inflicted was one of the bravest acts I have ever seen.

I continued on horseback from Kumul to Goroka. Pastor Kuso, a native missionary from the island of Mussau travelled with me to show me the way and to return the horse to Calvin. It was a small and often steep trail. Going down what later became the Daola Pass on the Highland Highway, in places the whole mountainside was covered with loose shale making it too dangerous to stay on the horse, and almost as dangerous to lead him because his feet constantly slipped on the loose rocks, bringing him right on top of me time and again.

Several days later—the morning after the Queen's Birthday weekend in June 1950—we chartered another of the little Auster planes to take our family as near as possible to Yani. As we boarded the plane, it was obvious the pilot had enjoyed his drinks over the holiday weekend because the plane reeked of alcohol!

Freda took the passenger seat beside the pilot and held the two children on her knees. We had included as much cargo as possible in the small plane. It was not much really, but it meant that I had no room to sit down. Nor was the plane big enough for me to stand. I had to crouch behind the pilot holding our dog, Socks, in front of me.

When God Calls, Expect Adventure

Because of the load, the pilot didn't attempt to cross the range, but skirted around its end and flew up the long Waghi Valley. It was a blustery day, making the plane twist and jump about, more than I have felt at any other time. Possibly the pilot's reactions were a little less acute than when he was sober. "Lord," I prayed as we prepared to land, "help us."

Medical missionary Len Barnard with Cessna 185 VH-SDA, and local highland warriors demonstrating their hunting prowess.

A MEMORABLE ARRIVAL

"Burst into songs of joy together, you ruins of Jerusalem, for the Lord has comforted his people, he has redeemed Jerusalem. The Lord will lay bare his holy arm in the sight of all the nations, and all the ends of the earth will see the salvation of our God" (Isaiah 52:9, 10).

The airstrip onto which we planned to land was at a 90-degree angle to the valley we were flying down and ran steeply up the hillside. To land, the pilot had to make a sharp left turn and give it plenty of throttle to make it up the steep incline. His second attempt was successful and we roared up the strip. It required a lot of engine power to climb to the top and even when we had reached the top of the airstrip, engine power was necessary to hold the plane in place while stones were placed behind the wheels to make sure the plane didn't roll back down the steep hill.

Just as the wheels were chocked, Socks—the dog—vomited down the pilot's neck. We had to inform the pilot because his mind was not yet sufficiently clear of drink to notice. We were certain God deserved more credit for our safe arrival that day than did the pilot.

It was now evening, so we set up camp in the rough grass house used by visiting government officers. The walls were made from tough plaited bamboo, the floor was dirt and a plaited pitpit platform for a bed. The only notable feature in the house was the toilet. One had to walk down a long 6-foot (1.8-metre) wide grass-roofed, pitpit-walled passage way until at last one came to a large, circular room, maybe 16 feet (5 metres) across, in the centre of which sat a lonely little box with a circular hole in the top.

There was no door, of course. One simply sat there at the end of this long, closed-in passage, staring down the full length of passageway to the main part of the house. There was no privacy from those in the house, only from those outside.

It was a bitterly cold night, and Freda and I cuddled the boys all through the night, trying to keep them warm. Next morning we found more than 50 men had come from Yani to assist us to carry our gear.

Our escorts looked imposing with their shiny dark bodies, wide bark belts pulled tightly around their lean abdomens. Over this belt hung a long, narrow string skirt reaching below the knees. Tucked in the back of the belt was a small branch with colourful leaves tucked upward, so the leaves hung down modestly. On their chests, they wore shells and strings of beads, while their tall headgear included long, colourful bird feathers. All this gave them a strong, tall and proud appearance, enhanced well by the long, dangerous-looking spears held by each man.

Two poles were lashed to a folding canvas chair to make a sedan chair for Freda. Clearly she was to be carried the whole way, as if she was a queen off on an expedition. For six-week-old Kenneth, we had made a canvas carrying basinet that hung from a central carrying pole slung across the shoulders of two strong men. Lyn sat astride the shoulders of one of the warriors and enjoyed his vantage point. It was a moving experience to watch the long line of laughing, happy men marching together. We had brought so few goods that many had nothing to carry!

The paths we followed wound between timber-fenced gardens stoutly designed to keep out pigs. Seldom were the paths wide enough for more than two people to walk together but the path was always steep, either up or down.

From the throats of the carriers poured forth a dirge that was nothing like music to my ears. But the more I heard it, the more it intrigued me. The leading group of men began singing, then the tune and words were picked up by the following group, then by the next. The song continued, but moved back along the line in waves. Before it had reached the tail-end group, the leaders had commenced a new verse.

Soon I began to recognise words here and there. I heard our names, then the places where we had worked. I heard the names of familiar people, and realised they were singing a history of Freda and me. As we walked, these men were singing a grand song, weaving in stories of us plus a promise of some of the things that were to come.

A Memorable Arrival

I turned to one man who could speak a language we both knew, "Are they telling our story in that song?"

"Yes," he replied, "they are telling everyone where you came from, how you got here, what they expect you to do and how they feel about it all. Your visit is a source of great joy and excitement."

It was humbling to hear such a song. I silently prayed that I might do all they expected while at the same time doing all that God wanted done for these people in the time we would be with them.

Later that day, we came to a transit across the face of a mountain that frowned many hundreds of feet down on the mighty Waghi River. More than any other part of the trip, this section caused Freda most concern and caused many silent prayers to rise heavenward. The narrow mountain track had been worn along the face of a cliff that dropped almost straight to a foaming river 1000 feet (300 metres) below. It was too narrow for the four men who carried her chair.

The man on the left front frequently slipped slightly over the edge of the track before pulling himself back from the brink. These slips were exaggerated for Freda, perched shoulder high in the carrying chair. All she could do was grasp the sides of the chair tightly and close her eyes, trying not to think of the tremendous drop below.

"You will pray to him, and He will hear you, and you will fulfil your vows. What you decide on will be done, and light will shine on your ways. When people are brought low and you say, 'Lift them up!' then He will save the downcast" (Job 22:27–29).

The Yani mission station was set amid glorious mountain scenery. The grass-thatched house we occupied looked north across a short section of garden land, then over the deep gorge of the Waghi River to almost perpendicular mountains that blocked any further view.

Following the river to the right, I could see a deep gorge set in a lovely valley, at the bottom of which lay "The Salt." My eye would follow down that valley until the majestic white cliffs of Mt Elimbari rose in the distance.

We must have gazed down that beautiful valley many times every day we lived there and it presented a different picture each time we looked. On many mornings, fog filled the valley as though angels had stuffed it full of heavenly cotton wool, then splashed its crests with golden sunbeams. We would watch as the morning mists rose until the mountains themselves were lost from sight, only to re-emerge in full colour. Should the mist be a little later, we had the glory of seeing the sun as a golden ball rising in a magnificent halo. Or there would be the times when the clouds hung like a protecting roof over the gorge, enabling us to look down the immense, cloud-capped tunnel.

Then there were the mornings when there was no cloud or mist. Instead, the sun enhanced with utter brilliance the colours of the hillsides and gardens, highlighting the columns of light blue smoke rising from the scattered hamlets. Never did we tire of admiring that changing vista.

Looking south behind the mission house, there rose a steep mountain range, the crest of which marked—at that time—the boundary of "controlled territory." Our house was part way up the mountain that marked the boundary. South of that mountaintop was an area known as

Amen!

Bomai. At that time, the government maintained no permanent control over the village people who lived there—and neither were these people being offered any opportunity to know our Saviour.

We were certain the Bomais must also be offered the news of a Saviour, who cared for them and wished them to be free from fear of spirits and superstition. I decided I must go over to see them, and bring to them at least the rudiments of the gospel story. My resolve was heightened when I heard that a Catholic priest had recently made a trip into that area. I felt I had as much right as he to go.

Our team was not large but it was essential we include some who had knowledge of the Bomai languages. I found the name "Bomai" interesting. It seemed to refer to a different area depending on where I was at the time I heard it. Finally I decided the name seemed to equate with our word "South." Each group of people spoke of those who lived south of them as "the Bomai people."

Going down the farther side of the range at the back of our house, we came to the first village. They welcomed us in their traditional manner, affording their uninvited guests with the highest degree of respect. One man came to each of us, knelt down and taking hold of our knees performed several suggestive, thrusting motions of his hips, intended as a very close welcome. Those village people were offering their greatest demonstration of respect and honour—and we accepted it as such.

In order to present the gospel story to the village people, we strung several picture rolls from the grass rooves of two houses. The pictures were intended to illustrate the story of Creation, the Fall, the Cross and the Earth Made New. To reach these people in their language, we found it necessary to have a line of four interpreters. I spoke in Pidgin, then the next three translated into languages they could each understand until the final interpreter spoke in a local language. It was the shortest language route available to us to reach these people.

The village people had arranged themselves in a semi-circle before us. The women sat cross-legged with their younger children on their knees and formed the inner semi-circle. The older boys and the men stood to form the outer, protective semi-circle. The men stood holding their spears and other war equipment at the ready. The older children

When God Calls, Expect Adventure

thought this was a great time for play and they took the opportunity to run in and out of the group making all the noise they could.

After telling the story of Jesus and what He has done for all people everywhere—including them—I explained how it was possible for us to talk to Jesus.

"We call it prayer," I said, "and this is how we do it. First, we close our eyes and bow our heads. I will talk to Jesus and you can listen. When I have finished, I will say, 'Amen.' When you hear 'Amen,' you can open your eyes again."

All of this had to go through the four interpreters and I was pleased to see the village people nodding their heads, indicating they understood.

As I began the important task of my first prayer with them, the adults all did as asked, but the children hadn't even listened. They continued to run around, yelling and squealing. With their eyes still closed and heads bowed, mothers shouted at these children, then flailed with their arms in an attempt to catch them. Also with eyes closed and heads bowed, the men yelled at the women, telling them—I presume—to keep the children quiet.

The women shouted back at the men. It was bedlam! When a mother did catch a child, she would pull him or her close to her chest and cover the child's eyes tightly with her hands. No child had ever experienced such treatment before, so they kicked and howled, trying to get free. With screaming children, and the yelling and shouting of the men and women, it was chaos—all still with closed eyes and bowed heads!

I tried to pray but not even the interpreters could hear. I shouted "Amen" but no-one heard that either. I shouted to the interpreters to help me and together we all yelled "Amen" as loudly as we could. Still no-one heard. We tried again but either they had not understood or they still could not hear. Something more had to be done, so we went from person to person. Using two thumbs, we physically opened their eyes, at the same time shouting "Amen."

Finally, some sense of order was restored. Our first public prayer in "Bomai" had not been a great success. Today, however, those same people do know how to pray.

INTO BOMAI

"He said to me, 'You are my son, today I have become your father. Ask me, and I will make the nations your inheritance, the ends of the earth your possession'" (Psalm 2:7, 8).

In faith that our Father in heaven wanted the gospel message spread and medical needs met, we patrolled further into Bomai. At one spot, we were shown where two months earlier a government patrol had been ambushed and attacked. It became necessary for the patrol to shoot their way out. No police were killed but 11 villagers died that day. By contrast, we had no man-made weapon. Our only weapon was the Word of God and everywhere we walked we were welcomed warmly—sometimes a little too warmly!

Late one afternoon, we had washed in a cold stream before climbing up to the village in which we planned to stay the night. I had left my shirt open hoping to dry off as we walked down a narrow track through a lower village. In that village, all the village people had formed two lines between which we were expected to pass

The women—in a line behind the men—held babies in their arms, while the men in the inner lines held the ever-present bows, arrows, spears and stone axes. As we squeezed between the two lines, I tried to communicate by a smile and a nod to each person we passed. But there was no hint of friendly response. Each man stood with a face set like stone.

As we reached the midpoint, the two lines of men closed in on us, making further progress impossible. They were not big men—none were as tall as my shoulder—but they were strong, forbidding and heavily armed. We would be no match for these fearsome-looking men.

What next? I wondered. *Protect us, Lord.*

A moment later, I was lifted and placed like a log on the shoulders of a dozen or more men. Their bodies were covered with rancid pig grease and various, coloured paints, much of which was now being transferred

When God Calls, Expect Adventure

to my freshly washed body. The smell was overwhelming and I did my best to lie still as I was manhandled.

In this manner, they set off along a track leading up the mountainside. It must have looked a bit like a caterpillar, especially when they came to huge fallen logs I was sure they would never climb over while carrying me. But they did.

At the time I had a cold that forced me to breathe through my mouth. Just below my face was a man with a dirty, greasy feather in his hair. Every time I opened my mouth to breathe that filthy feather popped in to tickle my mouth and throat.

I had no idea where they planned to take me or what they planned to do when they got there. Most of these men had never seen a white man before, let alone have one as powerless as I was at that moment.

There were many hands holding me aloft but for a few brief moments one hand felt distinctly out of place. Wondering if I could be imagining things, I froze. One of the men had felt it the perfect opportunity to find out if a white man had the same anatomy as they had. I could do nothing but assure myself that it was not immoral, he was just curious!

For about 20 minutes, they struggled up that bush track with me on their shoulders. At last we came to the village we had intended to camp in that night and I was allowed to get down. At last they smiled, and rubbed my arms and legs. The whole exercise had been the highest gesture of friendship and warm welcome. By now, of course, my body was about as greasy and painted as theirs had been, and there was no water with which to wash. Nonetheless, I feel sure God smiled as we spent the night among new friends with pig grease and war paint on our bodies.

We travelled on in a southerly direction until we began to get into a low-land malarial area. I was told that only a short distance further were the sago palm swamps of western Papua. A day or two later, we came across a lonely police outpost where I wrote a short note to the government officer, advising of the amount of malaria I had come across and suggesting that a medical patrol might prove helpful. The whole trip had been a positive one and we felt that we had been able to lift the name of the Lord before these needy people.

I was glad to get home again, only to find a policeman at the back

Into Bomai

door the next day, offering me a long brown official-looking envelope. I opened it to read something like this:

> *Dear sir, We note from reading your medical report that you have patrolled in the Bomai district. Regulations prohibit all but government officers, with proper police guard, from entering these areas under any circumstances. This is enforced for your own protection. By your own admission, you have entered a prohibited area without permission. It is to be noted that breach of these regulations is punishable with 12 months imprisonment, or 200 pounds fine. We require your presence at this station at the earliest to discuss the matter.*

A strange feeling runs up and down the spine when one reads a letter like that. Freda and I talked it over, decided on our strategy and then, after prayer, handed the policeman a written reply:

> *Dear sir, I note your request that I come to Kerowagi to discuss my recent patrol. I plan to call in on your office when I visit Kerowagi the week after next. Kindly expect me to arrive Thursday week, the 26th of this month.*

As it was December and I had planned to go over anyway, Freda and I had decided that the 26th was the best day to visit. We were right. He had partaken liberally of the "spirit" of the season, so was in no mood to make a big issue of my patrol. Instead, he simply pointed out that no-one but government officers were permitted into these restricted districts.

After accepting my apologies, he offered to show me around and share dinner. It seemed the day after Christmas was an excellent time to be reprimanded!

Freda and I had planned to relieve Pastor and Mrs Gilmore for the six months of their furlough. However, news that a medical problem with Pastor Gilmore's feet had not been resolved made our term of stay uncertain. *Well*, I thought. *I'm quite content to settle in for a longer stay if need be.*

When God Calls, Expect Adventure

The Gilmores had brought gladioli and dahlia roots to the station. The plants grew magnificently and brightened the station with their colourful flowers. Then the village people began to bring Freda rhododendron plants that grew in the mountains. Someone even brought in a lovely green parrot that became our pet. It would sit on my shoulder—or on the children's shoulders—as we walked. While sitting on our shoulders, it would talk into our ears. He could fly anywhere he wished, either inside or outside, but for some strange reason never flew through the door of the house. He always flew to some spot near the door, then walked out before flying again. If one of the dogs happened to be lying in the doorway, he would simply climb up over the dog's nose and continue on his way.

LEARNING THE CULTURE AT YANI

"Lord, you are the God who saves me, day and night I cry out to you. May my prayer come before you; turn your ear to my cry. I am overwhelmed with troubles and my life draws near to death" (Psalm 88:1–3).

Every morning, a long line of people waited for Freda at the dispensary, with all kinds of problems needing attention. One morning, Freda noticed that one imposing-looking man had been there several times. On his chest he wore the badge of a luluai, a government-appointed position similar to a village chief. He had brought his wife, who had a nasty gash on her head, probably caused by a bush knife.

Thinking back to the previous visit, Freda asked him, "Just the other day you brought a woman in with a broken finger, and you said she was your wife."

He grinned. "Yes, that was my wife."

"And the week before you brought another woman with a big sore on her leg. Was she your wife, too?"

His smile grew wider. "Yes, yes, she was my wife, too." A rising sense of pride was evident in the slight stiffening of his back.

"How many wives do you have?"

His pride took another lift as he threw out his chest and looked to make sure others were listening. But he had a problem working out how many wives he did have. He tried to calculate on his fingers,

When God Calls, Expect Adventure

then consulted with the one who was interpreting. Finally, he grinned widely, pounded his spear into the ground, stood tall and, waving the feathers in his headgear, he proclaimed so everyone could hear, "I have 12 wives."

Only a man of his standing could demonstrate such unbelievable wealth—12 wives!

One day we organised a party for the village people of the district—and hundreds of them came. The sports field was filled with people in all their finery of feathers, shells and paints. When a Chimbu man dresses up in traditional dress, he is impressive. Shells, feathers, beads and strikingly colourful paints were added for special occasions. Of course, no man was correctly dressed without his spear or his bow and arrows. Most also carried a stone axe pushed through the belt, ready for immediate use.

We organised our usual games, such as tug-of-war and foot races. While everyone enjoyed these white man's games, what they really wanted was to get onto the games of skill they knew so much better.

For the spear-throwing contest, we cleared everyone off the field. Then, each man in turn tried to throw his spear further than the others. The distances they could hurl a spear was most impressive. The first two-thirds of the spear's flight was absolutely straight but, at about that point, every spear lost direction, so much so that not one of the hundreds of spears landed point first. I often wondered if this just might have been a part of the art of spear throwing of which I was unfamiliar, perhaps to preserve the sharp point of the spear.

Next came the archery contest. A full double newspaper page was painted with concentric rings and fixed to a bank of soil for the target. The shooters' line was placed about 75 yards (almost 70 metres) away. Apparently this was too distant. As the arrows were made from pitpit grass stalks pulled from the roadside, the shafts were not really straight and therefore not balanced. Had they used their carefully guarded fighting arrows, the result could have been different but as it turned out, not one arrow hit the target, though some were close. One veered so greatly it struck a child in the thigh, almost causing a fight.

Learning the Culture at Yani

Money tied between split bamboo displayng "bride-price." In Highland culture, a young man would borrow money and pigs from relatives to purchase his bride. Recipients of bride-price would celebrate joyfully.

When God Calls, Expect Adventure

After this "party," a number of new people took a real interest in the mission and began to attend worship services. It served as a reminder that, in reaching out to others, we must embrace what they do well.

———•———

Like people the world over, Yani people found many reasons to have a gathering of one kind or another. A wedding was one good reason. In the past, bride-price had been paid in traditional items—agreed amounts of kina shell, pigs, plumes of the Bird of Paradise feathers, beads or stone axes—but cash was increasingly in demand.

We often met elaborately dressed groups walking along the trails carrying—and displaying—"bride-price." The method of display was to split a length of bamboo almost right through from one end to the other, then large denomination bank notes would be placed one above the other between the two halves of the bamboo. The bamboo halves were then tied together at intervals to keep the notes in place.

Sometimes it required five or more bamboo poles to display the bank notes to be paid. Each pole had to be decorated with colourful feathers or other brilliant display items. In some areas of the Highlands, pigs would join the procession, one foot tethered to their new owner—and following, one foot tethered to her new husband, would be the bride.

———•———

It is a truism of people all over the world that death is a time of deep significance, a time when people think deeper thoughts and listen more closely. And I believe it was by the Lord's leading that it became fashionable in the Yani district to request the missionary to come and conduct the funeral service for someone who had died, especially if that person was of high standing in the community. At such times, I found I never had a more attentive audience, and I was able to present more clearly the gospel story and what God would do for those who accepted Him. Jesus became precious to many a soul whohad given Him no thought until that time.

I never interfered with or suggested any changes to the method of burial they had traditionally used. Their cultural habits were every bit as good as those I had been brought up with.

Learning the Culture at Yani

For most burials in the Yani district the hole that was dug was up to 7 feet (about 2 metres) long. Having reached a depth of about 5 feet (1.5 metres), it was dug sideways so that a body could be placed under a shelf of solid earth, a little like a long cave running the full length of the grave. The grave was then lined carefully with a deep layer of leaves.

Carefully wrapped and tied in a large woven mat, the body of the deceased was lowered into the hole. Two men waiting below would tuck the body carefully into the "toe" part of the hole. The friends above, having collected large quantities of grass and leaves, would shower them down the hole to be pushed in over the body, until a carpet of leaves covered the body and the lower level of the grave. This was carefully tramped down. Then came twigs and smaller branches with the leaves still attached, all carefully trodden into place by the two men in the hole. Gradually the branches became larger and larger. Then a deep layer of rocks was thrown in until the hole was filled to ground level. Only then was the soil shovelled over the grave.

Under no circumstances whatsoever was soil to touch the body. But there was another aspect of the funeral that had no counterpart in my culture. In the Yani culture, it was expected that close relatives demonstrate the depth of their sorrow by attempting to commit suicide. This was to be carried out either by drowning or by hanging, at a time after the hole had been dug but before the final shovel of earth had been thrown over the grave. After that point, an attempt at suicide was no longer acceptable.

It was the responsibility of the more distant relatives to prevent the close relatives from committing suicide. So, at each funeral, it was customary to see a number of people with a rope tied around their waists, held securely by a stronger, more muscular young man.

Several times, when conducting a funeral service, there was an attempt by someone to struggle free. In most such attempts, the one holding the rope succeeded in his responsibility. One day, however, in the midst of my talk, a strong young man—probably a brother of the deceased—made a break and got away, with the whole audience after him, even those with a rope around their waists.

I was left standing there as the two men down in the hole shot out and were gone. Only a few of the elderly people, stood there with me.

When God Calls, Expect Adventure

Even my interpreter had gone. About 20 minutes later, with the glum-looking breakaway in tow, the whole group returned to listen to the rest of the funeral service. This time the man who had made the break had four men holding his rope.

As soon as the service was over and the last spade of earth placed, all ropes were removed and the whole group walked calmly back to the village.

"POPPA BELONG ALL"

"Bless those who persecute you; bless and do not curse. Rejoice with those who rejoice; mourn with those who mourn. Live in harmony with one another" (Romans 12:14–16).

I was helping Sealo build the first timber house occupied by a national church worker in the Highlands, when I noticed a large group of people passing by carrying the body of an old man on a stretcher. The old man had been propped up in a sitting position, and was decorated with all the traditional symbols of wealth—beads, feathers, shells and body paints. As I stood watching, someone spoke from behind me.

"Sir," the visitor said, "this old man was the biggest, most important father of all of us. We want you to come with us and take a service for him."

I raced up to the house to collect my Bible, reflecting on the fact that people from every corner of the valley would be coming to his funeral. He had been known as "Poppa belong all."

Clearly God was giving me a wonderful opportunity to present the gospel message to the leaders of every village in the valley. Freda said, "Let's have special prayer before you go that God will give you the right words to impress these important people."

It was late morning when I set off with them and I must have walked for more than an hour. Even so, I arrived shortly after the body, which meant I had opportunity to witness the complete ceremony—a ceremony I am sure had never been witnessed by any other stranger or outsider.

When I arrived, there were about 18 people present. The stretcher was resting on the ground with the body still propped up in the sitting position. I sat down with the group just a few feet away. We could hear voices of people approaching from all directions.

When God Calls, Expect Adventure

One woman—perhaps the "hostess"—stood and walked toward the approaching group. Each person she greeted held handfuls of grey mud that they smeared over their bodies as they wailed with sorrow.

As they came closer, men and women began to throw themselves on the ground. They would rise only to tear out handfuls of hair or break a branch from a tree before crashing to the ground again. Each fall seemed to be more desperate than the last and so violent I feared that ribs would be broken.

Until one has heard the wailing of Highland mourners, one could never imagine how heart-rending it is. It swells with notes of hopelessness, then screams with the sounds of utter finality and complete dejection.

Our little group responded with equally loud wailing, seeming to come as an echo or response to the wails of the approaching group. Of all those present, only the hostess did not cry out. She went to meet each approaching group and it seemed her duty to make sure they did not hurt themselves as she led them by the hand to the grave site. They came with every appearance of unwillingness, fighting and resisting all the way, but allowing themselves to slowly move forward until they were brought to the seated group.

The wailing slowly tapered off into conversation. Then another group would approach and the whole ritual of ceremonial mourning was repeated until that group also sat down. This went on for several hours as representatives gathered from all over the valley. They must have spent half the day alternately wailing and talking.

Meanwhile, a group of men began digging the grave. This was even smaller than others I had seen, no more than 4 feet (1.2 metres) long by about 2 feet (60 centimetres) wide. Its floor was sloping so that one end was about 3 feet (90 centimetres) deep, while the opposite end was about 5 feet (1.5 metres) deep, with another, smaller hole dug even more deeply at that lower end. Upon completion of the digging, the men drove four stakes into the floor of the grave, one near each corner. The tops of these stakes at the shallow end almost reached ground level, while those at the deeper end were quite a bit below ground level.

The old man's war shield was brought to the grave site and cut short so it would fit into the grave and rest on the four stakes to form a sloping bed.

It was now late afternoon and representatives from the whole valley had arrived. Amid more loud and desperate wailing, the old man's body was placed on the sloping platform, his head at the upper end and knees drawn up.

It was then my opportunity to present Jesus and the blessed hope of life again to those who accept Him. They listened closely and I am sure the Holy Spirit did His good work on many hearts that day.

Wailing began again as one after another of the men came forward to the grave side and tore from their necks the kina shell they treasured so highly. One such shell represented a whole month's wages for those lucky enough to find employment. The shell was then smashed with a blow of their axe and the broken pieces dropped on their ancestor. I know of no other time when such a valuable item would be deliberately broken.

Others tore strings of the much-sought-after red beads from their necks and dropped them in the grave. Many other items of traditional value went in as a sign of the loss the valley had sustained in the death of this greatly respected "father" of the tribe. Later, however, I saw some men retrieving the bigger pieces of shell and hiding them in their billums (string bags).

Bundles of bush rope and grass appeared while others drove a ring of light sticks into the ground around the grave. These sticks were bent over the grave until they formed a dome-like covering. Grass thatch was tied in place to form the roof. A short length of bamboo was placed centrally in the roof like a chimney, with all the internal segments of the bamboo knocked out.

"What is the bamboo for?" I asked.

"To let the stink out," I was told.

"Well, what is the hole at the bottom of the grave for?"

"That is to catch all the greases as his body breaks down."

Next a small opening was cut in the grass at the end nearest the old man's feet. Across this gap, a sliding timber door was placed.

"What is that for?" I asked.

"You see, when a member of the family comes along they can slide that door open and look at him while they have a good cry."

When God Calls, Expect Adventure

While this was being explained, a path was laid to the small door and colourful shrubs were planted along the pathway and all around the grave. By this time, it looked like an attractive miniature house.

"So, are you going to leave him like that?" I asked.

"Yes, he will stay like that until his body breaks down badly, then we cover him with earth, and he will stay like that for some months."

"What then?"

"He will remain buried until only the bones are left. Then we will dig up his bones and divide them among the close family members. They will look after the bones and keep them safely in their houses."

"Why?"

"These bones are very valuable to us because if anybody becomes sick a bone can be buried for a time outside the house. This will keep the evil spirits away from the house and allow the sick person to recover. Or if the gardens are not going well, a bone can be buried in the garden and that keeps the evil spirits out of the garden."

Because Christ is not yet accepted in all the houses of the Yani valley, the bones of the old man are probably still being treasured in some homes in the belief that they will protect the inhabitants against the evil one.

A HASTY DEPARTURE

"As you know, we count as blessed those who have persevered. You have heard of Job's perseverance and have seen what the Lord finally brought about. The Lord is full of compassion and mercy" (James 5:11).

We were enjoying our time at Yani and God seemed to be blessing our work. But, one Monday afternoon, the mail arrived. Included among the letters was a telegram that read: "A chartered plane will be calling for you and your goods on Friday the 23rd. Please meet it at Kerowagi Airstrip."

Freda and I looked at one another with our mouths open. Someone at mission headquarters had no idea how long it took to get from Yani to Kerowagi. Further, as usual they did not seem interested in asking us what we would prefer.

Freda was the first to speak, "That's this coming Friday! And it's already Monday evening! How can we possibly be there in that time?"

Together, we figured it out. We would have to be at Moruma mission station by Thursday—and to get to Moruma, we would have to leave Yani by tomorrow morning, Tuesday, no later than 10 am! Forget sleep. We would need to pack all night.

We looked again at the telegram. We just had to be there or an expensive charter flight would be wasted. There was no way we could send word asking for extra time.

We packed furiously most of the night. Early next morning, I went out to muster carriers but I discovered another major problem. This Tuesday had been earmarked by the local village elders for a big "Sing Sing." All the men were already dressed up in all their finery of feathers and paint, and none of them were going to miss out on such a special occasion.

When God Calls, Expect Adventure

"O Lord," I prayed from the depths of my heart, "You will have to help us this time. There is no possibility that we can carry everything and the plane is coming this Friday! Please, Father, You must touch some hearts. We simply can't do it of ourselves."

We didn't get as many carriers as we needed but we praised God for touching those hearts that He did. Many items had to be left behind but the essential items did get away with us, at about 9.30 am.

Yani is situated at an altitude about 6700 feet (about 2000 metres). The trail we had to take rose to 7000 feet (2100 metres), then plunged almost straight down to the Waghi River at 4400 feet (about 1300 metres). The "path" down that side was fine, loose shale that provided practically no grip for shoes. Two burly men each grasped one of Freda's arms and slid her all the way down that almost 3000-foot (800-metre) drop to the river. She was sure she had never gone down anything so fast.

We crossed the raging river on a flimsy cane swing bridge, then faced a 4000-foot (1200-metre) climb to 8400 feet (2500 metres). It was so steep. We had had no sleep and Freda was still breast feeding Kenneth at the time, as there was no other supply of milk available.

Native cane bridge in the Highlands of New Guinea. Such bridges were common and could be quite frightening

A Hasty Departure

We had climbed almost half way up when Freda's strength gave out completely. She simply sat down on the track and cried and cried. All this was too much for her. I endeavoured to comfort her and she did try to respond, but the human body has only so much to give. She was embarrassed that the carriers should see her like this but there was nothing she could do about it. Finally, the crying slowed to a stop.

From that time on, I noticed a decided change in the attitude of the carriers toward her. There was a sympathy that demonstrated itself in a determination to do all they could for her. Willingness replaced reluctance and we thanked God for that.

We crested the range at last, then dropped down to 5500 feet (about 1700 metres) for a late lunch. There was no time to rest, only lunch, then on again all afternoon and all the next day, climbing, then descending, knowing that every time we went down, we would soon have to climb again. There were mountains all the way, with rivers between. It was tough going.

On Thursday afternoon, we neared Moruma mission, thinking to ourselves, *Just one more river to cross!* But when we came to the river, our hearts sank when we found it in heavy flood. One glance at the clouds told us the river would soon be rising even further.

On the other side, Joe French from the Moruma mission had come to see what he could do to help us. Seeing the flood, he sent someone to collect a long rope. With a rock tied to one end, the rope was thrown across to us and, with the rope to hold on to, we were able to cross that chest-deep torrent before the clouds broke with the afternoon storm.

But Joe also had a message for us. We were standing there in our cold, dripping clothes when he said, "A message came through for you to say that the charter plane will not be coming for you for another two weeks."

You can imagine how we felt after all we had done to be on time!

In order to fill in the time profitably, we received a message asking us to go up to the leprosy colony at Togoba, just west of Mt Hagen. This enabled us to have a most interesting two weeks assisting Len Barnard in caring for a large colony of lepers.

The first part of the trip to Togoba was by air. We flew in one of Bobby Gibbs's Norseman planes. Hardly had we left the ground when

When God Calls, Expect Adventure

the passenger door flew open. I pulled it closed but it flew open again. It simply would not remain closed, so I stood beside it holding it closed. A storm had come in across our path, bringing some of the blackest clouds I ever saw. Unable to break through the cloud barrier, the pilot decided to land on the Banz airstrip to wait until the weather had cleared. I told him about the door. He fiddled with it a bit and put some oil on the locking mechanism.

An hour or so later, when the storm had passed, we took off but the door was no better. It flew open and had to be held shut again. While I held it closed, it caused us no problem and we landed safely at the Mt Hagen airport. But the next day as we were listening to the radio news, we heard an item that made us smile. The radio report was that one of Gibbs's Sepik Airways Norsemans had lost a door in flight over the Baiya River district.

Mission plane P2-SOC. In the remote Highlands, planes were the fastest method of travel, sometimes saving several days of difficult walking or driving.

LEPROSY CARE

"As you go, proclaim this message: 'The kingdom of heaven has come near. Heal the sick, raise the dead, cleanse those who have leprosy, drive out demons. Freely you have received, freely give'" (Matthew 10:7, 8).

Travelling the last few miles to the leper station was a most interesting and at times frightening experience. The only form of transport the hospital had was a small grey Ferguson tractor. For our convenience, the driver had fixed a steel scoop bucket to the hydraulic connections at the back.

"Do we ride in the bucket?" Freda asked.

"Looks like it," I said.

We placed our cases in the scoop, then got in with the cases. The road was little more than the common village trail. Rain earlier that afternoon had left the red clay as slippery as grease.

Our driver told me that the tractor often slid off the muddy road. When negotiating many of the steep downward slopes, he asked us to get off and walk. He would allow the tractor to begin to move, then apply the brakes to the back wheels until they locked, endeavouring to steer the machine and keep it on the track. It was nothing short of a miracle that he did so.

Before the next downhill, I talked with the driver. "Keep the tractor in low gear," I urged. "Keep the wheels turning slowly and you will have more control over the steering."

The driver indicated that he understood and set off confidently. He maintained power to the wheels but pushed full power on. He simply roared down that road, veering from side to side. Once again, the angels must have been working overtime looking after God's people and property, for somehow he managed to stay on the "road" most of the time. At the bottom of the hill, I encouraged him to return to his own driving methods for the present.

Upon our arrival, the most unexpected sight was the jail. Why would a church-staffed institution need such a fence? We discovered that the

When God Calls, Expect Adventure

government owned the hospital land and buildings, and had granted the Adventist church the responsibility of operating the hospital. The government had built a high-fenced prison compound to house the prisoners with leprosy while they received treatment.

After we had settled in and I had time to observe the government "prisoners," it soon became apparent there was no need to lock the gates. Rather, they were open all the time. The hardest part was trying to convince most patients that they could go home when their leprosy was under control. They were well fed and cared for. They were pleased to be receiving treatment for their ailment and to be supplied with a bed and blankets. They enjoyed the daily and weekly worship periods they could attend. Although government health workers had sent many

Lepers showing their damaged fingers and feet. The government built at least one Hansenide colony operated by the Adventist church.

Leprosy Care

of them and some had come fearfully, they were surprised by the level of care they received. It was a privilege to treat "prisoners" who refused to escape.

One of the sadder tasks each morning was foot inspection. Due to the nerve damage lepers experience, the patient often feels no pain when a part of his body is damaged—and the foot is the part of the body most subject to harm. The feet must be examined regularly and care given as soon as any injury occurs. A small fire in the centre of a room could have terrible consequences if a sleepy patient should allow their foot to fall into the fire. With no feeling to warn of the problem, the burn was sometimes severe. Similarly, if a rat decided to feed off the skin of a patient's toe, it might not even be noticed.

Frequently, the damage inflicted was so extensive it necessitated the removal of the toe. Hence, each morning it was normal practice to inspect feet for any new damage and amputate or treat the ruined part. Without such treatment, many of our patients might have died. Some patients had advanced leprosy that also affected their hands and faces.

While at Togoba, we saw many miracles of the spiritual kind. People came in dejected and hopeless, but before long a complete change came over them and they became true Christians. There is no question that the kind of ministry Jesus demonstrated—via the medical approach—is very effective. It reaches people at the level of their felt need.

The day came when several of the prisoners asked for baptism. One notable leper was Kai, who had bad feet but was determined to go back over the mountains to his village to bring the gospel to his people. He put his Bible and picture rolls in his shoulder bag and set off. Kai soon had a flourishing church operating in his village and the Lord richly blessed his ministry to his own people.

Other medical needs were also difficult to treat. "Pigbel" is a medical condition that few people have heard about. Until the 1960s, it was all too common an ailment in the Highlands of Papua New Guinea and many people died from this gruesome medical problem.

Pigbel is the result of a culture in which pigs were highly prized and rarely eaten. One of the main evidences of wealth in the village setting

When God Calls, Expect Adventure

was the number of pigs a man owned. Pigs were accumulated carefully, guarded zealously and used in significant events like the payment of bride-price or compensation. For most people, eating pig flesh was a rare treat and one anticipated greatly.

One significant event enabled the man to show off his wealth, when the village was to have "Sing Sing" feast and dance. At such events, I have seen as many as 30 pigs slaughtered and laid out for everyone to see. After slaughter, some of the pigs were cooked in stone ovens and consumed immediately but often there were not enough ovens to cook all the animals and the carcasses were quartered for distribution to the village people. Provision of extra portions to guests signified a successful feast.

Because pig flesh will spoil quickly in the warm weather of the tropics, all the pig had to be cooked and eaten without delay. Meat was a rarity in the village person's diet, so a second feast soon followed the task of dividing the meat among the family members and guests.

Unfortunately, this sudden change in diet can result in a blockage of the gut. The food cannot be digested quickly enough and begins to rot in the intestines. The bowel wall becomes infected and also begins to rot. The terrible pain and bloating that occurs is called pigbel, and it was common in the Highlands.

One day, a 40-year-old village woman came in complaining of pain in the lower bowel. It was clear that this was a case of pigbel and needed to be under the care of a doctor. We explained this to her and offered to take her the 20 miles (about 30 kilometres) to the government hospital in Kainantu but she refused. Part of the reason may have been a fear of leaving her tribal area. However, there was also a common belief that more effective medicine was dispensed at a mission hospital.

The people would say, "The medicine you give us is stronger because you pray when you give medicine. The prayer helps people get better." They were certain that it was the prayer that made medicine more powerful and this I believe came from traditional practices of healing where people viewed illness as a consequence of sorcery. Traditional cures often involved a spiritual dimension and this in their mind was lacking at the government hospitals.

Prayer is certainly powerful—but it is not just "a lucky charm." God

Leprosy Care

has granted humans wisdom and that wisdom is to be used in modern medicine. God does not do for people what they can do for themselves. So with reluctance we agreed to treat the woman at our clinic.

After three days on antibiotics, we persuaded the woman to take our offer of transport to Kainantu. It must have been a painful trip because jeeps are not fitted with soft springs to smooth out the ruts and potholes of a rough road.

At the hospital, the doctor was annoyed. "You should have called the police and forced her to come here for surgery," he declared.

A day or two later, the poor woman died. The doctor had tried to save her by operating, but a foot or more of her bowel had rotted so badly that the stitches would not hold in the tissue of the lower bowel.

The government-built Hansenide leper colony at Togoba, near Mt Hagen, was run by the Adventist Church.

THE REBELLIOUS MARE

"For rebellion is like the sin of divination, and arrogance like the evil of idolatry. Because you have rejected the word of the Lord, he has rejected you" (1 Samuel 15:23).

The day came when we left Togaba and flew to Madang, this time to relieve Pastor and Mrs Bert Grosser at Seure. We had become experts in relieving missionaries and carrying on their work while we waited for the Australian government to build the second leper colony. On one hand, it was frustrating but at the same time it was most educational for us to see how the different missionaries overcame problems. It gave us a tremendous opportunity to experience many types of work and contribute on different mission stations. Because of this, we were more effective missionaries than we would have been.

Seure (pronounced "se-oo-re") station was in the Saidor District. This was a new area for the Adventist work on the coast between Madang and Lae. It proved to be a difficult area in which to work because the results obtained in no way matched the effort expended. There were few students in the school and no adult baptisms, despite years of hard work by Bert and his team. Only a limited amount of work had been done on buildings. At the time we left Madang, four young men from the Madang district volunteered to come with us—and we were so glad they did. Without their help, things would have been nearly impossible.

The Rebellious Mare

We arrived at Seure late in the day and, next morning, we set out to make a round of the station and meet the students, only to find that all local students had simply walked away during the night. Only the four Madang boys were left.

We tried to take stock of the situation and an unhappy picture emerged. It seemed that Pastor Grosser, a new missionary to New Guinea, had been deposited in the area with only a few supplies and asked to set up a mission station. With no local help and only two or three Madang men to give him temporary help, Bert set to and located a plot of ground. Next, this small group had gone into the mountains, cut trees, hefted the timber on their shoulders and carried them back to build the houses.

The main house was located beside the ocean, with not one piece of sawn timber in it. Some time later, two pieces of sawn timber floated in on the waves. One of the planks served as a shelf in the kitchen. The other was a small boat's hatch cover that formed a level base for the kerosene fridge. A ramp of debarked timber served in place of steps. The best feature of the home was the roofing iron, sent from Madang. This enabled the rainwater to be caught in a tank for drinking water.

The walls of the house, made of plaited bamboo, were closed in to only 5 to 6 feet (1.5 to 1.8 metres) high, allowing air to circulate in the hot, humid climate. Because the floor was simply made from split palm trunks, we could see the ocean through the cracks and openings. Our son Ken often dropped spoons or other items through the floor. Despite the obvious drawbacks, we loved the glorious location.

Guano—the ever-helpful Solomon Island missionary and his equally helpful wife—lived in their grass house nearby, while the house for the students completed the entire station at the time. A quick review of the history of the area helps explain the problems the Grossers—and then we—faced in trying to get things moving.

About 60 years earlier, this area had been uninhabited. During the time of the German occupation of New Guinea before World War I, people who displeased the German administration were banished to Saidor. It was a kind of penal colony but without administration. Among the people who had been sent to the area there was no natural tribal unity and no historical attachment to the land. About the only

When God Calls, Expect Adventure

things they held in common were distaste for any kind of control or supervision and a deep dislike for the white man.

Soon after our arrival and their sudden departure, three of the local lads returned to school, so we now had seven students. We did our best for them by way of schooling and worship periods.

It was the wet season and the water from the roof of our house spilled over onto the steep ramp that served as our only access to the house. Many times when trying to negotiate the ramp Freda's feet would go from under her and she slid heavily down the steep and far-from-smooth ramp. We needed to replace the ramp with steps. I found a village man who was prepared to assist me in pit-sawing planks for the stairs. He only stayed one week before deciding the work was too hard for his liking. So the schoolteacher offered to assist me.

A few hundred yards from the station we had cleared a little area in the jungle beside a creek. No wind could penetrate the "cylinder" of clearing we had created. The sun sent its fierce rays down all day long, which meant we received all the heat but none of the cooling we so desperately needed. Pit-sawing is hot, hard work at the best of times, lifting and pulling that heavy 7-foot (2-metre) saw blade constantly, hour after hour as it bit into the stubborn wood and separated it into planks. But in the location where we worked it must have been at about its worst. Despite all that, we made the staircase, making our living conditions so much safer and more bearable.

Another major problem that limited our contact with the people was transport. Villages were well apart and a lot of time was wasted just getting to a village. As a solution, Pastor Grosser had bought an old ex-army mare that had been shot in the neck during the war, then set free on one of the plantations. For a nominal fee, Bert had been permitted to capture her and take her to his station.

The mare had a foal, which turned out to be one of the loveliest, gentlest horses I have ever dealt with. We called him Beauty. He would wander all around and under our house. Children could put their hands into his mouth, walk under his belly or between his legs and he just seemed to come back for more.

Freda did her ironing under the house and sometimes Beauty would wander over and just stand there, his large head a few inches from the

The Rebellious Mare

ironing board. A couple of times he playfully took a nice white shirt in his mouth and turned away with it, only to drop it nearby with green stains where his mouth had held it ever so gently.

On one occasion, I needed to go down the coast some 10 miles (16 kilometres) to the new station we were building at Kororo. So about midnight, when it was pitch-black, I placed the saddle on Beauty's back.

"Gee up," I said as I swung easily up into the saddle. But Beauty didn't want to go. He bucked a little, just enough to vent his displeasure at our midnight expedition.

"Gee up," I said firmly, urging him on. This time he bucked a little harder and broke the girth strap. This caused the saddle to fly loose and me to fall over his head onto the ground, extinguishing the light. Unable to see a thing, I reached out to see what I could feel and there he was standing and waiting for me to get up. I grinned as I thought to myself, *If it was light enough, I'm sure I'd see a devilish smile on your face, you villain.* Beauty was happy to make the trip to Kororo the next morning, but obviously he didn't want to go at night.

Another time, he did throw me and it was in daylight—but it wasn't his fault. Just as I mounted him that day, a dog bit him savagely on the

Mission house on the beach at Seure on the northern coast of Papua New Guinea between Madang and Lae.

heel causing him to lash out in fright. I landed on his neck, then the ground. My foot went through the strap that served in place of a missing stirrup. There I hung with my foot caught in the strap and Beauty's heels pounding down on my chest as he tried to get away from the irritating dog. I had very sore ribs for a few days.

The old mare almost killed me one day—and it was deliberate. It seemed foolish to have a horse on the property that was not being used. So I caught her early in the morning and brought her to the house where I tied her with a short rope to one of the house posts. I wanted to get the saddle on her and teach her to again take a rider. Getting the bridle on her took about 30 minutes of fighting. But it was a different matter when I tried to throw the blanket over her back. She reared terribly.

I stubbornly kept at it for hours until the mare finally accepted the blanket. By mid afternoon, I even had the saddle on her back. But when I tried to tighten the girth strap, she lashed out viciously and almost got my head with a forward kick of her rear leg. With no corral in which to confine her, I decided to tie her with a long rope to a tree that stood by itself. Positioning her at the full stretch of the rope, I tried to mount. She watched me unblinkingly and the moment I moved to mount her she pulled away. I don't know how many times this happened but I was determined to win.

Eventually, the wary mare tried a variation. Instead of bolting ahead as she had done on each previous occasion, she lifted her head, went around behind me and brought the tightened rope around my body, knocking me to the ground. Then she let fly with both her powerful hind legs in an effort to connect with my head, looking over her shoulder all the time. Her deadly hoofs lashed the air an inch or so above my face.

I got the message. The horse was too traumatised by its past to allow me close. Pulling myself up from the ground, I removed the saddle and let her go, grateful that God had delivered me from my own foolishness.

We did our best for the village people. I taught in the school to support the teacher. We showed picture slides in the villages at night. We tried everything we could think of to bring the story of Jesus and salvation to the people of the Saidor district. However, despite the eagerness of our efforts over many months, there was no real response. It seemed the people were like our untamed mare. Reaching them would take a miracle.

WARTIME REMINDERS AND GALIP NUTS

"All people are like grass, and all their faithfulness is like the flowers of the field. The grass withers and the flowers fall, because the breath of the Lord blows on them. Surely the people are grass. The grass withers and flowers fall, but the word of our God endures forever" (Isaiah 40:6–8).

Some of the final battles of World War II had been fought in this area. As Freda and I walked those trails and saw the cunning traps that had been laid by the Japanese soldiers, the well-concealed sniper nests and the diabolical positioning of gun emplacements, we marvelled that anyone could go through the area and survive.

For example, at one point in the trail a large tree lay along the ground. The trunk must have been more than 3 feet (1 metre) thick. The Japanese soldiers had dug behind it, creating a small "nest" with a slit below the tree, just enough to allow a rifle through. A man could walk right up to the log without knowing it was a trap. We saw complete bodies of fallen soldiers, still in their uniforms, lying where they had fallen, their guns beside them. The flesh had gone, but the bones were still dressed for battle, skulls with helmets still in place. Some of the local village people played little tricks by placing human skulls in trees overlooking the path. Ammunition and bombs were scattered all around. Some of the bombs were large. The local people told us that crocodiles caught after the war were found to have many human bones inside them.

When God Calls, Expect Adventure

Beached barges were lying here and there along the foreshore, their forepart on the sand, their sterns sunken under the water. In some, their compasses were still intact, tool kits still in the engine room. One blowlamp I retrieved from the salt water still had fuel in its tank. I pumped it up and lit it, surprised that it worked even after years of submersion.

One day I decided I should get a generator off one of the barges. I stooped under water to go through the engine-room door and found my way in. It was only a small space built for Japanese men, not a big Australian frame like mine. The huge diesel engine took up most of the room. I sat there, with my head above water, a snorkel tube in my mouth and goggles over my eyes. I was conscious that the last men who had been there were probably Japanese sailors fleeing from an air raid. In their quest to serve their emperor, they had brought death and destruction to New Guinea. Like grass in a field, they had withered and disappeared. I was determined to bring life.

Just below the ledge on which I sat, part of the hull had rusted out leaving a gaping hole through which I could see the sand. Only a few feet away was another shelf on which was resting a large black and yellow sea snake. Later I lifted my head just in time to see the snake slide off the shelf and swim across toward me, then dive between my legs and go out through the hole in the hull. It was a startling experience.

There were other hazards to avoid on land. Overshadowing our home was a huge galip tree, which produced a delicious nut that is prized in Papua New Guinea. The tree can be quite large and in season is covered with galip fruit, which vaguely resemble an oversized prune. Inside is a large hard-shelled nut, something like a large Brazil nut. It is so hard that it requires a hammer or a large rock to crack the shell and many a person has failed to open the shell even with such tools.

On this particular tree hung perhaps thousands of these sought-after nuts. The trouble was that the tree also became home to a myriad of stinging green ants. Not many people were prepared to risk the savage stings of the green ants to collect the nuts from the branches.

"I'll soon fix them," declared our teacher as he walked off into the

Wartime Reminders and Galip Nuts

nearby bush. He located a small nest of black ants on the branch of a low shrub, broke off the branch with the nest intact and leaned it against the trunk of the infested galip tree. Immediately the black ants swarmed angrily off in search of the green ants.

By morning, the ground was littered with dying and dead green ants. There was no problem now climbing the tree to knock the delicious nuts to the ground. A little later, someone used the story to illustrate the point that we can never succeed in the Christian life if we try to pick off our bad habits halfheartedly, one by one. Success in the Christian life is assured when we seek outside help to replace bad habits with good ones in a concerted, well-planned attack. I could imagine Christ making a comparison like that.

However, there was another popular method of collecting galip nuts for which it is less easy to draw a spiritual parallel. That other method was to locate the roosting tree of certain birds. Throughout the day, the birds gorged themselves on the fruit, then flew to their roosts for the night. The fleshy outer part of the galip was easily digested but even the bird's acidic gut was unable to digest the hard nuts inside. These simply passed through the digestive system and were unceremoniously deposited on the ground below.

Collecting the nuts from the ground, even if it meant sifting through bird waste, was much easier than climbing the tree and facing the green ants' stings. Perhaps if any parallel can be drawn it is that we may often find good things in the detritus of life. It really depends on our attitude and how determined we are.

———•·•———

We always tried to find blessings in difficulties and worked hard to improve our situation. We did have some modern conveniences. At the Seure station, we put in our first electric lights. We had a 12-volt truck battery for the radio, plus a small 12-volt generator to charge it. I managed to locate some globes from behind the dashboard of a wrecked army truck and these were wired over the bed head. They were poor lights but more convenient than lighting lamps every night. We could simply switch on our tiny electric lights whenever we wanted.

When I went down to Kororo to see to the building work, my

When God Calls, Expect Adventure

quarters were much more challenging. All the students and I slept in a shelter shed that was no more than a few poles to hold a leaf roof over a bamboo platform we used as a large communal bed. All around our small clearing was thick jungle. Even here, there were treasures to be found in the hardship.

In the daytime, a group of cream-tailed Ragiana Bird of Paradise danced in one particular tree. It was glorious to watch them parading about in all their splendour. They were lovely dancers, too. In contrast to their good looks, they must be the noisiest fliers I had ever heard. Each beat of the wings sounded like a person exhaling explosively through clenched teeth. It was a heavy, noisy, almost-can't-make-it kind of flight.

Like the Ragiana Bird of Paradise, we also tried to be beautiful. Our dance was the construction of a school but, like our performers, getting off the ground was quite an effort.

Nadzab airfield, about 60 miles (100 kilometres) from Lae on the New Guinea north coast, as it appeared at the end of the war.

EARTHQUAKE

"Nation will rise against nation, and kingdom against kingdom. There will be famines and earthquakes in various places. All these are the beginnings of birth pains" (Matthew 24:7, 8).

One night the students and I had been asleep only a short while when the ground began to shake and heave violently. It was an earthquake—and a severe one. From the ground came a roar like the muffled scream of mighty jet engines racing from north to south along unseen tracks far below the surface of the earth. What had been solid earth bucked and twisted along the great fault that runs the length of Papua New Guinea and feeds the great volcanoes on this part of the Pacific "Ring of Fire."

We could see nothing in the darkness but huge trees began crashing to the ground all around us. My instincts screamed for me to run, but my mind reasoned that I could just as easily run into the path of a crashing tree. So we stayed huddled close, praying, listening and waiting for the aftershocks to subside. My thoughts were with Freda and the children. In the morning, we found the path blocked in many places where trees had fallen. I had no way of knowing if my family was safe. All I could do was trust that God had heard our prayers.

Later Freda told me her experience. She had put the children to bed but she had stayed up to complete a domestic task. The kerosene pressure lamp hung on its nail in the doorway where it gave light to two rooms. Built as it was on high stumps, the house suddenly began to sway violently. Freda rushed for the children. Taking Kenneth in her arms, she tried to lead Lyn out of the house. The house was shaking so violently that she was bumped heavily from one wall to the other in the hallway.

Freda and the boys had to half-crawl all the way to the door and down the stairs. From the ground, she looked back to see the pressure lamp swinging wildly.

We had always said that if an earth tremor came, we must put out

When God Calls, Expect Adventure

the flame under the kerosene fridge, then put out the lamp. Such flames could easily cause the house to burn. Freda started to go back to extinguish the lamp but the students warned her it was too risky to go back while the tremor was so violent.

Inside the house, things were not as she had left them. When our fridge had been delivered, it came in a large wooden crate, which had been too valuable to simply store. It had been given shelves and became our glass and crockery cabinet, where all our precious crockery was stored.

Now the crate and all it contained lay face down on the floor. Almost every piece of our crockery and our few glass dishes were smashed. This was not easy to take for a woman who had worked so hard trying to turn the house into a home. The scene was heart wrenching for Freda.

———•———

But we grew used to the earth shaking. Mt Lamington—some 260 miles (420 kilometres) south-east of us—had become a regular source of tremors, with speculation that it might erupt.

One morning I was out milking the goats to obtain milk for the children and as I squatted to do the milking I simply could not keep my balance. I was sure the billy goat must be butting the sides of the small shed. At the same time I heard a roar like a huge express train passing just beneath me. It was then I noticed the coconut trees. They were whipping their heads about so much they almost bowed to the ground.

On the news later that day, we heard that Mt Lamington had erupted. A huge amount of the mountainside had blasted out, sweeping the forest, villages and their occupants before it. An estimated 4000 people were killed in a blast that devastated everything for 14 miles (22 kilometres) on that side of the mountain.

Sadly, one of my college friends died in that blast. Maynard Lock was living in the Poppendetta area and decided that morning to climb the mountain with his father-in-law, a judge in the New Guinea courts. The two adventurous men intended to snap some pictures, and collect evidence that the enormous volcano was becoming active and might erupt. Sadly, they were never seen again.

———•———

Earthquake

Other dangers were less conspicuous. Daily practice on the mission station after worship each morning was that the students would line up to be given the work to be carried out that day. Our son, four-year-old Lyn, considered the students as his friends so would often line up with them.

One morning I had detailed most of the students to go down the coast a short distance to collect some timber poles for a planned building. Lyn started to go with them, so I called him back, telling him not to go with them. He was most unhappy and persisted. I reminded him it was for students only to do that kind of work.

He countered with, "But I lined up with them."

I smiled, then thought to myself, *They'll care for him, why not let him go?* So I said, "OK, you go with them."

By this time, the boys had rounded a clump of trees. Lyn knew the way and ran after them as fast as his little legs could go. I thought no more of it until about 30 minutes later when Lyn came in soaked to the skin and crying.

When we heard what had happened, we were horrified. The students had hurried so much that Lyn had not caught up with them before he reached a small stream that had to be crossed. He plunged in but there had been rain in the hills and the water was too high. In a few moments, he was being swept downstream to the ocean.

Somehow, Lyn managed to stay afloat and some distance down he bumped into a rock or log to which he managed to cling. Then he dragged himself out and found his way through the bush back to the mission station. Surely the angel of the Lord had stepped in to correct the damage I had created by my thoughtlessness!

Our second son, Ken, was to have his first birthday during our stay at Seure. We decided to make it an occasion when we could invite some of the village people to join with us. As a "special," we gave the students a large goat to cook and prepare. Much of the preparation was carried out under our house, but the actual place for dining was on a grassy patch that the boys had covered with leaf shade above and with clean banana leaves for the tablecloth.

When all was ready, we were called to take our places at the "table." Freda was invited to sit at the place of honour and as soon as she

When God Calls, Expect Adventure

was seated she looked at the table. Directly in front of her was the cooked head of the goat with its eyes staring directly at her, positioned deliberately as a mark of honour. It was intended that she could then enjoy the greatest delicacy they knew—the eyes. Freda declined.

The Hawkes family (circa 1953): Freda and Ken on left, Lester and Lyndon on right.

LEAVING SAIDOR

"But now I urge you to keep up your courage, because not one of you will be lost; only the ship will be destroyed" (Acts 27:22).

Jesus had said that His followers were to become "fishers of men." But somehow things were not going that way in the Saidor area. Our mission saw no success in its "fishing" in the area.

Neither did the Catholic mission. They actually recalled their priest. However, good man that he was, he refused to go and held his ground. His superiors reluctantly accepted his stand but advised him that when he did move on, they would not be replacing him.

Nor were the Lutherans gaining converts, to the real discouragement of the local Lutheran pastor. Sadly, he became so disheartened and discouraged by the indifference of the people that he became depressed. It is not possible to understand why people do such things. He committed suicide, using his own rifle, and his church decided not to replace him either.

The Adventist Church mission office discussed the situation with us—by mail, of course—and it was decided that a different approach had to be tried. Kororo—some 10 miles (16 kilometres) south—had been leased for a future school and to retain the lease on that land we were required to erect a building there. To satisfy this requirement, we would have to move from our home on the beach. We collected the timber on the Kororo station and split palms for the flooring. Half the roofing from our house at Seure was removed and transported down by a Papuan-style double-log canoe.

After completing the new buildings at Kororo station, our work would be done. We had arranged with Pastor Ward Nolan—acting president of the Madang Mission—to come and collect us on a given Tuesday so we could begin our journey to our next posting. The house at Kororo was completed on the Friday before that deadline.

On the Sunday morning, the students and I sailed back to the Seure mission in the canoe. We normally would call on the village people

When God Calls, Expect Adventure

to help us drag the heavy double canoe up the shingle beach. It was about 7.30 am when we approached the beach and I was apprehensive because the village people rarely rose early and went to the gardens before noon. They seemed to prefer to spend the morning talking and chewing betel nut. I feared they might resent being called to assist so early.

As we came nearer, we saw all the people walking toward their gardens with their gardening tools. Never before had I known them to go to work at that time in the morning, so to me this could only mean one thing. The villagers knew we were about to leave the district and they didn't want to give any more help. We had served them well, yet they were absenting themselves when we needed assistance.

Most of the local students had gone back to their villages, so we only had a few boys from Madang and a couple of men who had been teachers. Without the help of the village men, it was impossible to drag the heavy 50-foot (15-metre) canoe up the beach, nor was it going to be possible to carry the goods from the station to the beach where we were to meet the mission ship on Tuesday. I could sense serious problems ahead.

The only thing we could do was to try to anchor the canoe out at sea, but we had no true anchor and the seas were heavy that morning. Neither could we stay on the canoe, so we dropped a heavy object to act as anchor and all but one student—Nenel—dived overboard and swam to the shore. I went home to assist with the packing. Some of the staff began to burn the poor quality houses we would no longer be using. Others removed the remainder of the roofing iron from our house.

No more than an hour had passed when Nenel came running in to say that the anchor had dragged and the canoe was breaking up on the beach. We raced down, but it was too late. The two great logs were intact, but all the cross timbers had smashed and most of the lashings were broken. The decking was washing in and out with the waves. The goods we had left on the canoe were now somewhere under the ocean, including the generator I had salvaged from the Japanese wreck.

It was Sunday morning and we had a smashed canoe, with no hope of repairing it before we had to leave. We had no roof over our head and no carriers to transport our goods to the beach when the mission boat

Leaving Saidor

called for us on Tuesday morning. And there was no way to get word through to Pastor Nolan to tell him of our problems. Without help, it would be impossible to make a fresh start.

We sent for the Luluai—the village leader—and a group of village men came meandering through the plantation with him. There was no friendliness on their faces and I was not looking forward to this meeting. I thank God Freda was there. She was so upset at the way things had turned out that she said the things I should have said to them.

"No, no, please don't tell the government," they pled. "Truly, we promise to repair that canoe this afternoon."

"This afternoon?" Freda asked.

"Yes."

"Not tomorrow?"

"Yes, yes, we'll go and do it now. We promise!"

And off they went. I felt Freda was saying too much but God must have put the right words in her mouth for she had said what needed to be said, and the village men were sorry for what they had done or—more accurately—were afraid that an adverse report of their activities would get to the government.

Repairs to the canoe commenced that afternoon and, to my surprise, the canoe was fully seaworthy the next day. In addition, the village men offered to carry our cargo to the beach for us. We gave them presents as a token of thanks, marvelling that God had turned a disaster into a blessing. Had that canoe not broken, we would not have had the assistance of the village people.

We had removed the rest of the iron from the roof of our house and burned down all unwanted buildings. We wanted to leave the place as tidy as possible and it would not do to have derelict dwellings littering the land. Only the native missionary's house and a building for a church were left.

About mid-morning Tuesday, we stood on the beach waiting for the arrival of the mission ship, totally unaware of the events that had been unfolding in Madang. Pastor Ward Nolan had been acting president while Pastor Stan Gander was on furlough. Knowing he had the *M V Lelaman* at his command, Ward had made the promise to collect us from the beach that Tuesday morning.

When God Calls, Expect Adventure

Unexpectedly, Pastor Gander had returned earlier than planned. He immediately announced that he must get up into the Sepik area as soon as possible and, on Monday afternoon, he informed Ward Nolan that he would be taking the *Lelaman* the next day.

"No, you can't do that," Ward said.

"And why not?" Stan demanded.

"I have promised to collect Lester and family on Tuesday."

"You can collect him when I return."

Ward refused to back down. "I can't just leave them there."

"The boat must go to the Sepik!"

"I said I was coming to get them," Ward declared. "And get them I must!"

These two good men were standing on the wharf at the time. Stan was determined that he was about to take off for the Sepik. Ward was just as determined that he had to fulfil his promise. The argument—I was told later—became even more heated.

Stan Gander must have seen something in Ward's face that worried him.

"I can't swim," Stan protested, backing away. "Truly, I can't swim. Be careful, the boys are watching."

Thankfully for Freda and I, Ward had won the day and Stan agreed to postpone his urgent missionary work to pick us up. I often wonder what might have been the outcome if Pastor Gander had undertaken the journey to the Sepik, while we were sitting on the beach with all our worldly goods in a few boxes beside us. But God had His hand over events and all turned out well. The boat arrived. Our goods were loaded, and the double canoe was delivered to the people in the town of Saidor who had agreed to purchase it.

BOGIA

"Then I said, 'Here I am, I have come—it is written about me in the scroll. I desire to do your will, my God; your law is within in my heart'" (Psalm 40:7, 8).

Back in Madang, there was still no word from the government regarding the second Hansenide leper colony, so we were still "up in the air." We had a place to live in Madang, and we were able to assist Pastor Stan Gander in some things. But we were missionaries! That meant we wanted to feel we were accomplishing something worthwhile for our Lord. It was decided that I should take a few national men with me and proceed to the Bogia district, where our church's message had not yet penetrated.

Pastor Gander was again taking the *M V Lelaman* to the Sepik, so our group travelled with him. Our first stop was at Manam Island, located a few miles out to sea from the Hatzfeldhaven District, a little south of Bogia. The island is a classic, cone-shaped volcano that rises impressively out of the warm, tropical water. As it rose from the deep, its lava cooled rather quickly, forming a thick pillar. But once the pillar rose above the ocean the lava would cool more slowly, allowing the flows to spread wider, giving the island its peculiar mushroom shape.

Finding a place to drop the anchor was difficult. When we did find a place, it had to be uncomfortably close to the rocky cliffs and white surf. I spent the night in one of the several villages on the island with a native missionary who had been sent to the island a few months earlier. He was greatly encouraged by our presence and we had a blessed time with the people. Freda and I had experienced real isolation ourselves and we knew the importance of a visit by someone who took an interest in the work we were doing.

As the boat began to leave the next morning, we looked on what must have been one of the loveliest scenes one could ever witness. The deep sea was the brightest of blues. The conical island was swathed with the loveliest green, while from the top drifted a beautiful plume of white

When God Calls, Expect Adventure

smoke. And at the top of the cliff stood a group of happy people, waving us goodbye and inviting us to return again soon.

An hour or so later, we went ashore by dinghy to meet with the village people of the Bogia district and see if any villages might be happy to have a missionary stay among them. The whole area had been under the care of another church for decades. However, the people had not advanced as much as they should have. Healthy competition is good in mission work, just as it is healthy in business. With no competition in this area, the village people had not advanced.

We gathered the different village groups together and talked with them. One village quickly requested that one of the missionaries be located in their midst. I went to several other villages and talked with them until I found another that would like to have a missionary live among them.

The problem was that the second man who had come with us had shown less and less interest in taking up a posting. All he seemed to want to do was sit with his back to a coconut tree and strum on his homemade ukulele. When I told him of the village he had been invited to work with, he said he had no interest. No amount of talking would get him to change his mind. I was so disappointed!

This was not the first time I had seen a good worker lose interest in the Lord's work after they began to strum a ukulele. I began to dislike the instrument, a dislike that even extended to guitars and other stringed instruments for a time. I have learned better, of course! But it was disappointing to have a village make the request, for me to have a person right there to take up the post, but for that person to turn the work down. He dropped out of the Lord's work. Despite all that, today the Adventist work in the Bogia district is strong.

The arrangement was for Pastor Gander to collect me as he returned from the Sepik. We were to meet at the Potsdam Plantation.

Talking with the Potsdam manager and his wife while awaiting Pastor Gander, I heard an interesting story. Only a few miles down the coastline, living as the manager of a plantation, lived an Australian who went under the historic name of Oliver Twist.

It was well known that Oliver enjoyed his drinks. A few weeks earlier had been Christmas, and Oliver began to celebrate on Christmas Eve. The next morning he was still "enjoying" himself. All plantations and

Bogia

government outposts were tied together by a "Radio Sched" on which messages could be passed by radio at nominated times each day. Oliver turned on his radio and transmitter, and with a heavily slurred voice began to pass out Christmas messages to the various operators of the different stations. After completing that list he began to give them a concert of very questionable songs. For hours and hours, he simply sat with his radio transmitting, giving messages, telling stories between drinks, singing or whatever else came to mind.

As long as Oliver Twist's set was transmitting, no-one else could transmit. Station after station tried to tell him to get off the air, but he wasn't listening.

Some of the top government authorities were called to transmitters in a vain effort to get him off the air but he never gave them a chance. He never listened. He simply transmitted. People everywhere were getting increasingly mad with him and someone finally had to take a boat to his plantation and deliver a stern message!

Missionaries can easily fall into the same trap. It can be easy to transmit our ideas without really listening. It is not enough to have a message that we impose on everyone else. We need to listen. We need to acknowledge their needs. And we need to respond.

Pastor Stan Gander giving injections to a Highlander.

DEALING WITH THE UNEXPECTED

"*If you spend yourselves in behalf of the hungry and satisfy the needs of the oppressed, then your light will rise in the darkness, and your night will become like the noonday. The Lord will guide you always*" (Isaiah 58:10, 11).

While travelling with Pastor Gander on the *Lelaman*, we had an unusual experience where the Lord's hand could be clearly seen. It was evening when we set off from Potsdam Plantation going south to Madang. It was very dark and we had to travel by compass. As light broke next morning, we could not recognise the shoreline. The shoreline we could see was unfamiliar and even the compass bearing was wrong. We reluctantly came to the conclusion we had overshot Madang during the night and were now well south of the harbour.

But it still didn't look right. The direction we were forced to travel did not correspond with the charts. At last we decided the only way to know whether we were north or south of Madang was to go ashore at a village and ask. We made our way into a convenient bay and some of the crew went ashore in the dinghy while we waited.

When the crew returned, they told a strange story. No boat had ever entered the bay where we were because there are so many dangerous reefs. We were well north of Madang, and had hardly travelled far at all during the night. From what they had learned, we estimated we still had about six hours travel to reach our destination. To make matters

Dealing With the Unexpected

even more confusing, the last leg of the trip into Madang should have required about two hours travel, but we did it in about one hour!

I thought about it and studied the maps for some time after getting home, concluding that there must have been an unusually strong current against us for most of the trip, but after holding us up all night it actually assisted us for the last part of the journey.

Listening to the local 7 pm radio news, I heard that a government barge on its way back from Karkar Island (out to sea from Madang) with a large group of people aboard had broken down at sea and disappeared. Despite searches all day, no sign of the barge or its passengers could be located.

Having had our experience that day with these unusual currents, I reasoned that they had affected the barge. I rang the Marine Department and reported our experiences, quoting times and speeds. I even suggested where I believed the barge might be located.

Despite the scepticism in the voice of the man listening, they eventually sent out a ship in the direction I indicated and the barge was found right where we had worked out it should be. I felt the Lord had again used us to save the lives of some who might otherwise have been lost altogether.

Sometimes God can teach us profound lessons in the simplest of incidents. Pastor Nolan—now the new president in the Madang area—had gone away on patrol when we arrived. One evening his wife, Ora, asked me if I would start the generator engine to get the lights going.

"Sure, where is it?" I asked.

"It's over in that shed near the mango tree," she replied.

"Are there any tricks needed?" I queried, knowing that many mission generators were unique and temperamental.

"Yes, Lester. It's an old Japanese Yanmar engine. Ward always calls it 'Grandma' because he said it sleeps on its back all day and only does a bit of work of an evening. It's a diesel engine and is sometimes hard to get started. When it refuses to start, Ward puts a bit of petrol on its breather and it starts easily. The petrol is in a small oilcan in the shed."

Sure enough, it was an old-style engine with the open big ends and the long connecting rod lying naked in the opening between two rather

When God Calls, Expect Adventure

large iron flywheels. I tried to start it by turning it over, but there was no response. With a smug grin, I said to it, "OK, old girl, I know how to get you going."

I hadn't done this before, but felt confident I could handle it. I poured a little petrol onto the breather, where air was sucked into the cylinders. To make sure it would really start, I poured more petrol on until it began to leak out the bottom. Then I gave the wheel a spin.

There was an ear-splitting "BANG!" and the engine took off. With each revolution, the bangs seemed to get louder and more violent, until the engine was fairly screaming. Panicking, I turned off the fuel but it made no difference. "Grandma" still screamed even louder, her normally sedentary pistons flying up and down with such force that she threatened to explode. Then I noticed the whole huge concrete block that served as Grandma's bed was lifting and falling, sending out clouds of dust from underneath.

I took off for the safety of the bush, expecting the engine to explode behind me, fragmenting into little pieces. Instead, it finally slowed down, then stopped. The dust ceased to rise. The only continuing evidence of the experience was in my racing heart, as I left the safety of a tree and went to investigate.

In my inexperience, I couldn't understand what had happened, so I went back to the house and rang the town's engineer. After giving him a short explanation, he asked one question.

"Son, did you put any petrol on the breather?"

I began to justify myself, "They told me . . ."

The engineer cut right through, saying, "Son, learn this lesson. Always follow the maker's instructions. Don't listen to anyone else. If the maker says use diesel, use only what he says." And he hung up.

Many times I have told that story. It has illustrated many talks on health, particularly with regard to diet. If we humans hope to get the best out of life and avoid many of the illnesses common around us; if we wish to have the happiest and the longest life, we can do no better than to "follow the Maker's instructions." We are wise to use only the fuel for our "engines" that our Maker assigned to our fore-parents. Any attempt on our part to operate on any other fuels can only result in damage and our malfunctioning.

HOUSE FIRE

"When you walk through the fire, you will not be burned; the flames will not set you ablaze. For I am the Lord your God, the Holy One of Israel, your Saviour" (Isaiah 43:2, 3).

It was now 1952. After a time of impatient waiting at Madang and without any sign yet from the government that the second leper colony could open, we were invited to return to the Highlands, locating this time at Kabiufa in the Asaro Valley, about seven miles (11 kilometres) west of Goroka.

Here was located the new Coral Sea Union Mission Training School, only in its infancy at that time. We were invited to help teach at the school. In Goroka, Pastor Eric Boehm was the local mission president, while Kabiufa High School was under the care of Lyn Thrift. Kabiufa would become one of Papua New Guinea's leading private schools, a vital institution that trained church leaders, prominent businessmen and even politicians.

The house we were assigned was small but nice, built of bamboo walls with a thick grass roof. It contained a small "lounge room," one small bedroom and a tiny room we used for dining. At the rear and semi-detached was the kitchen and bathroom, also made of the same materials. Just out the back of the kitchen ran a small water race, bringing water from a creek to the school gardens.

Most mornings we were up and about the day's duties by dawn. But one particular morning we had opportunity to "sleep in." Of course, we didn't sleep—we were too accustomed to being busy in the mornings—but we did stay under the cosy blankets while we heard the kitchen boy come and light the wood stove, then go off to his other duties. It was a cold morning and we luxuriated in the warmth of the bed while listening to the crackling of the fire in the kitchen. It was a rare privilege.

I remember saying that morning, "Doesn't it sound great to hear the fire crackling away so merrily?"

When God Calls, Expect Adventure

We enjoyed it for a few more minutes, lying in our bed, enjoying the warmth and comfort.

"He certainly must have used the right sticks in the stove this morning," I commented. "The fire seems to be getting better, don't you think?" And we rested there a few moments longer.

"It almost sounds too good. I think I'll go and have a peep." The bedroom was located at the far end of house, farthest from the only exit.

One look into the kitchen and I shouted, "The kitchen's on fire!"

The entire under-side of the thick grass roof was burning. Smoke billowed upwards and the greedy flames threatened to consume the whole house if left for even a minute longer.

On the kitchen bench stood a 10-gallon (35-litre) drum in which we kept our drinking water. Grasping the aluminium dipper, I began tossing water up at the fire. Thankfully, the grass was damp from the morning dew and the water I frantically threw up was enough to quench the flames. Had we waited any longer it would have burned like fury!

When the fire was out, still wearing my now-sodden pyjamas, I went to find Freda and the two boys. They were on the safety of the lawn. But, to my amazement, our large camphor-wood chest was also out on the grass.

"Why did you bring this out?" I queried.

"It has all our south clothes in it." Freda replied, referring to the treasured items of clothing we would wear when we returned to Australia. Freda had been working on the sewing machine for weeks making clothes for the boys and herself to use on our forthcoming furlough. They were among our most precious possessions at that time.

"OK, I'll take it back in."

I tried to lift the heavy chest, but hardly budged it. I tried again and failed.

"How did you get it out here?" I asked, checking to see if she had received help.

"I just brought it out. Why?"

"Freda, this chest is so heavy I can hardly move it! How did you do it?"

"I don't know," Freda replied, as puzzled as I was. "I just did."

I needed Freda's assistance to move the trunk back inside because

House Fire

it was impossible to move it on my own. It's amazing what the human body can do when it is sufficiently motivated. It makes me wonder how much more we could have done for the Lord if only we had put our complete energy to the task.

———•———

Marvellous to us, in a different way, was the opportunity to return to Australia for furlough. According to mission policy, we were entitled to return home for six months. Three months were to be for church work and the other three were for holidays. Freda was terribly excited. Our children had been born in Papua New Guinea and this would be the first opportunity for loved ones to meet them.

Our trip home was on the *Malaita*, under the command of "Wild Bill." We called at Samarai where Bill regularly collected large numbers of tropical fish and placed them in the many salt-water fish tanks installed all over the deck of the ship. Someone in Australia must have been buying the fish, probably for sale to folks with small aquariums in their homes.

Furlough was a special time and I chose to assist evangelists in their campaigns and duties. On one occasion, I worked with Pastor Burnside in the role of truck driver. My job was to drive a mobile advertisement through the city and try to gain as much attention for his campaigns as possible.

"See if you can stall the truck at every corner," Pastor Burnside instructed me with a grin, "so that people can have ample time to read the large advertisements on the back."

But after our time in Australia, it was not difficult to return to Papua New Guinea. We loved the work there!

OMAURA

"Praise be to you, Lord, the God of our father Israel, from everlasting to everlasting. Yours, Lord, is the greatness and the power and the glory and the majesty and the splendour, for everything in heaven and earth is yours" (1 Chronicles 29:10, 11).

Even after our furlough, the government had not yet moved to set up a second leper colony. We returned to Kabiufa where I helped with the building program—classrooms, then houses. Next I was given a team of Mussau builders and asked to build the mission house in Goroka. Because finances were tight, the plan was that on Monday morning I would ride my bicycle the seven hilly miles (about 12 kilometres) to Goroka, spend the week building, then return home again Friday afternoon.

After a few weeks of this work, the mission committee met in Goroka. Shortly after the committee closed for the day, Eric Boehm called me aside and told me that the mission had decided not to wait for the government to set up a second leprosy hospital. Instead, the mission had decided to establish its own nurses training school and hospital at Bena Bena. Freda and I were asked to head up the institution. This was great news. We were tired of constantly moving and doing work on other people's mission stations.

To scout things out, I went the 12 miles (20 kilometres) by jeep across to Bena. I shifted some of our goods using a trailer, revelling in the thought that soon we were to settle down in one location for a reasonable period of time, rather than be in another temporary posting. While anticipating and waiting to do leprosy work, we'd had 15 moves in the previous five years!

We returned the next day to Goroka for the last of our supplies. The mission committee was still in session when Eric Boehm, the president, came out and called to me.

"Lester," he said. "The committee has decided that Omaura would be a much better location for the nursing school than Bena Bena. We are asking you to go there instead."

Omaura

"Why?" I asked. "We have just moved most of our things."

"Bena is near a large government hospital," came the reply, "and it would constitute a duplication of services. Omaura is not at all well served medically, and it has better gardening possibilities."

It was a month before we actually moved down to Omaura so Freda decided to make the most of our situation in the short time we had in Bena. I installed the generator in the hydro-power plant Laurie and I had been working on months earlier and built the switchboard to go with the unit. This was a help to Jack Aitken and his wife who followed us at Bena when we left. Under Jack's leadership, Bena Bena became a great school. It is always pleasing to have the opportunity to make things a little better for those who were to follow.

Omaura lies in an undulating grassy valley at about 4800 feet (1400 metres) above sea level and some 18 miles (30 kilometres) south of Kainantu. That stretch of "road" was simply dreadful most of the time and especially so when there was or had been rain. But the station itself was attractive with its long avenue of pine trees leading to the house, from which we so often looked out over the valley to Yonki Mountain.

1955 Graduating class at Omaura Nurses Training School.

When God Calls, Expect Adventure

Within a few weeks, 24 hopeful medical students arrived, about half of whom were men. It was great to think that we had been granted the privilege of establishing the first nurses training centre outside of Port Moresby itself. But we had nowhere for them to sleep, no classroom in which to teach them, no hospital, no medicines, no syllabus, no books, no precedent to follow! All we really had was faith that if this was God's will, He would find solutions we could hardly imagine.

To add to our challenge, Omaura—established several years before the war—was an operating mission station, with its own district and a string of village churches to care for, plus its own school of some 100 boarding students. All these needed care in addition to major renovations on the station. The roof on the school had fallen in. The sleeping quarters for the students were way below standard. Everywhere we looked, there were jobs demanding immediate attention. And, of course, our budget was limited. How, we wondered, could all this be achieved? Nevertheless, this was God's school and we knew God would find a way.

It seemed the most important task was to build a new dormitory for the boys, and re-pitch and replace the roof on the school. The building also needed a room where the nursing students could meet. All this

Patients waiting for medical care at Omaura. The building at rear was the temporary hospital.

was managed in a surprisingly short time, giving a place for some of the medical students to live and a classroom in which they could be given their medical lectures.

Pastor Ward Nolan, then health director at the church's head office, visited soon after we had settled in. We showed him the plans we had drawn up for the hospital we intended to build.

"We have only just converted a disused bamboo house into a temporary dispensary," I explained. "And for a short-term measure, we have taken over a deserted village, situated some distance away. That is where we are housing our patients."

"I see," Ward replied noncommittally.

"When do we get the money to build the hospital?" I asked. "We can't go on like this."

"Sorry, Lester, there is no money." Ward shrugged his shoulders helplessly. "We talked about this in committee last week and the decision was that you would need to put up a temporary hospital. Later, when we get more money we can erect a permanent building."

I became upset. "I'm sorry too, Ward, but there will be no temporary building put up on this station! I don't believe in them. Invariably they become permanent. I suggest you go back to the committee and tell them there will be no building put up on this station until we can put one up that is of permanent material. I'm sick of temporary buildings!"

Freda stared at me, surprised at my outburst.

"Well, I'll pass on your message, Lester," Ward promised.

"Thank you for coming," Freda added diplomatically. "Please come inside. We can eat soon."

After all I'd said, I felt guilty. I don't usually talk like that!

A couple of weeks later, I received a letter from the church's treasurer saying that a sum of 500 pounds (about $1000) had been "found" and had now been allocated for the proposed hospital building. In the same letter, we were informed that no builder was available to do the work. We would have to manage the entire building process on our own.

That was OK with us. So long as we had the money, we would do the work ourselves. I now think God put those frustrated words in my mouth and used them for His purpose. Without them, I doubt any money would have been allocated at all!

When God Calls, Expect Adventure

The first step was to update the derelict station sawmill. Most of the circular saws hanging on the wall were buckled and unusable, so we sent for a book on "Saw Doctoring" and ordered a kit of saw-doctor hammers so we could restore them.

The engine that drove the mill was an old 8-horsepower Ruston Hornby diesel that needed a complete overhaul. It was hopelessly underpowered, but someone before us had overcome that by reversing the drive pulleys, meaning the saws would now "tear and growl," rather than "sing" through the logs.

Tamangei—the teacher in charge of the day school—took over the operation of the mill, assisted by another teacher and a few students. Those men worked heroically. They worked so hard that, one day, the heat from the engine exhaust set the grass roof of the mill ablaze. Everyone raced onto the roof, taking anything they could grab with which to beat out the blaze. We thank the Lord the whole mill did not burn down. Its loss would have been a terrible blow.

With the assistance of the male medical students, we began the task of building the hospital. One of the students was taught to be our window-maker; another learned how to level off the stumps for the new building. Each learned some new skill. All the skills I had acquired working on different stations were now put to ready use and slowly the hospital took shape. Each afternoon we also provided class time where medical skills were learned.

A visiting government official reminded us of how much progress we were making.

"You have your own little kingdom here," he exclaimed on his visit.

"Why? What do you mean?" we asked.

"Just look around you. You have your own school, your own hospital, your own electricity, your own sawmill, your own church, your own store—you've got it all. And to top it off, the whole thing is set in such a peaceful, park-like atmosphere."

Freda and I looked at each other for a moment before saying, "I suppose he's right."

It was a busy and a happy station. Trouble was that—like all other stations—we always needed just a little more finance. There was so much more that should be done—and could be done—if we could only

Omaura

pay for it. We sold sawn timber to government stations and plantations for their building programs. This brought in a little cash, but never enough. We operated on an annual budget of 100 pounds, which had to cover the operation of the sawmill, the school, the jeep and upkeep of the whole station plus the hospital.

Omaura trainees treating "outpatients" in the great outdoors. Men rarely came to clinics with women and children.

BELLY SPIRIT

"'On that day, I will banish the names of the idols from the land, and they will be remembered no more,' declares the Lord Almighty. 'I will remove both the prophets and the spirit of impurity from the land'" (Zechariah 13:2).

Freda took on a heavy load at Omaura. With the assistance of the female nursing students, she would sometimes care for hundreds of patients who came to the dispensary each morning. She had to watch over the obstetric cases that invariably came only when the women were in deep trouble. On top of all this, Freda took the jeep and timber trailer out into the bush and down into the gullies to haul in the pine logs she would buy from the village people.

A problem that had to be faced was the terrible fear all Highlanders had toward what they called "poison." Highlanders would allow nothing personal to be left where another could get it, because that substance, they believed, could be used as a basis to "poison" the original owner.

For example, a Highlander would never allow the chewed remains of his sugarcane to drop on the road where an enemy could come along and use it to work "poison" on him, possibly causing his death. Waste materials could be made safe only by throwing them in a running stream. No paring of his fingernails was allowed to drop carelessly; no blood could be left on the trail; no hair was allowed to drop where it could be found. These and many other items could be used to "poison" one to death.

Looking at this with our understanding of germs, it seemed a rudimentary method of controlling the spread of disease. However, their fear was more deep-seated. It included the fear of evil spirits that could be used by an enemy to inflict illness and death.

As a foreign medical worker, it was difficult to know what our patients thought about their treatment. Although not something we encourage, it is possible that some thought that medical power was actually power over the spirit world. Wherever possible we taught people about preventative health.

Belly Spirit

Doing the rounds of the hospital patients one morning, we stopped by the bed of a woman who had come to us only three days earlier with pneumonia. Antibiotics had worked their cure on her.

"You are almost ready to go home again," we told her. "Just one more day of medicine and you can go home."

She was elated and gave us a lovely wide-mouthed grin.

During the afternoon rounds, we came again to the small grass hut in which she slept. We were shaken to find the woman unconscious, with almost complete loss of blood pressure, no discernible pulse at the wrist and very shallow breathing. It was glaringly obvious to us that this woman was dying.

I called for Freda to see if she could pick some clue I had missed, but she was as puzzled as the rest of us. There was no obvious reason.

"Has she eaten today?" Freda asked.

"How could she?" I replied helpfully. "She is unconscious."

"She has to have food if she is going to have strength to fight back." Freda declared, determined to do what she could for the woman. "I know—we'll use a stomach tube."

Freda raced off to prepare something nutritious, while I readied the tube. A stomach tube, made of rubber hose about the size of a small finger, is more than 3 feet (1 metre) long with one smooth end protecting the outlet hole, with a rubber funnel at the other end. The tube is inserted down the throat until it is inside the stomach, then the nourishment is poured in via the funnel.

We noticed some resistance as we inserted the tube. We had thought that being unconscious she would not have been aware of what we were doing. Proceeding with the treatment, Freda poured some eggnog down the tube.

Turning to the night-duty nurse, I said with resignation, "I have no idea what is wrong. But it does seem she might die tonight. If she does, please call me." At that moment, I was wondering what I would write on the death certificate.

But there was no call during the night. As soon as morning worship was finished, I hastened to see the woman. To my surprise, I found her sitting with a group of her friends around the small fire, laughing and devouring a chunk of sweet potato.

When God Calls, Expect Adventure

We were mystified. We called Esther, the local nurse who spoke the woman's own language. It seemed an eternity as they talked back and forth, until Esther nodded the well-known nod that closes such interrogations.

"This is what happened," said Esther. "After you saw her yesterday morning, she learned that the previous occupant of this bed had died here. And less than three days later, she was placed on the same bed."

"Go on," I urged.

"It is commonly believed that the spirit of the dead person stays nearby for three days. That spirit enters the belly of any person foolish enough to lie on the bed before the three days are expired. When she found out about the previous person, she knew she was going to die. Nothing could save her from the spirit."

Esther added, "Then, last night, you pushed that tube down into her belly. That tube gave the spirit a road to get out, and he went. That's why she is alright again today."

The power of the mind! In the first instance, it was a faulty belief that was killing her. Then, when the mind changed beliefs, she became well again almost instantly. Within the space of less than 24 hours, this woman had changed from dying to very much alive, all because of the power of "mind over matter," coupled with a dread of the power of evil spirits.

"If only we could persuade people to have as much faith in Jesus, what miracles we would see," I murmured to myself. "The trouble is that our faith is not decided enough, only partly developed. If our faith was more solid, surely we would be seeing more miracles than we are now seeing. Not just more miracles in the medical field, but in the area of the Spirit."

My mind went to Jesus' oft-repeated statement, "According to your faith, be it unto you." We receive only in proportion to our faith. I determined that I would work more closely with God than I had in the past.

TEARS OF THANKS

"When he saw the crowds, he had compassion on them, because they were harassed and helpless, like sheep without a shepherd. Then he said to his disciples, "The harvest is plentiful but the workers are few. Ask the Lord of the harvest, therefore, to send out workers into his harvest field" (Matthew 9:36–38).

We felt sure that there were still many people in the villages who would be helped if only they would come in for medical care. So we decided to call in a representative from each of the surrounding villages and give that person a basic course in what was little more than first aid. They were to come one day a week for a period of time. Then they would be given basic supplies and given the position of "Medical Officer" for the village. They were intended to be the liaison between the village and the hospital-to-be, becoming the hospital's representative in the village.

To add to their feeling of position, we conducted a final examination and a graduation service. None of them could read or write, so we conducted an oral exam. We invited the government doctor from the Kainantu hospital to take part in the examination and graduation. He duly presented them with their graduation certificates.

For several months, the scheme worked wonderfully. Then I noticed that there seemed to be fewer of these hospital representatives in the villages, until at last there were none. It was then that we worked out what had happened. I spoke to the Kainantu doctor when I discovered that all our village representatives were now working in the Kainantu hospital as medical staff. I wanted to know why.

His face lit up in a slightly embarrassed grin. "They are my best workers in the wards," he said. "In fact, they are better than some who

When God Calls, Expect Adventure

have been here for years. The really good ones are superior to many we get from the Port Moresby Training School. They came seeking a position with this hospital. How could I say no?"

Those we had trained were all church members and anyone who has the Lord in his heart should be a better worker, especially in one of the caring professions. So, in a sense, even this loss on our part added to the Lord's glory in the overall picture.

Yet our first village representatives were sorely missed. Over centuries, a strong fear of entering the territory of another tribe had built up in the minds of the Highland people. This meant many needy cases simply would not come to the hospital if it meant traversing the land of another clan.

In an effort to overcome this barrier, we arranged medical patrols into villages around our region. At the same time, these patrols gave the medical students first-hand experience in locating, diagnosing and treating the diseases common to the area. Any condition too complex for simple treatment was brought back to the hospital. For some patients, it was the first time they had left their small tribal area and

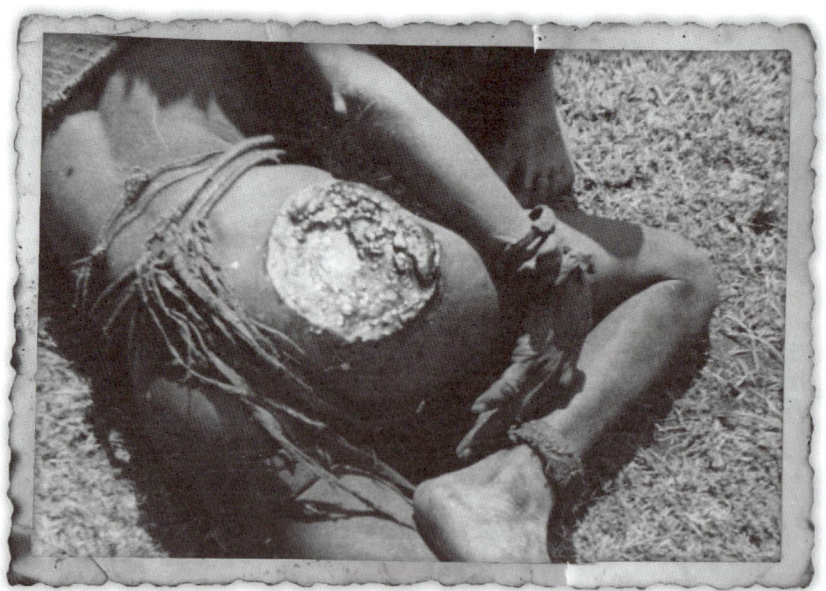

Some ulcers were huge, but disappeared with one injection of penicillin. Known locally as a "shoot"—the people would come with a request, "Masta, mi laikim shoot?"

they would not have dared come without an escort.

The students brought back an interesting report from one such patrol. As they entered a village, they noticed all the inhabitants hurrying in the other direction.

"I wonder where they are going—and why?" someone queried.

With no obvious answer, they suspected a sick person was being hidden. The medical group followed as quickly as they could. However, the village people had scattered in all directions, causing the students to stand and ponder.

"Hey, what's that dreadful smell?" one medical student commented.

"It's terrible," another exclaimed. "What could it be?"

The students followed their noses, and were led into a long grass area where they found a 14-year-old girl, alone and shivering with fear. This was where the smell was coming from.

One of the team had a closer look. Examining her gently, he discovered she had a maggot-filled ulcer that extended all the way from the small of her back to the calf muscle of her leg. She had suffered this terrible condition for so long, with her legs drawn up in the foetal position, that the knee of the affected leg was locked stiff. The flesh appeared to have joined between the calf muscle and the buttocks. Filled with pity, the men brought her into the hospital on a stretcher, watched no doubt by the clan members who had attempted to hide her in the grass.

It was many painful weeks before the girl was able to return home. She had to learn to walk again. However, in the end she was restored to health and she returned happily, eager to show her family that she was healed. Without the intervention of the medical students, she would either have died or lived a life of disability.

One of the most common ailments of the district was yaws, an infection that caused unsightly ulcers and frequently with it a change to the shape of the shinbones. The condition could be absolutely debilitating, leaving sufferers unable to walk and sometimes leading to death.

One injection of penicillin would give complete relief from yaws and eradicate the disease from the person. The effect was dramatic. People suffering from the disease came every day with the request in Pidgin,

When God Calls, Expect Adventure

"Me laikim wanpela shoot"—translating roughly to "Please give me an injection."

Within 12 months, yaws had completely disappeared from the district. It was a terrible condition and the tragedy is that so many people had suffered for the want of a simple treatment. No doubt the arrival of Western medicine had a profound impact on the health of many people in the district. But belief in the power of spirits to bring sickness and death remained strong.

Yaws was common and resulted in terrible sores, bone and joint infections. Just one injection of penicillin often cured the condition but could not remove the scars.

AMAZING ESCAPE

"Hear my prayer, Lord; listen to my cry for mercy. When I am in distress, I will call to you, because you answer me. Among the gods there is none like you, Lord; no deeds can compare with yours" (Psalm 86:6–8).

"There goes a large part of our budget," said Freda one day when we went in to Kainantu to collect the three drums of fuel, delivered by chartered plane. As in most countries, it was illegal to load fuel on planes also carrying passengers or other cargo, so the only option was to charter a plane especially for fuel or other supplies.

We were discussing this one day at Kainantu, when Syd Stocken asked, "Why not charter into Gusap? Gusap is only 1000 feet (300 metres) altitude. The charter costs are lower, which means you'd get the fuel for a much more reasonable cost."

"I wonder if we could?"

"Let's go down and see," he suggested.

Between us, we arranged a day and a time to have a look. It sounded simple. All we had to do was ride to the top of the last hill, then descend the Kassam Pass. Today the Kassam Pass has been remade and tar-sealed, and is used constantly by all sorts of vehicles, including large trucks. But at that time, the road was little more than a widened walking trail that descended precipitously down an awe-inspiring escarpment into a vast plain below.

I will never forget that trip. Syd had attempted to save money for his station by buying a motorbike, reasoning that a bike would use less fuel than a jeep. His brother in Sydney, trying to be most helpful, had bought for Syd a fairly large machine, one better suited to long, open roads. It was too heavy and too fast for New Guinea's "roads."

This "road" had not been maintained or used for years and was in its

When God Calls, Expect Adventure

worst condition. It was a twisty, extremely steep descent of more than 4000 feet (1200 metres), all of it covered with rocks or washouts. It was bump, bump, bump, with brakes hard on all the way. As pillion rider, I was constantly bounced forward until the muscles of my legs chafed and ached more than I had ever felt in my life.

Finally, we reached the valley floor at the junction of the Markham and Ramu Valleys, and followed the Ramu River to the disused wartime airstrip known as Gusap. Here the motorbike could at last show its paces as we raced over the thousands of neatly laid Marsden Matting—a metal matting that locked together to form a safe surface for hastily built wartime airstrips—where only a few years earlier fighter planes and bombers had taken off and landed. The metal surface was now partly hidden under a growth of grass.

There seemed no reason a plane could not land fuel here at a fraction of the cost we had been paying. We could come later and collect it by jeep ourselves. It seemed a great possibility and we could have our fuel for less than half the price.

Going back up the Kassam was 10 times worse than coming down. The bike's low gear was nowhere near low enough for this road. Every bump and ditch we crossed lifted me up to land down on the steel bar that was supposed to stop the pillion rider sliding off the back of the seat. It was weeks before I was able to sit down without pain from my tailbone.

A week or so later, we arranged for a planeload of fuel to be dropped at Gusap. The pilot simply unloaded it onto the strip and left it there for us to collect whenever we were to arrive. We knew it would take the whole day, so Freda decided to take the two children and come with us. Aga—a local teacher—also came to help with the lifting. Hooking the heavy timber trailer on the back of the jeep and storing a few ropes, we set off after an early breakfast. The plan was simple. All we needed to do was load the drums onto the trailer and climb back up the steep road.

It was lovely along the Markham flats as we returned from the airstrip with the three drums of fuel. But the steep climb through the numerous hairpin bends was ahead of us. The first was not too bad. But the second was just too steep. The jeep's engine simply did not have the power to haul those three drums up through the bend.

Amazing Escape

We had to stop, roll the three 44-gallon drums off, drive the jeep and now-empty trailer up and around the bend, then roll the drums up the steep road, round the corner to the back of the trailer where Aga and I lifted each one onto the trailer to be tied down. It was heavy work.

But this was just the beginning. This procedure had to be repeated for every one of the sharp hairpin bends up this zigzag track. A jeep in its lowest gear is a powerful brute—but even a jeep did not have the power to make those bends and pinches.

Each time it was the same painfully slow ritual: unload, roll the drums up the road and around the bend, lift them up with brute force and tie them securely. The process had to be repeated every few hundred yards.

By the time we had repeated this dozens of times, the drums seemed to accumulate weight. They were really only about 400 pounds (180 kilograms) each, and there were only three of them, but by afternoon they seemed to weigh double that.

Such heavy work on the engine meant it was hard on engine oil. By midafternoon, the amount of oil in the motor had dropped dangerously low. To enable us to make the rest of the trip, we had to redirect the path of the oil through the engine. Doing this enabled us to reach the top with just sufficient oil.

It was not long before sunset that we approached the last of these now-despised hairpin bends—and this was one of the worst. Everyone got out and, exhausted, I decided to do my best to make it through the bend without unloading the drums. On the right rose the bare embankment reaching up to the road above, while on the left was an awesome drop where the excavated soil had been pushed over, forming a slide down to the gully hundreds of metres below.

To make matters worse, the jeep had no brakes. The chains we used in muddy conditions had a bad habit of wearing out in a short time, breaking and ripping the hydraulic brake lines out. On this vehicle, we drove using gears to slow us.

As anticipated, the engine did not have enough power. I swung the wheel to deliberately jack-knife the jeep and trailer. It worked, but the trailer wheels stopped only about a foot (30 centimetres) from the road's edge. The tyres were almost rolled off the trailer rims, and the tail of the trailer protruded ominously out over the edge. Had the trailer gone

When God Calls, Expect Adventure

over it would have taken the jeep and me with it. Instinctively I lifted my heart to God with a fervent "Thank You."

Again, we had to off-load the drums, move the jeep, roll the drums up to the repositioned trailer, re-load them and tie them down.

It was about 8 pm when we rolled into the government stock station at Arona, where manager Steve Baxter came out to see if he could do anything. We borrowed a little engine oil. Because the night was quite cool, Steve—in his kindness—brought out a blanket and threw it over Freda, who was nursing two-year-old Kenneth on her knees, then tucked the blanket tightly in under her seat.

Ahead, we knew, was just one more short, steep pinch, this time without a bend, not far from the Omaura mission station. I told Freda I would try to make it, but if we failed I'd run the trailer back into the bank and we'd leave it there until morning.

We gave it all we had as we climbed. The motor roared, then chugged and almost faltered. My foot was flat to the floor. We were almost to the top—just a little more and we would be over and home.

"If I get out, you might make it," Freda called. But the engine stalled a moment later. In her haste to get out, Freda forgot the blanket was tucked in. It sent her and Kenneth crashing to the ground. Because it had no brakes, the jeep began to roll back and it was at that moment that I heard Freda scream shrilly, "THE WHEEL IS GOING OVER KENNETH!"

I managed to stop the jeep's further movement.

"You've stopped it on his chest!" came the next scream.

What I saw struck terror into my soul. The back wheel had run up his legs to his chest and stopped there. Kenneth's life hung in the balance.

"I can't go forward. The wheel will tear him to bits," I yelled.

Under my breath, I prayed, "Lord, please don't let him suffer. Please!"

The jeep could not go forward and there was no way of lifting it off his chest. I let the jeep roll further back—it was all I could do. Freda was quick to pull his head to her so the wheel ran up over his left shoulder and arm. Then she pulled him aside.

We rushed Kenneth's limp body around to the lights at the front of the jeep to see what had happened. His left shoulder was dislocated, but we heard it snap back into place. There were no obvious injuries

Amazing Escape

or broken bones but there was a real possibility of internal injuries. We dropped the trailer where it was and sped home those last few miles.

We examined Kenneth under the electric lights at the mission. He was grazed and bruised. His left arm could hardly move and the tyre marks ran all the way up his abdomen to his chest. But he was alive. And not only that, he was almost unharmed. It was a miracle.

How we thanked the Lord! I don't know how many times we said "Thank You" to the Lord that night— and for a long time afterward. The tyre marks soon vanished, and within a fortnight Kenneth began to use his left arm again.

We never tried having fuel delivered to Gusap again. It might have saved money but it was not worth it.

Missionary Syd Stocken near Kainantu on a tractor and early-model Howard rotary hoe. Gardens were an important part of mission life.

SNAKES ALIVE!

"The people came to Moses and said, 'We sinned when we spoke against the Lord and against you. Pray that the Lord will take the snakes away from us.' So Moses prayed for the people" (Numbers 21:7).

Snakebite cases were so frequent—and our success rates with their treatment so improved—that we began to think we had perfected the treatment. Most bites were from the small, sluggish death adder—some people called them the "deaf adder"—a short snake with a stubby tail. They do not move quickly so were often still crossing the almost invisible path through the grass when trodden on. This was usually when they struck their victims.

One afternoon as Freda glanced out the window, she saw—for the second time that day—a group of men running while carrying one of their number on their shoulders. She knew immediately this was another case of snakebite. She sent a message to the dispensary: "Prepare for another case of snakebite." At the same time she prepared first aid items and stood ready at the gate.

"Snakebite," they yelled.

"Where?"

She administered first-aid treatment, then together they raced over to the "Outpatients" where the antivenene injections were ready.

Having dealt with scores of snakebite cases in Papua New Guinea, I knew the treatment taught at that time in first-aid books and lectures was not correct. In all the classes I had attended to maintain my first-aid certificate, the suggested plan was to put a tourniquet on tightly for as long as 20 minutes, then release it for short periods before tightening it again. I had even been taught to use a short stick to twist the tourniquet very tightly.

The people near Bena Bena would place a tourniquet below the knee and leave it on for days. I reasoned that a sudden, periodic release of a tourniquet would allow too large a dose of the toxin to be released for the body to deal with.

Snakes Alive!

The more suitable treatment we had learned to use had come to us partly from our own numerous cases and partly from the local people themselves telling us how they treat such cases. Combining what I had learned from the local people with scientific advances, like antivenene injections, meant we were able to save almost every case that came to us.

I wrote to the first-aid trainers outlining the reasons why the treatment they were teaching was flawed and suggesting a better approach. I received no reply, but later editions of the official first-aid book changed its suggested treatment.

———•———

One day our seven-year-old son, Lyn, came running up the road, dragging something on a string and yelling, "Mummy, look what I got here. Look, I did it myself."

He sounded so excited and Freda went out to see what he had. They met on the back veranda. On one end of a 3-foot (1-metre) piece of bush creeper was this grinning lad. On the other end was a not-too-happy death adder!

Lyn presented his catch so proudly, only to be shocked by the look on Freda's face. His friends had shown Lyn how to pin a snake down with a small forked stick while slipping a string over its head. Now, here he was—proudly showing off his handiwork.

Lyn's timing was actually very good. A government doctor in Kainantu had talked to me about his interest in arranging for production of a specific antivenene for this local snake. He had asked me to send across a live snake should I have the opportunity.

Here was the opportunity. We placed the snake in an empty powdered milk tin, sealing the lid with sticky tape and a note of warning. I also wrote a covering letter explaining the unusual gift.

When the doctor received it, he was at home with his family. Placing the tin on the table, he turned to read the letter. His five-year-old son thought he would help his daddy by opening the tin for him. It took a few moments to pull the sticky tape off and he was just removing the lid when the father read that the tin contained a live death adder. He was just in time to slam the lid back down on the tin.

As it turned out, the experts in Port Moresby were not at all interested

When God Calls, Expect Adventure

in developing an antivenene, so the scheme lapsed. Even so, we were grateful for the advances that had been made.

The help we received from the doctor was much more pleasant than the gift we sent him. At about this time, Freda was having trouble with one of her eyes. We went to see the doctor and he immediately diagnosed a growth—a pterygium—spreading across her left eye. We set a date to return and have it removed, pleased to discover he was an eye specialist from Hungary.

Somehow he and his whole family had managed to escape the Communist nation, bringing nothing at all with them. But because of the government policy in Australia, such doctors were not accepted automatically into the Australian medical system. The only job this great man could find in Australia was preparing jam tins in a Victorian factory. Finally, he was granted the chance to again practise medicine if he was to work for a given number of years in a small hospital in Papua New Guinea and that was how he came to be at Kainantu. On the other hand, Kainantu and Papua New Guinea were blessed to have such a man to care for their medical needs.

His "surgical theatre" was no more than a small grass-roofed bamboo hut. In an effort to make it a little safer for such delicate work, a wartime silk parachute had been strung up under the grass roof to form a litter-proof ceiling. The "operating table" was no more than a wooden kitchen bench. However, to his credit the operation was a success and the eye did not bother Freda any further.

Because no other dental service was available in the Highlands—a dental service was available only in the government hospital in Port Moresby—our dental services were much sought after. Some, particularly the Europeans, travelled long distances to avail themselves of our service. Our knowledge was limited, but the Lord blessed our efforts with many successful restorations.

One day a man of some importance brought in two of his wives. It seems they had had a fight over something. One woman had a broken

Snakes Alive!

arm, the other a split skull. The looks they traded during treatment were enough to make anyone laugh, while keeping them well apart. At the same time, we felt sorry that the Lord had not yet had opportunity to make the wonderful changes in their lives He will always make when allowed His way.

Success in treatment of many cases was only because of the Lord's unseen help. One Sabbath morning, I had gone to the grass-roofed church but Freda stayed in the dispensary because she had a childbirth case to attend to. Sabbath school had ended. In another 15 minutes, I would need to take the sermon for the day. But someone ran to me with a note in hand.

The note was from Freda, saying that an urgent case had just been brought in and she needed me to assist. I ran to the dispensary's small birthing room. But the woman lying on the bed had a different need. She had given birth to her child in the village but had been brought in because the placenta had not come away, known as "retained placenta."

If the placenta does not come away, it dies within the womb and begins to disintegrate. Without correct treatment, this invariably causes death to the woman. Freda had already prepared the woman and had

Dental work at Omaura. It was very common to extract teeth.

When God Calls, Expect Adventure

anaesthetised her before I had time to scrub up and prepare. Together we worked and—thank the Lord—we were able to manually remove the placenta. When the woman woke, her face had a look of profound gratitude. She knew that without the operation she was doomed to die. But now, she would live. I was even back to the church in time to take the sermon for the day!

While sermons had their place, we also preached by our actions. Because the work of a hospital was not yet understood by the village people, too often they brought the sick person for treatment only when death was just around the corner. For some, that was too late.

One woman was brought in by other village women on a homemade stretcher and simply dumped at the door, the carriers leaving for home immediately. We tried to save her but she passed away less than an hour later.

Because hers had been a problem associated with childbirth, none of the men from the village would have anything to do with her. A village man would excuse himself by stating simply, "I don't want to get women's disease."

No man was ever able to explain to me exactly what the "women's disease" they feared so much really was. But there was no doubt they feared it deeply, and it affected their lives profoundly. No man would walk under a building where a woman could be walking on the floor above. Somehow the "women's disease" might fall on him.

It was late on Friday afternoon when the patient died. The village carriers had gone home. Four of the male medical students volunteered to carry her body back to the village. Culturally, this must have been a hard thing for them to do.

When the group arrived at the village carrying the body of the deceased relative, the village women cried over those four men and offered them garden produce as a thank-you gift. That one act of love did as much as almost anything else to bring the people to think about the changes they saw and respected in Christians. As Jesus had shown that medical help opened doors to the gospel in His time, so we found the medical work opened doors in ours.

TAMBU!

"A voice of one calling: 'In the wilderness prepare the way for the Lord; make straight in the desert a highway for our God'" (Isaiah 40:3).

I felt honoured when I was invited to become a member of the executive committee for the Eastern Highlands Mission. This required that I attend committee meetings at least twice a year in Goroka, almost 50 tortuous miles (80 kilometres) away! That trip required about 160 gear changes per hour, about one new tyre every trip and at least one broken spring. In the wet season, mud chains were required on all four wheels.

On my way to Goroka in June 1954, we came to a point where the so-called road was no more than smooth sloping rocks forming the hillside. It was doubtless because of the underlying rock that no attempt had been made to cut a track. Inasmuch as the hillside was steep and normally flowing with a smear of water, I always feared the jeep would slide sideways into the creek below. It was one area every driver took very cautiously.

Freda in a Willis jeep on her way to Goroka.

When God Calls, Expect Adventure

But as I came to the top of the pass this day, I found a barricade of drums and saplings barring the normal track. Instead I saw that a new road had been dug down the north side of the valley. This new road descended to the bush along the creek. Presumably the road crossed the creek to join the old route further on.

So I started down the freshly dug road, but found it so soft and muddy it was essential to use low ratio, four-wheel drive to get down. I wondered how I was ever going to climb back up with gravity working against us.

Sure enough, the road entered the bush at the bottom of the hill, made an s-bend across a newly constructed sapling bridge and finished the s-bend as it rejoined the old road.

The committee meeting lasted for three days, during which we had constant rain. Pastor Eric Boehm asked me if I would take an American visitor home with me so he could see a little more of the work of God in Papua New Guinea. He was a friendly person, and we got along well, even though he found conditions so vastly different from any he had known. Especially did he question the ability of jeeps to do all they were said to be able to do.

As we neared the spot where we were to climb back up the "new" section of road, I explained what to expect. I swung the wheel to enter the s-bend, but there was a small tuft of grass in the middle of the track. I immediately swung out again and returned to the old path.

"We can't go that way," I declared.

"Why not?"

"Well, did you see that tuft of grass?"

"Yes."

"That is a tambu. Roughly translated into English it means 'law'."

"So, people just go around making up laws do they?"

"Any place where Highland people leave a tuft of grass should be avoided. Tambus are placed on paths that are not to be used or on trees not to be climbed. I don't know why they put a tambu there but there's probably a good reason."

My visitor laughed. "This jeep can't even climb over a tuft of grass!"

We were climbing steadily up the old tilted "road," being careful we didn't slide off the side. About halfway up, I was able to look back and see down through the trees to the section of new road. What I saw frightened me.

The rains during the previous few days had completely washed out the new bridge. Not having brakes on the jeep, I would have tried to get all the speed possible to commence the fresh-mud climb. I would have come around the trees only to find no bridge where a new one was expected. Just what damage might have occurred I don't know. But a jeep with two passengers aboard dropping some 10 feet (3 metres) onto the rocky bottom of the creek was not the way to health and long life!

Knowledge of local customs and a confidence that the local people do not "fool about" with such signs saved us from serious injury. The warning that had been left for us had to be obeyed. Many such "laws" set down by the people of that time were sensible and deserved respect by all.

God has also established certain laws for humanity. Some of His laws are to be found in His book—the Bible—and one transgresses those laws at the peril of happiness on earth and loss of eternal life. Other laws God has favoured us with have to do with health. Again, the quality and length of life are greatly affected by our respect for those laws. God does not give arbitrary laws just to make things difficult. Every law He places before us is intended to add quality to life, and ultimately eternal life for those who respect His laws. By the time we made it to the mission station, I think my visitor had a new appreciation for jeeps without brakes and the warnings issued by uneducated Highland men!

———•———

It was most encouraging to watch Omaura mission station change. We built weatherboard houses with timber floors for the teachers. Several standards of housing were made available to the students. When students first came to us, their understanding of hygiene was no better than that practised in the village. So they were placed in houses just one step above those of a village situation. And the student wanted no more at that stage.

However, before long they began to see that others lived at a higher standard and they began to want to join that group. When they had demonstrated they had learned certain hygiene criteria, they were

When God Calls, Expect Adventure

allowed to move into houses that had individual beds and blankets. Later they moved into even better accommodation. It was most interesting to watch as they developed, each at his or her own speed. Nothing was forced on them. They moved as they made up their own minds. Being their own choice, they made much more permanent decisions. It was their own decision, one they owned—and it stuck.

Tamangi, who was the head school teacher and also the senior sawmiller, expressed his desire to have a better house, so we sat down and drew up a design that pleased him. He was permitted to mill the timber himself and his house began to take shape. I helped some of the time, but Tamangi did the majority of the work, after normal work hours. At times I heard him hammering away as late as 11 at night.

This was the first national house in the Highlands made all of sawn timber, with an iron roof and even glass windows. The house had a bedroom separate from the living room, plus a spare room for visitors. The kitchen was separate again but also constructed in sawn timber. Tamangi was the proudest man I ever saw when at last he and his wife were able to move into their new house.

Tamangi and his wife in front of their new timber and iron house at Omaura.

SOWING SEEDS IN THE MARKHAM

"I planted the seed, Apollos watered it, but God has been making it grow. So neither the one who plants nor the one who waters is anything, but only God, who makes things grow. The one who plants and the one who waters have one purpose, and they will each be rewarded according to their own labour" (1 Corinthians 3:6–8).

Far below us in the Markham Valley were hundreds of villages with people who had not yet had opportunity to hear God's message. *What can we do about it?* I wondered.

The answer came in mid 1953 when we asked a young man from Mussau—one of Papua New Guinea's islands—to see if he could raise any interest among the Markham people. With the passing of years, I have forgotten his name, so I will call him Mark. He was an enthusiastic young evangelist and started off soon after. All he had was his Bible, plenty of faith, and a rucksack on his back with some essentials and a picture roll sticking out the top.

We gathered around him for prayer, bowed our heads and asked the Lord to bless his efforts. Then he marched off and we didn't see or hear from him for about two weeks.

After descending from the mountains, Mark found a village. He knocked on doors until late at night, before a family allowed him to stay with them. The next day he set about using his simple medicines. People began to take a little interest in him, but the interest seemed

When God Calls, Expect Adventure

to be mainly for what he could offer to them, not the message he was presenting. Mark discovered that much of the valley was under the influence of another church denomination and they didn't want any other mission.

Yet Mark persisted. He continued going down the valley and talking with a few people until he gathered a few he considered friends and he felt it might be time to make a bolder approach.

One sunny afternoon, Mark and I arrived in the mission jeep, having made the twisting descent down the Kassam Pass. The people were different to the Highlanders—taller, thinner and darker-skinned. The Markham women wore colourful, dyed grass skirts that had a pleasant "swing" to them as they walked. Many of the men had a length of coloured cloth that they wound around their waists. But the thing that stood out clearly to me was how many men, women and even children were slaves to tobacco and betel nut.

That night, we decided to show pictures of Jesus, projected on a sheet strung between two houses. We positioned the jeep so its bonnet would serve as the table for the 12-volt projector, and the jeep battery provided the power. Crowds of people arrived to view the filmstrips and a few slides. We told the story of Jesus and they watched, wide-eyed. To them, it was exciting to see real moving pictures Yet, of all the hundreds who were present, not one came to talk to us. They were afraid. To sit there in the dark was alright, but no-one would risk being identified and reported.

We went down there on several occasions to show more pictures and I used a small 16-millimetre movie projector I had acquired. It had a 12-volt projection globe and was powered by turning a small crank handle. The crowds grew larger, and in time became friendlier. Even so there were no conversions to Jesus.

One evening, I sat in the jeep in prayer as I waited for the crowds to arrive.

"Lord," I prayed. "Are we really doing your will here? Is this where you want us to expend our efforts? Not one person has been converted to you, God. Not one. Is there to be any result at all?"

I am not one to have great faith in "signs" but that night I asked the Lord to give me an answer from His Word. I closed my eyes and laid the closed Bible on my knees. Then I let the Bible fall open where it would. With my eyes still closed, I placed a finger on the page, then opened my eyes to read the text under my finger. Here is what I read:

Thus saith the Lord, Thy labour of Egypt, and merchandise of Ethiopia, and of the Sabeans, men of stature, shall come over unto thee, and they shall be thine: in chains shall they come over, and they shall fall down unto thee, they shall make supplication unto thee, saying, Surely God is in thee (Isaiah 45:14, KJV).

No message could have been more direct. The "men of stature" described well the height of the people, "in chains" also described their addictions perfectly; even the naming of ancient dark races was most fitting. In this text, I believed God told me that they would come and bow before Him.

Yet I was to be disappointed. Although we continued our visits over many months, we found no evidence that our efforts made any difference. We saw no baptisms at this time. But, like seeds planted in a garden, some sprout quickly, while others seem to take their time. As God says in His word, no seed planted for Him and His work goes to waste.

———•———

In the 1980s, our son Kenneth and his wife Kaye were working as missionaries in Papua New Guinea. One Sabbath, they went to visit a few of the churches in the Markham Valley. In one place alone, there were about 1000 worshippers. The membership was growing rapidly and the pastor was not there that day. Ken was informed by the village people that the pastor cared for 18 churches in his section of the Markham!

God had certainly fulfilled His promise to me that night years earlier. He always does. We can never know the impact of our work and words as each of us makes a small contribution in the Great Commission. Sometimes it takes generations for change to become apparent. So often we want a quick result but God wants a good result and work on hearts can take time. This has been true through history. Sometimes results have been remarkably quick, while at other times the seeds don't germinate for quite some time.

"NOW I CAN SCRATCH, TOO!"

"Do not conform to the pattern of this world, but be transformed by the renewing of your mind. Then you will be able to test and approve what God's will is—his good, pleasing and perfect will" (Romans 12:2).

Our boys, Ken and Lyn, had a great time at Omaura. There was space to play, including room to ride their bikes. They had a wonderful dog as their mate. Under one tree, we had built a glass-fronted beehive and the boys spent hours sitting there among the bees, watching all that went on inside the hive.

We laughed the day Lyn came in, having discovered he could ride his bicycle using only one hand. He informed us with great excitement that, "Now I can scratch and ride at the same time."

Our boys had another hobby they really enjoyed. They collected all the caterpillars and cocoons they could find and placed them on our poor citrus trees. One day Lyn was keenly watching a particular cocoon, sure the chrysalis was about to emerge. He pleaded for just a few more minutes when Freda called him to do his schoolwork.

Finally, Freda went down to see what he was watching, impatient at the delay. Lyn explained that he had never actually seen a butterfly emerge from its cocoon but was sure this one was ready. He begged for more time. To Freda, the cocoon looked like any other and she told him he had to get his schoolwork done before he could come back. Lyn came in reluctantly, with many a backward glance. He did his assigned work as quickly as possible, then raced back to the tree.

"It's gone, Mum," Lyn cried with frustration and disappointment. "I knew it would open. Now I haven't seen it come out!" He was upset and Freda went to try to console him. She did her best but it was a long time before he stopped crying.

"Now I Can Scratch, Too!"

Unfortunately, the only part of the day Lyn disliked was school time. He found school difficult and developed a decided distaste for it. There was so much more of interest outside.

Freda had many other responsibilities around the mission station, some of which were impossible to ignore. She had the care of the maternity section of the hospital—and the outpatient section much of the time—plus responsibility for the small trade store. She also spent time teaching the female students cooking, the making of clothes, home hygiene and numerous other subjects, all of which took large amounts of time. Trying to fit "school" between so many pressing responsibilities was not easy.

Not long after the cocoon incident, Lyn did something that made us think seriously. Freda had spent a whole day trying to find him so he could come and do the day's schooling. He had disappeared. Toward evening, Lyn walked in to greet two relieved parents. When asked where he had spent the day, he admitted having climbed a tall tree and staying there the whole day.

"Why did you do that?" I asked.

"I didn't want to do my schoolwork," he answered.

Freda and I talked things over that night. We remembered how Mrs Mitchell, wife of the Papuan Mission president, allowed nothing to distract her household during the period of the day marked for schoolwork. She would not even answer the phone or a knock on the door. Freda could do something similar but not with all her responsibilities. And if things went on like they were, we feared the boys' education would suffer.

There seemed to be just one answer. Lyn must somehow be placed in a regular school. My retired parents in Brisbane said they would gladly take him in, until we returned for furlough.

We agreed that he would fly south in January, 1955. The mission's administrative meetings were in progress in Lae at the time and I was down there for the meetings. Freda placed Lyn on the plane in Kainantu and I collected him in Lae. A huge lump filled my throat as I watched my son, who was just about to turn eight, step off that plane with his little case in his hand.

That afternoon, I introduced him to Mrs Campbell, who was to fly

When God Calls, Expect Adventure

on the same plane and keep an eye on him until they reached Brisbane. I found it hard to watch as he boarded the plane to leave Papua New Guinea. How much harder it must have been for Freda!

In Brisbane, the passengers went through Customs and Mrs Campbell continued on to Sydney. Unsure what to do, Lyn sat waiting. Soon he was sitting alone with not one other person in the Customs lounge. Outside, my parents waited and watched at the door as passengers emerged—but there was no Lyn. Finally they found someone who would allow them to go into the Customs lounge, where they found a frightened and shaken eight-year-old. It was such a shattering experience that Lyn was reluctant to leave home for any reason for years.

Lyn started school in Brisbane, but six months after he arrived, my mother became ill. Freda flew down to care for both Lyn and my mother in July, 1955—two days after I was ordained to the gospel ministry. Before she left, we spent quite some time discussing our future. Neither of us wanted to go back to Australia to work but it seemed unfair on the children to stay. With much prayer, we decided we had to go. In having children, we had taken on a great responsibility. If we were to be faithful to them, we had no choice!

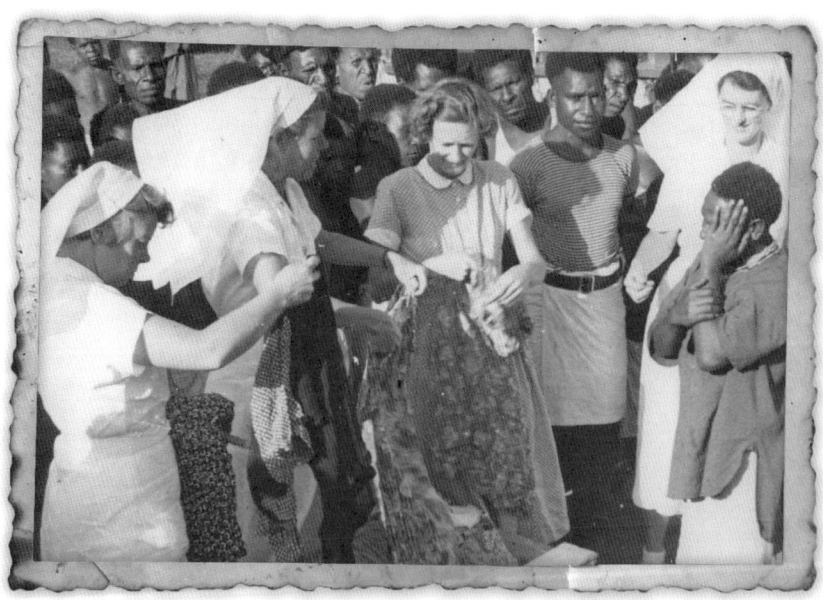

Mavis Barnard, Essies Petherbridge and others distributing clothes sent from Australia, probably at Togoba Hansenide Leper Colony.

"Now I Can Scratch, Too!"

I stayed on in Papua New Guinea for a further two months. One of the great highlights was seeing the first class of trainee nurses complete their course and graduate. This was the first group outside Port Moresby to have completed a nurse-training course and it was a wonderful day, full of celebration and pride in their accomplishments. We had done it!

As I looked back on the nine years we had served in Papua New Guinea, we could see the hand of the Lord had blessed our work in so many ways! We had loved the people with whom we were working. We had toiled with them side by side and we had the satisfaction of knowing we had given of our best for the people of Papua New Guinea—and for our Master.

CANNIBAL COUNTRY

"Dear friends, let us love one another, for love comes from God" (1 John 4:7).

Before leaving Papua New Guinea, there was one more place I wanted to visit. Many miles south of Kainantu was an area known as the Fore (pronounced "for-ray") country. The inhabitants belonged to the large group of fierce people commonly known as the Kukukuku. Little was known about them other than they were almost small enough to be called pygmies—and they were cannibals.

Syd Stocken of Kainantu Seventh-day Adventist Mission had begun to work among these people by sending in a brave native missionary, whose name was Arunki. Arunki was equipped with some trade items, a couple of blankets and some clothing, plus a picture roll.

This was a tremendous step of faith on his part for he was going to meet a group of people about whom he knew little. Apart from the presence of the Lord with him, he had one decided advantage: he could speak a language they also knew, so could communicate with them.

The first time Arunki opened the picture roll to try to tell them a Bible story something unexpected occurred. One of the men grabbed the picture roll and slipped the string over his head. Then, while Arunki looked on with astonishment, he began to perform a jig to the extreme merriment of the rest of the villagers. In the view of the village people, this sheet of colour was so much better than the feathers or tin lids and labels they often used as ornamentation.

Most of us accept a picture for what it is. Our eyes gather colours and shapes on a two-dimensional surface and our minds represent them as three-dimensional pictures we can understand. According to Arunki, all these people saw was a maze of blotches of colours. It required time before they could read these two-dimensional colours as three-dimensional pictures.

———•———

One day in early September, 1955, Arunki heard much shouting and the sounds of men running through the village. Obviously there was a tribal fight that he felt duty-bound to stop.

Arunki raced out, calling on the men to stop but an arrow hit him in the leg, penetrating deeply. He fell and the concerned men gathered around. They explained that an unknown pig had made its way into the village and they were trying to catch it. Unfortunately, Arunki had only succeeded in getting in the way.

Clearly Arunki's wound was going to become infected if he did not seek medical attention right away so he was taken into Kainantu and placed in the hospital, where he had to stay for some weeks. Now he was unable to bring his villagers to the first Adventist camp meeting in the Fore District.

I was asked to care for the three days of camp meetings. Len and Mavis Barnard had been asked to replace us at Omaura when we left, and they had arrived in late September, bringing their two little girls with them. I asked Len if he might like to come with me to the first camp meeting among this cannibal group and found him more than eager. Len would never turn down such a challenge. Mavis, on the other hand, was not enthusiastic about the idea.

Our ex-wartime jeep was loaded with six people and all their camping gear, including cots, blow-up mattresses, blankets, food, lamps, clothes and all the materials required for a three-day camp meeting.

Groups of village men waited for us along the way. Each group had the same basic message for us: "Please, can you send a teacher to our village? Our people want to learn. Our children have no school to attend. We want a teacher."

"We are sorry," we could only reply. "But you are welcome to come to our camp meeting." It made my heart break to hear such requests and not have qualified people we could send.

Several hundred people gathered for the camp meeting, every one of them deeply loved of God, many having walked great distances to be present. The little church had no hope of holding everyone, but they crowded in, or around, so eager to be part of something new and exciting. We held meetings Thursday afternoon and Friday morning.

Len and I decided the free afternoon was a great opportunity to visit Arunki's village and take a picture of the first grave ever to be dug in that area. This represented a significant breakthrough in God's work among these people, when Arunki had convinced the villagers to bury a deceased 14-year-old, rather than eat his body, as was customary.

The Fore people's tradition was to make the loved one a part of themselves! Even the bones would be burned, ground and used. Under no circumstances would they think of placing their loved one in the dirt, where insects, worms and even pigs could feast on them. No higher expression of love was available to them than consuming the dead—but this came at a terrible cost. Disease was readily passed on, including the terrible laughing sickness with symptoms similar to modern "Mad Cow" disease.

We searched for someone who could speak the language of that village but we could only find one man who claimed he could speak a language they would understand.

Some time later, our guide and interpreter finally told us to stop at a given point because the village was "over there." Leaving the vehicle on the road, we traversed about 100 yards (about 100 metres) of tufted grassland where there was ample evidence of the rooting of pigs. Next we entered a band of forest before entering the village.

Obviously no-one had heard us coming, nor had they expected us. When they saw us, every woman screamed and grabbed their terrified children as they raced into their huts. Every man snatched up his bow and arrows or spear, and held them at the ready.

"Speak to them," I told our interpreter.

"They don't understand," he said fearfully.

No other white person had ever entered this village and they had no idea what to expect. We put out our hands and advanced toward them, trying to make ourselves appear friendly.

The situation was tense. They were terrified but at last we came up to them and they surrounded us. The weapons were lowered slowly. We tried sign language. Little by little, it seemed that our request to be taken to the grave had been understood.

A young boy was pushed toward us and it was indicated that we were to follow. His whole body was covered with black soot. The last thing we noticed as we left the village was that all the men grasped their weapons and ran off into the bush. Only one man remained. He climbed a dead tree in the centre of the village and made it to a spot high up, where he could shout our movements to everyone.

Our young guide took us past some of the village gardens, then down a washout where a bank had been formed by the running water. The bushes hung over in such a way that we felt we were walking down a leafy tunnel. It was a creepy feeling, walking in known cannibal country with our heads bowed, eyes fixed on the ground, almost waiting for an arrow or a sudden strike from a stone axe. At each point in our journey, the sentry broadcast our movements.

Finally, we came into the village's sacred area, set aside for ancestor worship. The main feature was a unique type of "headstone" made of a tree trunk. The long trunk lay between two large stones and sported many small branches cut off about 6 inches (15 centimetres) from the trunk.

The small branches formed a row of pegs, on which the skulls of the deceased persons had been placed. As we viewed the scores of skulls, we noted many were so small they must have been from children. Others were green with age, indicating they had been on those pegs for many years.

When a family member wished to do so, they could come to this area and mourn over the lost relative before whose skull they were standing. We even saw the remains of some skulls that had fallen onto the ground and had not been restored to the position of honour. Possibly there was no-one still living who mourned that long-departed village member.

A short distance from us, we saw it. The attempt to fence the grave had been futile and the village pigs had furrowed the ground viciously. They had not dug deep enough to disturb the boy's body but we wondered if such desecration must have been hurtful to the family members. We re-arranged the fence and took our pictures. We were now ready to return to the village and the jeep.

At this point, we realised we were alone. Our guide had disappeared, leaving us feeling decidedly uneasy. Now we were doubly aware of the unfriendly reception of the fighting men. The disappearance of women and children always precedes a tribal fight. The village men had vanished with their war implements. We could no longer hear the constant shouting of the treetop sentry. And now, our guide had disappeared, too.

We prayed, then took stock of our situation. Going in the direction we had come seemed to be heading into an ambush. We could follow the creek bed down to our right and around back to the jeep, but we had no idea how far that would be, and, in any case it was just as suitable for an ambush. Neither idea seemed wise.

We prayed again. Higher up the grassy hill, we could see the deserted village. Going straight up that hillside through the long pitpit grass seemed our best option.

Pitpit grass resembles sugarcane but with one nasty added characteristic. Its leaves and stalks are covered with hairs that become miniature barbs that can penetrate human skin like thousands of tiny arrows. Our hands and legs soon looked like velvet. We struggled on until we came to the narrow band of trees at the edge of the village, then entered.

The man sitting in the sentry perch slid down the tree, grabbed his bow and arrows, and ran off into the bush. A squealing pig shot out of a house, ducking between our legs before fleeing into the bushes.

So far, so good. We only had the band of trees and the patch of grassland to traverse and we would be safe. Suddenly the sound of dogs barking and men shouting came from the direction we were headed. Now we knew the warriors were waiting for us at the jeep. We stood there with the deserted village behind us and a band of trees hid us while we prayed anew.

We moved slowly through the bush to a position where we could see the men without being seen. It was chilling. Fifteen men plus older boys held long killing sticks or hefted large clubs. The normal bow-and-arrows set were evident on every man's shoulder and stone axes hung from their waistbands. Even the boy who had been our guide was now armed.

We had a final prayer and decided there was only one thing to do. We had to go out, trusting the Lord, and show no sign of fear.

For the third or fourth time, Len said to me, "Things are decidedly sticky, Lester."

As soon as we were spotted, a huge shout rose. Everyone turned and lifted the sticks and clubs above their heads as they began something that sounded like a kind of dirge and a whoop mixed together. For a moment, they stood looking at us while giving this mixed cry.

Then, with another lifting of implements they began to race toward us, still yelling and whooping. They bounded over the pig wallows and grass tussocks. There was nothing we could do except stand in shock and await our fate. Running would show weakness—and would be futile anyway.

My mind went blank. Then, just in front of me, within striking range, was a bearded face with a toothless smile on it. It seemed quite wrong as he brought down the stick on me. I felt my right arm to see if it was broken and was mystified that it wasn't. I looked again at the face before me. It was still grinning. He was bringing down another killing stick

The first camp meeting in the "cannibal country" of the Fore district.

When God Calls, Expect Adventure

and something began to "ring a bell" in my mind. It looked familiar, like a stick of sugarcane. That was even more mysterious. Then I looked at the club in his other hand. It also looked familiar. A second glance showed it to be a large taro. On the ground, I saw a large yam.

All this happened in just a moment. Then it dawned on me as I looked around that all the men were offering yams, sugarcane and other foodstuffs. They were not out to kill us. They never had been! They had actually rushed away to gather gifts, the best of their gardens and their headlong rush to greet us was not the attack of warriors, but the enthusiastic advance of friends.

———•———

The camp meeting was a success. A few days after the camp, I sorrowfully returned to Australia. Little did I know that I was just beginning my missionary career or that God had an even more remote destination in mind.

PITCAIRN ISLAND

"Sing to the Lord a new song, his praise from the ends of the earth, you who go down to the sea, and all that is in it, you islands, and all who live in them" (Isaiah 42:10).

In Australia, Freda and I soon became restless. I was invited to visit Pastor L C Naden at the South Pacific Division headquarters and he informed me that he was looking for someone who could go to Pitcairn Island. I walked out of Pastor Naden's office dejected. Pitcairn was possibly the most isolated mission posting in the world!

Norman Ferris had served on Pitcairn and, great storyteller that he was, he made life there sound wonderful! If Norm had been a salesman,

The Hawkes family back in Australia—for a short time—with Aunty Mary Dunlop in back seat.

When God Calls, Expect Adventure

he could have sold anything. But as we listened, we began to see how the Lord had prepared us to fit into the particular needs of the island. The pastoral work also required dental, medical skills, and engineering ability. It all seemed to fit.

To obtain another point of view, we went to see Fred and Myrtle Ward who had been missionaries on Pitcairn for a period of some 14 years, many years earlier. They gave us a picture of the less-glamorous aspects of life on Pitcairn. By now, we could see both the potential and the possible problems. We returned to Pastor Naden and told him we would be happy to take the position.

During this time in Sydney, as we pondered our next move, our daughter Robyn joined our happy family.

Getting to Pitcairn proved difficult. In June 1956, we travelled to Wellington, New Zealand, on the old *Wanganui*. After three days of blustery weather, we were booked on the *Rangitata*, which set sail on Sabbath afternoon. During the night the ship crossed the date line, so when we woke in the morning it was the Sabbath again!

Among the passengers was elderly Parkin Christian, Pitcairn Island's chief magistrate. Parkin was returning from Norfolk Island where he had represented Pitcairn at the centenary of the transfer of all Pitcairners to Norfolk Island in 1856. This transfer had been carried out at the instigation of Queen Victoria because, at the time, Pitcairn Island was overcrowded and was threatened by a severe drought.

Because the Norfolk Island penal colony off the coast of Australia was closing, it seemed logical to transfer the Pitcairners there. Norfolk had good houses and community buildings, plus plenty of land and cattle. And it would be much easier to administer.

For some of the new settlers it was misery. Finally, a few families decided they could take it no longer. They chartered a ship to take them back to Pitcairn Island and remained there. It was to the descendants of these few families that we were called to serve.

We had been a week into the trip when Captain Hopkins called for me to meet with him. Captain Hopkins was a big man with a prominent jaw, a man of few words, but woe betide anyone who failed to listen.

Pitcairn Island

He came right to the point, "Mr Hawkes, weather reports from Pitcairn suggest there is a high possibility we will not be able to put you ashore on Pitcairn. There are storms in the area, and I doubt the island boats will be able to get out of the harbour. You should prepare to stay with us until we arrive at Panama, then take another ship back to Pitcairn."

I felt excited at the thought of seeing another part of the world but, when I went to tell Freda, she was not at all thrilled. The thought of "camping"—as she called it—who-knows-where for weeks or months in a foreign country, while trying to care for a new baby raised no enthusiasm whatsoever. Of course, I should have thought of that myself.

———• •———

Late in the afternoon of that Sabbath, July 7, 1956, we had our first glimpse of Pitcairn through the mist, rain and clouds. As predicted, the seas were quite heavy and white-topped. Word had come through to the captain that the boats would be out to meet the ship. And they were—but how they leapt about on the huge seas! The oarsmen struggled valiantly to draw close.

It was becoming dark when the boats at last were able to tie up to the lee side of the *Rangitata*. Huge lights were slung out over the side of the ship to illuminate the dancing boats on the water below. The transfer of cargo in these savage conditions took a long time. The small boats rose and fell about 20 feet (6 metres) with each wave and extreme care was essential to be sure the descending cargo didn't crush one of the men below.

It must have been about 10.30 pm when a coal basket was placed on deck and lined with sheets to make it somewhat clean. A wooden chair was placed in it and Freda was asked to occupy the chair. Then the three children were given to her.

Many of the passengers were leaning over the side to see all that was going on.

"They must be very dedicated," one commented.

"Absolute fools," suggested another.

I noticed that the second suggestion had more outspoken believers than the first. Due to the blackness of the night and the sheeting rain, no-one could make out any sign of the island. To all appearances, we

When God Calls, Expect Adventure

were being cast adrift on the open ocean many miles from land and in a heavy storm. Wisely, the captain had not risked his ship by coming close to a rocky island when he could not even see it.

The spectators gasped as the basket was lifted by a ship's cargo crane and swung out over the side. I was asked to climb down a rope ladder—called "Jacob's Ladder"—and hold the basket to prevent it crashing against the side of the swaying ship. In the pitch-blackness of the night, the ship's side seemed like a great cliff of shiny black that went down forever. As the ship rolled and pitched in the heavy swell, I desperately hung on, trying as best I could to help Freda and our frightened children.

As we neared the small boats, another danger presented itself. The boats would rise and crash with tremendous force against the rope ladder on which I stood. Then the boat would seem to sink some 20 feet as though retreating and gathering momentum to leap up and make another grab at my feet. At that moment, the basket was dropped into the boat and sank with it. Freda and the children scrambled into the small boat and, on the boat's next "grab," I also jumped in. Looking back up the same wall of steel from the instability of the island boats, it seemed an awesome height.

As soon as the ropes dropped and we were free, the ship began its journey on to Panama. Our three little boats began their fight toward the island, for the winds and seas had driven the *Rangitata* miles past the island before they had completed the transfer. Oliver Clark, the local church elder, took three-month-old baby Robyn and tucked her inside his rain coat, keeping her dry. We sheltered as best we could from the rain and the drenching spray as we battered into the waves. We were in the only boat with an engine, so our boat was trying valiantly to tow the other two boats into the storm and wind. To avoid the worst of the seas, the men steered the boats first into the lee of the island then along the north side toward the little dent that they called the harbour.

I could hear the sound of waves crashing against a rocky cliff-face only a few yards away. I yelled above the roar of the wind to warn the crew of the danger. They simply smiled. Only later did I learn that waves do crash against steep cliffs, but the water itself hardly moves. Later, I would watch men swimming right alongside the cliff face, rising

Pitcairn Island

and falling as each huge wave crashed and turned over on itself, but the swimmers just lay there with their faces in the face masks looking for fish they might spear.

It was quite some experience going in through the rocky entrance to the harbour that night. The women of the island had taken up positions around the small "harbour," holding kerosene lamps so the boats would be better able to gauge where to aim for. For quite some time, the captain of each boat waited and watched the breakers. They believed there was a rhythm to the waves—three large waves followed by seven smaller ones. Even knowing this pattern granted no certainty that this was the case in every instance. Suddenly the captain shouted "Nausataim" ("Now is the time") and the engine was gunned to maximum to ride a selected wave into the tiny harbour.

The other boats were powered by 14 oars and one sweep oar. They had to pick the right wave and give the oars all they had at the right moment. Our boat raced like a surfboard on the front of the selected wave, but only for long enough to enter. Then the engine had to be reversed equally as heavily to stop the boat crashing into the rocks on the far side. Men seemed to be everywhere, carrying their saturated

The 14-oar boat at Pitcairn Island.

When God Calls, Expect Adventure

cargo into the dubious shelter afforded by the boat sheds, where it was left for the night.

It was about midnight when we stepped out of the boat onto the shore. It was raining as we climbed "The Hill of Difficulty"—a climb of some 200 feet (about 60 metres)—but never had firm land felt so good!

The famous *Bounty* Bible.

"P" FOR PASTOR

"My righteousness draws near speedily, my salvation is on the way, and my arm will bring justice to the nations. The islands will look to me and wait in hope for my arm" (Isaiah 51:5).

We spent what was left of the night in the home of Oliver and Jessie Clark. Like the others, it was a simple structure with a series of verandahs, each of which had been closed in as the need arose. We loved those rambling houses.

In the morning, we walked through the only village on the island—the population when we arrived was 125—past a number of unpainted but interesting homes, each clearly reflecting the different personalities of its owner. From "The Edge," we could look down on the tiny, bright-blue harbour, now quiet, with its fan of grass-roofed boathouses facing the timber boat-slide. Just outside, and to the right of the pint-sized harbour lay the rocky area where the blue of the sea was shattered into white foam. This was the place where the famous *Bounty* had been driven ashore, stripped and later burned.

Looking beyond to the farthest point on our right, we saw the twin-spired rocks known as St Paul's standing in the pulsating, deep-blue water with a white collar around their bases. From the rocks of St Paul, our eyes followed the rise of one of the mountains of Pitcairn until up in the clouds was the pointed rock known as Ship Landing Point because it gave direction as to where the harbour was to be found.

Beside us stood a shed reeking with the smell of diesel and oil. It housed the engine that hauled the "flying-fox" up the steel cable stretching steeply down to the harbour. The flying-fox itself was no more than a small wooden platform hanging from a pair of wheels on the steel cable.

Clarence and Langford were getting the machinery ready to haul up the cargo. I saw a smile cross Clarence's face as he pulled his hand out of a large tin of golden-black waterproof grease and held it out, offering to shake.

When God Calls, Expect Adventure

The Lord seemed to whisper to me, "Take his hand. This is a test to see if you are prepared to dirty your own hands." I took the hand, met his eye and shook it vigorously, grease and all. We both smiled, sizing each other up, then I stepped back to allow them to continue their work.

May I be forgiven for feeling a little unjustified pride when I heard Clarence say in the Pitcairnese dialect—which he thought I would not understand—"It's alright. He's a man."

Being a man did not spare me from the islander's unique sense of humour. Among the cargo we had brought were two foam-rubber mattresses for the boys. Because they were dripping wet, they were laid out to dry, cellular side up. From their vantage point on the underground water tank, a group of the island men watched with interest. The foam mattresses caused the greatest merriment.

"What could these funny things be used for?" asked Desmond.

Each man gave the most outlandish suggestion he could think of, causing great peals of laughter. At last Andrew had what he thought was the best idea.

"I know," he shouted, "the foam hollows are to keep the eggs in. That way they won't get broke." Everyone roared with laughter.

If you can't take mockery, don't go to Pitcairn. Mockery is a way of life and forms the major part of local humour. In some cultures, it is polite to compliment your friends and affirm them. On Pitcairn, it was every man's mission to find something to jest about. However, it was good-natured humour, which seemed to be always received with a laugh.

The house we were to occupy had not been used for decades. Creepers and bushes had hidden it for so long it had almost faded from memory. But all that had now been cleared away, leaving only the now-drying remnants of the creepers thrusting out between the wall timbers. The house seemed to emerge like a butterfly from its cocoon. There was no paint on the outside but the walls inside had been lined with Masonite sheets painted gloss white. Over each window hung lacy,

"P" for Pastor

green-spotted curtains. Furniture was minimal but adequate. A large flat stone formed the one step up to the front door.

There were no flower beds or lawns but several huge mango trees gave shade to our home. The outer walls of the house were made from precious Miro wood, cut with an axe. The roof consisted of all sorts of lengths of rusty iron and the water it collected was channelled into a large underground cement-and-sandstone storage tank.

On the wall of the hallway hung an ancient telephone. It was a polished wooden box with a mouthpiece protruding from the front, while a heavy earpiece hung from a single hook on the side. A small crank handle powered the ringing. It was a party-line phone system, with every phone on the one circuit. When someone wanted to ring a certain person, the ring would sound in every connected home.

We had to learn Morse Code because each home had its own special signal. Because I was the pastor, we had the letter "P" as our code. I had to listen to each call to pick out the "dit-daa-daa-dit"—Morse Code for P—call. The phone seemed to be ringing all day long.

Then there were times when someone had news for all 125 of Pitcairn's residents. On these occasions, one long call was given and everyone would lift the receiver to hear the message. Next came an

Students of the Pitcairn Island school in May, 1958.

When God Calls, Expect Adventure

animated discussion of the news during which everyone would try to get his or her comment heard.

Some of the good folks loved to pick up their receiver and eavesdrop on the conversation of others. One day, the schoolteacher rang. I answered and we were talking for a while when we heard the sound of a dog barking. "Do you have a dog there?" Mr Wotherspoon asked me.

"No, we don't," I replied. "But it does sound like Oscar's."

There was an immediate click on the line as Oscar's earpiece was hurriedly replaced on its hook.

Despite such small inconveniences, we were very happy.

Even the children were impressed with school hours. Mr Wotherspoon kept hours that varied according to season. In summer, school would commence as early as 6.30 am. In winter, it would generally commence at 7.30. Children returned home for breakfast at about 10 am and school closed for the day at about 1 pm.

Pitcairn Islanders were early risers and made the most of daylight hours. If I was not at the dispensary by 6.30, someone would be down to knock on our door, complaining that they were wasting the whole day. Six to 10 am was precious gardening time and the work in Pitcairn's rich, volcanic soil could not be interfered with!

Cabbages and carrots prospered. Pineapples, pawpaws and coconuts flourished. The grapefruit was as sweet as many an Australian orange, not to mention the large, loose-skinned mandarins. Situated just north of the Tropic of Capricorn, Pitcairn's climate and geology provided a hilly agriculturist's paradise.

When mango season came, there was so much of the sticky fruit that we had to dig trenches to bury hundreds that fell to the ground. Watermelons of gigantic size grew in abundance, often each weighing in excess of 70 pounds (30 kilograms). Avocados by the basketful were brought to us. And, whenever we had a need, a single comment would result in the arrival of produce. The people were kind to us.

Impressed with the island and its people, I prepared for prayer meeting on Wednesday evening. Every person on the island turned up to hear me speak on the subject of prayer. I tried to divide the people into two smaller prayer groups but this had not been done before and the idea failed.

"P" for Pastor

How did I go? I wondered. *Am I making a good impression?*

Next morning the retiring nurse told me the islanders were quite disappointed with me! They had come expecting to hear stories about where we had worked previously and what had happened in those places. Instead, I spoke about prayer. Not only that, but I had tried to make a change. The historical ways of doing things had a certain sacredness or tradition about them and I would have to be careful to tamper only carefully and slowly. They accepted changes only after they had seen for themselves the advantages that might come.

There was no other church on the island. No-one had to do personal study to be able to defend his or her beliefs. Some were among the most ardent followers of the Lord I had ever met and were prepared to support the Lord to the point of great sacrifice. But for others, religion was almost like clothing they were required to wear. This presented Freda and I with a reason to work hard to bring the love of Jesus right into the lives of the people.

THE UNSINKABLE FRIDGE

"Great is the Lord and most worthy of praise; his greatness no one can fathom. One generation commends your works to another; they tell of your mighty acts" (Psalm 145:3, 4).

This was 1956 and, like many of the places we visited in Papua New Guinea, moving pictures had never been seen on this island. The first films to arrive were black-and-white *Faith for Today* films narrated by Pastor Fagal. The church was well filled for the first moving pictures, which consisted of a short story, sermonette and several musical items.

Outside the church, after the showing, a gentle giant approached me. Fred Christian had to split his size-14 boots from tongue to toe in order to get his huge feet into them and now he stood before me looking desperately worried.

"Pastor Hawkes, how did Pastor Fagal know where I was going to sit? He just kept looking at me. Why didn't he look at someone else?"

Anderson—who had been sitting on the other side of the church—broke in, "But, Fred, he wasn't looking at you. He couldn't have been, because he looked at me the whole time. I felt like God was staring right through me. I even moved along the seat to get away, but he still kept looking at me!"

The islanders' discomfort with moving films soon settled. Some weeks later, a batch of Family Films arrived from the United States.

The Unsinkable Fridge

Mostly they were story films with a strong moral in each. The people loved them.

Also new to the island were visitors determined to stop off on one of the most remote destinations in the world. Louis Marden, a photographer and writer from the National Geographic Society arrived. He had been sent for six weeks to do an article for the December, 1957, issue and, when it was published, it was the longest article ever printed in *National Geographic*.

Louis soon learned something we already knew. To his consternation, the Pitcairn people were never idle. Some months after he had gone, I was able to obtain a picture he had never been able to take—a picture of a group just sitting during daylight hours, doing nothing but talking. It was the only time I ever saw people doing nothing but sit and talk.

For this reason we had to ban sanding wooden curios or plaiting baskets in the hall while films were being shown. Such activity made it impossible to hear the sound track!

Perhaps one of the reasons for this constant busyness was the taxation system. Pitcairners paid none! In lieu of taxes, they were expected to do public work as required by the elected Clerk of Works. Jobs included making or repairing roads, erecting or repairing a public building, or work on the boat-slide or on the boats themselves. It could be anything of value to the entire population. To call the men to work, the Clerk of Works had to ring the bell at about 6 am and all the men had to then appear within about 15 minutes for duty.

Sometimes, as soon as the clerk began to allocate duties, someone would call out, "No. I'sa gwin' fishin'." Others would agree and before long all the men were "gwin' fishin'"—the Clerk of Works with them. Public works could wait!

How they loved fishing! Every man had a wooden, flat-bottom canoe in which they paddled out to a selected spot. Baited hooks were dropped to depths of as much as 500 feet (150 metres) and any man who came home with less than 40 fish would consider he'd had a "dry" day.

Maybe the good fishing accounted for the state of the island jail.

"Do you have a policeman on Pitcairn?" chirped one eager visitor.

In his slow, easy drawl Parkin replied, "Yeah. Course we's god a

When God Calls, Expect Adventure

poleecemaaaan." His drawl was distinctive and extended, making it hard for an outsider to understand.

"Well, what does he do?"

"Ooor, he makes oot gun licences."

"Well, do you have a jail on the island?"

"O'course we's god a jail."

Warming to the topic the questioner asked, "Does anyone ever go into the jail?"

"Oooor, plarnty."

"They do, eh? What do they go in for?"

Parkin took his time as he drawled slowly on, "Oooor, they's goes in t' sweep it out. What else?"

One day I went to see Floyd, the island's policeman. We talked for a few minutes, then I suggested we go down and have a look at the jail. We walked beneath heavily scented orange trees until we arrived at a simple, unpainted, one-room building with a small veranda on one corner. The door was ajar slightly but wouldn't open wider. Neither would it shut. I looked for something that might be catching under it, such as a stone or stick. Nothing. I then looked for something above that might be holding it tightly. Again, nothing. No amount of force would budge it.

Then I looked at the hinges—just one huge mass of rust. The door hadn't been moved in years. Nor had anyone swept the building in who knows how long!

Those rusted hinges spoke volumes for the century-old Pitcairn law that forbade alcohol in any form on the Island. God had performed a mighty work on the mutineers of Pitcairn!

Instead of collecting prisoners, Floyd collected stamps, at least one copy of every stamp printed anywhere in the world each year! He obtained huge albums and filled every one. To see a stack of those stamp albums made me wonder just how much they would be worth on the stamp collectors' market.

My service to Freda was obtaining a new kerosene-operated fridge. Andrew, the island's cashier and secretary, was asked to order one for us.

The Unsinkable Fridge

He was convinced we would do best to order from England and we had to borrow money from the church offering account to pay, and record it as a debit against our wages account in Fiji.

When the *Athentic* arrived off Pitcairn, two island boats were tied side-by-side against the ship where they bobbed up and down as they waited to collect the cargo being lowered by sling. When our fridge, still in its wooden crate, was down to about 6 feet (2 meters) above sea level, it suddenly toppled sideways out of the sling and fell with a mighty splash between the two longboats. There it floated for a few minutes, long enough for the island men to jump in and run a line around it. This line was then tied to the empty sling and the fridge was hauled up out of the salt water, drained, then lowered into one of the longboats.

This of course was terribly disappointing! I wrote to the shipping company outlining the incident and requesting that our case be considered for insurance. I hardly expected the reply we received. I don't have the exact words of their reply, but the sentiments were as follows:

> *Dear sir, Thank you for your letter regarding insurance on the refrigerator which you reported as having been dropped in the sea while being unloaded. We wish to advise that the insurance policy clearly states that insurance coverage ceases the moment an item leaves the ship's slings. Inasmuch as the said item had left the ship's slings before it fell into the sea and was damaged, insurance no longer applies.*

The fridge was taken home and washed out as thoroughly as was possible on an island where no running water existed and where a water hose could not be seen. The fridge did operate, but before long it began to rust badly. By the time we left Pitcairn, our unsinkable fridge was worthless.

APPENDICITIS

"Jesus turned and saw her. 'Take heart daughter,' he said, 'your faith has healed you.' And the woman was healed at that moment" (Matthew 9:22).

A few years before we arrived on Pitcairn, a young island girl had developed appendicitis. Finally, a ship arrived and took the girl on board, but she died before reaching New Zealand and was buried at sea.

"What would you do if someone got appendicitis?" the islanders often asked me.

"I'd operate, of course," was my reply. During my nursing training, I had spent many extra hours in the theatre watching at close range all that a doctor would do during surgery. We had illustrated books on surgical procedures and some surgical instruments.

The day came when Beatrice (not her real name), an unmarried woman of about 40 years of age, presented with severe abdominal pains. Every test normally given for appendicitis indicated that we had a serious case on our hands. The island's radio operator, Tom Christian, began calling all shipping, endeavouring to locate a ship that would be able to take her to a recognised hospital.

At the same time, Freda and I began to make preparations, should surgery become necessary. It was clear that time was not on our side. Something had to be done—and done quickly.

There were two main things to do. First, we believed we had to have as many as possible of the island people praying and, second, we had to prepare for an operation. We set a time for 10 am, hoping that a ship would be located by radio before then.

With just 20 minutes to spare, a ship was found. What a relief. We had no sterilisation equipment, no retractors and for anaesthetic there was only a little nitrous oxide and a bottle of chloroform. There was only one good scalpel. We were so glad to hand the case over to a doctor.

Beatrice was taken on board and treated with antibiotics. Upon arrival in New Zealand, she was admitted with "Acute Appendicitis"

Appendicitis

and urgently wheeled into the operating theatre. Upon opening her abdomen, the surprised surgeons found a serious case of ovarian abscess. I often thank the Lord that He took over and saved us from having to face such a problem.

———•———

Unfortunately, we were tested more seriously one Sunday. I was on the south side of the island when a young man came running and shouting for me. Between gasps for air, he told me that Jessie, the wife of the church elder, had been found collapsed and unconscious on the pathway outside her home.

By the time I had run the mile or so back to the village, Freda already had Jessie in the house and on her bed where she lay totally unconscious. Examining her, we immediately noted her extreme pallor. The only blood test we had was the old Tolquist test, which showed her haemoglobin to be dangerously low.

Clearly, Jessie had suffered internal blood loss and urgently needed a blood transfusion. But no blood bank was available on Pitcairn, nor had we even the beginnings of a blood transfusion set. There was also no way to determine her blood grouping or to indicate who might be able to supply suitable blood.

With a little improvisation, we managed to infuse some saline directly into our patient's muscle tissue. However, with a woman as large as she was, two pints of fluid was nowhere near sufficient.

Something more had to be done. We tried several methods.

We need blood, I said to myself. *Mine is the universal type—but how can we collect it and administer it to her without equipment?*

I felt utterly frustrated, even angry, in my helplessness. Several times we called for sessions of prayer. I actually cried tears of despair on several occasions. I knew what to do. I knew what she needed, but we were completely incapable of doing anything more for lack of basic equipment.

Tom had already tried the ship-to-shore radio but the nearest vessel to answer was just leaving the Panama Canal, still 10 sailing days away. Tom had just received a new "Ham" radio set and offered to set it up to see if we could contact a doctor somewhere.

When God Calls, Expect Adventure

Tom ripped open the packing cases and pulled out the radio set. He began to set it up in his house in a hurry. There was no time to check each part. He just plugged each wire into the position marked for it and began to call.

Someone answered from the United States and Tom explained the problem we were having. The American grasped the problem quickly and asked us to wait while he contacted a doctor. We had waited one or two minutes when Tom looked up to see smoke drifting up from his transmitter. He turned it off quickly.

Something had not been connected correctly. Imagine the frustration as a doctor came on the line and called us via the receiver. With no transmitter, we were not able to reply. For more than half an hour that doctor called and listened, called and listened, before finally deciding he could not reach us. We just sat there feeling discouraged. Help was reaching out to us but we were unable to accept it.

We tried all day to get assistance. We radioed Fiji, asking them to have a plane drop some blood for us. The answer from them was that they had no plane available that could do so. "In any case," they added, "it is not possible to drop blood."

"But it is possible to drop plasma," we radioed back—but we received no help from them.

We radioed to the United States military, asking if they could send a plane with blood and a giving set. Their reply was that they had no plane capable of flying the distance to Pitcairn and back without a refuelling stop. They could not help either.

That evening, I went to see Floyd who had an even smaller radio set. It was so small we doubted it could do what we required. He called out "CQ" several times. An American voice answered. Again we told the story, and this stranger volunteered to get a doctor "on the patch," as he called it. A few minutes later a doctor came on air. When he realised it was Pitcairn Island he was talking to, he told me he had trained as a doctor at the Adventist Church's Loma Linda University.

"Do you have transfusible blood?" he asked.

"No, nothing. We have given the only saline we had."

"Do you have a transfusion giving and receiving set?"

Appendicitis

"No, nothing like that either."

Every question he asked had the same negative answer.

Finally, he said, "Then all I can say is that the woman will die and there is not a thing you can do to stop it. I'm sorry."

On Tuesday morning, Jessie was still in a coma. We called every person on the island to a special prayer meeting in the church. It was one of the most earnest prayer sessions one could ever witness.

Early Wednesday morning, Tom called shipping again. This time the captain of a ship named the *Scherzo* called in, saying, "I have been listening to your messages. We have no doctor or medical person on board, so can't help that way. But we do have some bottles of something called 'Plasma.' I wonder if they could be of any assistance to you?"

Tom rang me and I told him to answer yes. The captain replied, saying he would be passing the island about 8 am and would let us have the plasma.

We were out at sea when a most decrepit, hulking, rusty cargo vessel came around the island. It did not stop, but travelled straight past us, dropping a huge canvas bundle into the water near our boats. Instead of stopping, the captain swept past with just a wave of his hand.

We sailed back as quickly as we could and eagerly opened the bundle. Inside were six bottles of plasma—each with its own sterilised "giving set." A few minutes later, the plasma began to drip into Jessie's body. By the fourth bottle, she was awake and talking to us. The plasma had saved her life.

Jessie made a good recovery. Months later, she went to New Zealand and was diagnosed with an internal ulcer that had been the cause of her collapse.

Some weeks later, I received a letter from the captain of the *Scherzo* in which he apologised for not stopping. He explained that he had had an accident leaving the Panama Canal and his rudder was not operative when the ship's speed dropped below 75 per cent of full speed. Had he stopped, he might not have been able to steer away from any dangers. He explained that he was Norwegian, his first officer was Chinese and all other members of the crew were Indian,

When God Calls, Expect Adventure

none of whom could speak English. No-one on the ship knew how to use the plasma, so he was happy to donate it where it could be used.

That night, we again met as a church and discussed the way the Lord had been present. We had given our problem to Him and He had answered.

LOST AT SEA

"I know that the Lord is great, that our Lord is greater than all gods. The Lord does whatever pleases him, in the heavens and on the earth, in the seas and all their depths" (Psalm 135:5, 6).

One Sabbath evening, most people were sitting around the village square. The *Rangitiki* had called late that afternoon, bringing supplies and mail, so everyone was in good spirits. The evening was balmy and the islanders sat in groups around the square, talking and enjoying each other's company.

Some of the younger boys were having a great time racing around the various buildings, chasing one another and throwing stones. Twelve-year-old Noggie raced around from the back of the dispensary just in time to be struck in his left eye by a stone. His cries of pain soon filled the square.

In the clinic, I observed that the whole coloured section of Noggie's eye had been damaged and was now concertinaed into one corner. This was serious!

Tom ran to the radio shack and requested that the *Rangitiki* return to collect Noggie. The wounded boy's father gathered clothes and a few items to take with them. Others readied our transport. Within hours, we put out to sea in the motorised long boat, shrugging our shoulders against the rain that began to fall lightly.

We headed straight for the lights of the returning liner and met the ship several miles out to sea. They lowered a unique stretcher into which Noggie was strapped. Then the stretcher was hauled up, much as a fish is pulled out of the ocean by fishing line—headfirst and spinning. Meanwhile, Len, captain of our longboat, ascertained from the ship's navigator the exact compass bearing of the island, because by now the rain had set in, blanking out the land completely. We waved the ship goodbye and watched for a few moments, as the *Rangatiki* got under way. It was about 3 am and very dark.

"Whar dah kumpass?" shouted Len. "We's mas a gwin." ("Where's the compass? We must get going.")

When God Calls, Expect Adventure

The men looked in the expected place, but the compass was not there. Others just stood in shock, dumbfounded. In the rush to get to the ship, no-one had thought to see that there was a compass on board. Without it, we would be lost at sea!

The liner was beginning to pick up speed. All the Pitcairn men shouted to the passengers and crew who lined the rail of the departing ship but no-one heard. They probably thought the men were offering an enthusiastic goodbye.

Aboard the longboat, pandemonium broke out as everyone blamed each other with angry words. We were miles away from the island. Even in daylight, it would have been but a speck on the horizon. In the dark and the rain, it was impossible to know which way to go. We had no idea how many times we had turned and twisted as we lay alongside the liner and what direction we had drifted. We could not see the moon or even a single star to navigate by.

Suddenly, the solution occurred to me and I immediately thanked God. I pointed decisively and shouted: "There is no problem. The island lies in that direction."

The men wanted to know how I could be so certain.

"The liner returned to Pitcairn for Noggie and now it is returning to New Zealand. It must be going away from the island. All we have to do is keep the lights of the liner directly astern of our boat and we'll be heading straight for home."

They saw the reasoning immediately. At about 5 am, when the lights of the liner could no longer be seen behind us, the drizzle seemed to part and there, looming out of the semi-darkness and thousands of square miles of Pacific Ocean, lay Pitcairn, only a mile or two ahead.

What shouting broke out in our small boat! What a relief. We thanked the Lord for the thought He gave me that night.

To the islanders, the sea was moody and ever-changing, a beautiful, dangerous, and sometimes unpredictable friend. It had to be treated with the utmost respect!

"I've seen many strange things in my 70 years on this island, but never anything like we had last night," Parkin said one day.

Lost at Sea

Several others agreed.

"Only the hand of God could have saved so many people from death," Parkin concluded.

We had gone out as usual to meet the ocean liner *Ruahine* on a warm March evening. There was nothing to indicate that this rendezvous would be different from the many other times when we had visited a passing ship. Handmade curios were sold to passengers, while cargo was off-loaded into the island boats. This included two tons of cement in sealed drums, enough to pave the entire village square.

It was about 9 pm and very dark as we approached the harbour. The island women were there as they often were with lamps, waiting for our return. But tonight the lights winked and blinked confusingly. Clearly they wanted to convey some message, but just what that message was the boat's crew could not make out.

It is the job of the boat's coxswain to select the right wave before the boat attempted to enter the turbulent waters of the treacherous "inlet." Believing he had selected the right wave, Len yelled, "Now, alogetter, lay to."

Fourteen oars began to work as the men threw their weight into the task. What we did not know was that inside the harbour the water was unusually turbulent and reached higher than ever seen before, maybe as much as 13 feet (4 metres). The level was so high that it reached up and into the boat sheds, as though it would drag the housed boats away and suck them out to sea.

A wave drove us forward, out of control, faster than any of the men had gone before. Panicked cries rang out as the confused coxswain struggled to regain control. There was no point. We were as helpless as a discarded matchstick flung into a raging river. First, our boat smashed into the rocks on the starboard side of the harbour. Next, with a loud, jarring thud we collided with the rocks on the other side of the harbour. Next we were spun sideways and were driven up to the housed boats in the sheds. Miraculously, the heavily laden boat stayed upright but it was filled with water from the waves.

I regained my balance as quickly as possible and peered into the darkness to see what the next wave was going to do to us. To my shock, instead of water, the harbour was empty, and a few fish flapped among

When God Calls, Expect Adventure

the exposed stones. In the minutes that followed, the men leaped out and struggled heroically to unload the boat.

Soon the next of the tsunami waves began to come and the second boat, not knowing what had happened, began its run in.

"Go back," we shouted. But our men were too late to halt its progress. It too was smashed against the cliff face on the right, then spun savagely around. A few of the men grabbed valuables and jumped into the water but it was deeper than expected. Chester was almost crushed in the mayhem but his boat stopped just short of his legs.

Immediately a message was sent to the third boat, warning it not to attempt to come in. They stayed out all night, while the island people sat on the hillside, flashing Morse Code messages to the men at sea.

In the morning, we inspected the harbour. The sea level had returned to normal but there was significant damage. Great boulders lay on the small pebbly foreshore where they had been thrown by the ocean surge. The timber boat-slide was undermined and two boats were badly damaged.

For days the people marvelled over the fact that no-one was hurt. Time and again folk came to me and said that God must have been there, that He was so good to them. And they were right. Few people ride to land on the crest of a tsunami and come out of it unscathed, especially when the landing is the treacherous "harbour" of Pitcairn Island.

A CLOSE CALL

"Blessed are those you choose and bring near to live in your courts! We are filled with the good things of your house, of your holy temple. You answer us with awesome and righteous deeds, God our saviour, the hope of all the ends of the earth and of the farthest seas" (Psalm 65:4, 5).

Danger was never far away on Pitcairn. Many locations were named after individuals who had experienced serious accidents or who had died.

One Sunday, I took nine-year-old Lyn to the far side of the island to an area known as Tedside. The tide was low, so we went down to look at the Pacific Ocean waves as they crashed onto the shoreline.

The rugged coastline on this side of the island consisted of a massive rock face, which at water level, reached out into the ocean like a series of 30-foot (10-metre) fingers on a giant, rocky hand. Between each finger were deep chasms loaded with huge lengths of brown kelp. Waves boiled and churned through the chasms with awesome fury, then sucked out at a terrific rate. It was mesmerising watching water batter the kelp beds and crash into the immovable volcanic rock in a battle that had been going on since the island had first risen above the surface of the sea.

Lyn and I stood on one of the exposed fingers, awed by the power of the water as it pounded in and roared out. Detecting a different sound, I glanced seaward. What I saw struck fear into my heart. A huge, rogue wave was coming inexorably at us with tremendous power. It crashed across the fingers of rock.

"Dad!" Lyn cried.

"Hold on!" I yelled. With no time to run, I held Lyn on the lee side of my body and turned side on to present the smallest possible drag surface to the wave.

The wall of water knocked my legs from under me, dragging us along the rocks.

"Help us, Lord!" I cried.

When God Calls, Expect Adventure

My left hand found a crack in the rock large enough for my fingers. My right hand was locked on Lyn's as his body was swept parallel to mine in the mass of white, foaming water, which tugged him toward the boiling chasm below. Somehow, my left hand held until the water had passed over. Then, with a tremendous sucking sound, it poured down the chasm on its way past the swaying kelp and back into the ocean.

Lyn and I scrambled to safety. From a safe distance, we stood and wondered at our escape. There was no-one on this side of the island, there was no place to climb out of the sea and, had we been swept in, the alarm would not have been raised for hours. Thank God we were not taken with the water for if we had there would have been no hope of making it back to land safely.

On another afternoon, our family was walking along a rocky foreshore. I heard an urgent call and raced ahead, fearing the worst.

Lyn and Ken were standing on a rock bridge. Beneath them, the surf surged in and out. In the foam-filled pool below, Roger—a 12-year-old Pitcairn boy—was desperately grasping at rocks to stop being carried out to sea.

During a lull in the waves, he managed to scramble up and we pulled him out.

"What happened?" I asked, relieved that all three of them were safe.

"We were standing on the rock bridge when a wave came from nowhere," one of the boys said.

The wave would have washed all of them into the water. It had grabbed at them, sweeping around their bodies. Without thinking of himself, Roger had thrust out both hands, pushing Lyn and Ken back to an upright position as he himself was sucked away.

Roger was a much better swimmer and he knew it, so had taken the risk himself in order to save them. Thankfully, the brave boy had been able to hold on to the rocks below and scramble back to safety.

The sea provided other challenges, too. In a shed in the village, I had come across a four-cylinder marine petrol engine that was not being

A Close Call

used. Many times, I had heard one or more of the islanders complain about the huge bulk of the whaleboats they had to drag in and out of the water at times when there was only a small job to be done. So I began advocating for the building of a smaller boat that would be adequate for many of the smaller tasks that needed to be carried out around the island. With just the right engine for such a boat, this seemed to me to be the answer to their prayer.

Not being a member of the island council, I was not privy to their discussion but a meeting was held and afterwards the chairman came to me.

"The council has decided to build a small boat, using the spare petrol engine," he said.

I began to smile—but he had not finished his speech.

"And they want you to design a suitable boat."

In mission service, one never knows what strange request might come—and this was one of those times.

"Here are the specifications it must follow," continued the chairman. "It must be capable of carrying a big load. It must be able to go through waves without shipping water. It must be capable of going backwards into waves just as successfully as it goes forward. It must not have a deep draught because it must be capable of going over shallow water. It must have the propeller deep enough not to come out of the water when going in and out the harbour. It must be capable of turning quickly in heavy seas . . ."

It was quite a list—and it seemed that most of the requirements were contradictory. One would surely deny the possibility of another.

I had never built a boat, nor did I know anything about designing one. But that made no difference: the job was mine, they told me, and I decided it would be a good challenge. So I sent to England for books and materials on designing boats. I studied hard and, little by little, I began to incorporate the essential features into a plan, until at last a design emerged.

The boat was about 25 feet (almost 8 metres) long. It had a flared bow to deflect water and a spoon stern to give it lift when hit by a following wave, while at the same time allowing the propeller to be tucked well under the boat where it would not lift out of the water as

When God Calls, Expect Adventure

we passed over a wave. The design was fairly flat-bottomed and wide-beamed. Like all boats on Pitcairn, the rudder was quickly removable, allowing the use of a sweep oar in tight situations.

The council studied the design carefully and voted to build it. On the floor of the public hall, I drew the shape of each rib in full size. We cut out a piece of plywood the shape of each rib and gave one to each man with the instructions that he go into the bush and find two limbs of suitable wood with exactly the same shape as the plywood pattern.

"Cut them and bring them in," the supervisor instucted. "You others can find timber for the keel, the gunwale, the seats and so on."

The timbers came in and formed a large pile. Then came the work of shaping each piece. A suitable location had been selected within the village area and building began. The only tools used were axe, adze, brace and bit, hammer, saw and plane. I guess someone had a ruler, but I didn't see it being used. Nor did they use a spirit level—a weight hanging on a string was their plumbob. Much of the accurate work depended on the fantastic eye of John, who seemed to be able to detect any small variation.

It took many weeks of work but the boat stood finished at last, with the engine installed and even fuel in the tank. On launching day, the boat was dragged by sheer manpower along the path to The Edge. Everyone from the village came to watch the action.

The men gave a tug that pulled the boat over the edge onto the steep downhill path. Immediately everyone scattered as the boat bounced its way down several metres until it stopped against a rock. Another nudge and it bounced further downhill over rocks and stone steps, finally reaching the water's edge. No Australian boat owner could have watched the pounding this new boat received. But Pitcairn boats are built to take rough handling.

The maiden voyage had to be out through heavy seas. We started up the small engine and set off for the harbour entrance, but the boat was making way so poorly that several oars were pulled out to assist in getting into safer water outside. The clutch clearly needed to be adjusted. When that was done the boat performed well, even making circles in an arc little more than its own length. It rode the seas well both backward and forward. Only one problem was evident: it was slow, only

A Close Call

capable of doing about four knots (about 7.5 kilometres per hour). But in the short distances it was designed for that was not a major problem.

Because of its slightly barge-like shape, it became known as "Dumpy" and became a favourite for such jobs as collecting sand and local supplies. One day it brought 40 sailors ashore from a naval vessel. Heavy seas were running that day but not one of the standing men got so much as a splash on his uniform.

It seemed amazing to me that a non-sailor missionary with career experience in the Highlands of Papua New Guinea would be called to Pitcairn Island to design and help build a flat-bottomed boat named *Dumpy*. But I was proud that God could use even a novice like me!

Pitcairn men building *Dumpy*, a general purpose craft.

THE BOUNTY ANCHOR

"We have this hope as an anchor for the soul, firm and secure. It enters the inner sanctuary behind the curtain, where our forerunner Jesus, has entered on our behalf" (Hebrews 6:19, 20).

The *Yankee* was the personal yacht of a retired United States naval admiral by the name of Irving Johnston. He and his wife made regular world trips and, on one visit to Pitcairn, a student crew member was testing his scuba gear when he spotted the fluke of a huge anchor down on the sea bed. Taking into consideration the position in which it was found, and the lay of the anchor, it was clear that only the *Bounty* could have placed an anchor in that position and at that angle. It must have lain there unseen for 168 years.

Excitement ran high on the island. Plans were made to bring it up and, with the *Yankee* present, such a venture was possible. Divers descended to the bottom of the sea. The *Yankee* was able to position itself above the anchor and winch it to the surface. Holding the anchor in that position, the *Yankee* motored to a quiet alcove where the huge anchor was transferred to one of the island longboats for the trip ashore.

There was great excitement as this historic anchor was landed on the boat-slide. After two weeks of anti-rust treatment, it was hauled to the village square and positioned in a bed of concrete outside the public hall where public functions were held. Its great mass was a reminder to the people of their heritage. Like the anchor, they too had endured.

———•———

We learned to enjoy the lifestyle of Pitcairn. On rare cricket days, everyone who could walk went to the almost level area in Aute Valley. Every person—young, old, woman or man—was assigned to one of two cricket teams, each of which boasted as many as 30 people.

A pitch was prepared by cutting the grass, and the "wicket"—a drum—set up. Any batsman seen to simply "block" the ball was automatically "out." A batsman had to strike hard at every ball. If he missed, and the ball struck the wicket, he was immediately out. The same applied if he was caught on the full. If however the ball was struck and lost, the batsman had to keep running until it was found. On rare occasions as many as 15 or 20 runs could be made. There were no fours and no sixes, just a great deal of hilarity when the ball was hit into a shrub that housed a vicious nest of wasps!

Of course, with as many as 20 people fielding, there was a strong chance of being caught. If you were bowled out, there were at least two or even three innings per side for the day.

It was a fast and furious game. As the school teacher was called to take the bat on one occasion, he was a bit slow getting there, so the bowler simply bowled him out before he reached the pitch. No-one took much notice of the score. That wasn't the point. It was a day for fun, and they made sure they had plenty of it.

Most evenings had some function scheduled. Tuesday nights were for the first-aid class. The members always arrived in full uniform and, at

The *Bounty*'s anchor in place oustide the public hall on Pitcairn Island.

When God Calls, Expect Adventure

the completion of their course, would receive their certificates from the captain of a visiting ship. Wednesday evenings were set aside for prayer meetings. Thursday was for the brass band. Saturday evenings were for pictures, if there were some to be viewed, and Christmas was celebrated with gusto, with pomp and ceremony and lights moving all over the village for hours as stockings were filled.

By Christmas Day, the village square was filled with newly "planted" trees decorated with balloons and bunting and small gifts. It seemed to be a custom that every family would give gifts to each other family, mostly handmade or homegrown. In 1958, we required five wheelbarrow loads to carry our presents home—and almost every present was a pineapple!

Some islanders would give their friends pandanus leaves from which the recipient would later make a basket. Another might present a length of raw Miro wood, which could be turned into a carving. Another might give a live chicken or a woven hat.

Late in the afternoon, all islanders would gather around the loaded trees in the village square. Several men and women would go to the trees and begin pulling the presents off while calling loudly the name of the intended recipient. It was all confusion and excitement until all presents had finally been collected and everyone sat down in the square admiring their gifts and expressing their thanks to the givers.

We had been on Pitcairn almost three years when the church leaders in Wahroonga suggested it was time for us to move on. Pastor Rex Cobbin accepted the request of the church leadership to replace us and a fortnight after the Cobbins arrived in 1959, we were able to obtain passage on the *Athenic*.

Our daughter Robyn's third birthday occurred during that trip home. The ship's kitchen staff prepared a special cake for her birthday and a party was held for her in the ship's dining room.

Our two boys had the run of the ship, as any normal child would have back then. Without our knowledge, they discovered the area where the poker machines were located. They watched various passengers playing the machines and somehow worked out a "system."

The Bounty Anchor

Just before we docked in Auckland, some of the passengers told us what had been happening. Lyn and Ken would watch the machines, then at certain points they would say, "Next time you will get some money."

And they were right. Money would pour out. The passengers told us it was uncanny how the boys were right each time and they thought we had a real treasure to be capitalised upon.

We felt differently. We were embarrassed and felt our witness for the Lord had been somewhat compromised.

In Sydney, we were given the responsibility for the Auburn and Guildford churches. We built a house in Pendle Hill, near the railway station so the children could go by train to school in Auburn. For a time, we also cared for the Penrith church. Then one night in 1961, Pastor Bob Frame rang asking us to return to Papua New Guinea to head up departmental work with the Bismarck–Solomons Union Mission. Church leader, Pastor Naden, also spoke to us, assuring us we could do such work. The call surprised us, so we prayed about it. It seemed the Lord was again calling us to more mission adventures, so we accepted!

RABAUL

"You who are young, be happy while you are young, and let your heart give you joy in the days of your youth" (Ecclesiastes 11:8).

The Bismark–Solomons Union Mission had its headquarters in Rabaul and cared for the New Guinea islands plus all of the Solomon Islands. We arrived in Rabaul in December, 1961, and were allocated the residence in Attar Street, right behind the church. This was to be our home for the next eight years, by far the longest time of any position we had previously held. But it proved to be a happy time. There were other missionary's children in town and our youngsters had a wonderful time with them. Indeed, we had the privilege of some of the missionaries' children from outlying stations boarding with us most of the time. Being able to do this meant those children were able to attend a school, at the same time as living in a Christian home, plus have the opportunity to go home to their parents several times a year. Our house was always full of teenagers and we enjoyed it.

The hills around Rabaul were a maze of tunnels, dug by the Japanese army during the war. In these tunnels lay hidden many "treasures" to be discovered by adventurous youngsters. They would come home telling of the new caves they had discovered and how there were radio parts here and ammunition there. In another part of the cave system, they would find what had been a command post with about a 7-foot (2-metre) long cement-lined slit for observing any enemy ships that might try to venture too close. Immediately behind the observation slit was a dirt ramp, down which the observers could slide quickly away should it be advisable to do so. There were so many of these tunnels that the youngsters were always finding new ones and new "treasures."

Another delight for the youngsters was their dugout canoe that had been sent to them by one of the Solomon Island pastors. And they also had a small "yacht." The canoe was fitted with a mast and a sail, and was really intended for use only in calm weather. One day a real storm had come up in the harbour, with high winds and heavy seas. Ken and his

Solomon Island friend Gibson—who later became one of Papua New Guinea's first airplane pilots—were out in the canoe enjoying the thrill. Gibson sat at the front where his back was used to divert the water from coming into the canoe.

The winds were so strong they were unable to turn the canoe around. They simply had to drive on further out to sea. Finally, a moment arrived when a turn was possible so they turned and drove back again at break-neck pace, shouting with excitement. There was a certain amount of fear, of course, but that only added to the excitement of the trip. They came home absolutely bubbling over with the news of the trip and how they had mastered it all. We could understand their excitement, but down deep we thanked the Lord that their guardian angel was alert at the time.

Volcano climbing was another excitement. Rabaul is situated in the centre of a caldera, a huge old volcano. The original volcano is no longer active, but situated on its rim are several active smaller volcanoes. These have been known to erupt from time to time. In 1937, there was a huge eruption that caused serious damage. Again in 1994, the city of Rabaul was destroyed. But during the time we lived there, we experienced no major eruption. We did, however, experience constant tremors to keep our minds sharp.

One of the smaller mildly active volcanoes situated on the rim of the old caldera was Matupit.

Matupit volcano was quite exciting to visit. It was constantly smoking and steaming, but only from numerous, small vents here and there within the crater. One could climb to the lip of the crater, then let oneself down inside by holding onto a rope, which had to be renewed frequently due to the corrosive effect of the sulphuric steam. Inside, one could walk all around looking down into vents from which hissed super-heated steam or blasts of super-hot air. Around these vents were beautiful lace works of crystallised sulphur. Provided one was careful where one walked, one could go all around inside the volcano. Not everyone has had that kind of opportunity and the mission young people loved it.

At the base of the volcano, near the sea, were several creeks of extremely hot water. To fall out of the canoe when paddling in them

When God Calls, Expect Adventure

would have been disastrous, probably fatal. But the boys went there because in the area the wild bush hens made their nests, relying on the heat of the ground to incubate the huge eggs they laid. The boys would dig these eggs out and place them in the creek until they were cooked, then have a feast.

Volcanic tremors were common in Rabaul. Some were serious enough to cause the water tanks to actually dance from toe to toe, splashing large quantities of water over the top. But we had so many tremors that life without them—on furlough, for example—seemed somehow wrong, as though something was missing.

I remember the day Ken came back with a huge grin on his face. He told how he had seen a major tremor coming. He saw it coming because the road was undulating in his direction, like a wave coming toward a swimmer on the surface of the sea. He immediately jumped on his bike and rode as hard as he could into the on-coming undulations, just to feel the "waves" under his wheels. He assured me it was exciting.

Another interest was what we called our "TV." Lyn had made a large fish tank using the windscreens from an old army truck for the front. This tank was filled with seawater obtained by dragging their canoe down to the water, on its pram-wheel trolley, where the canoe was filled with water, then slowly drawn back to the house, usually arriving with about 50 per cent of the water they started out with. Every so often, they would have to replenish or replace the whole tank-full of water due to some disease or fungi entering it.

On Sunday afternoons when I was home, the boys and I would go to the reef to collect fish and other marine creatures for the tank. Each of us had an inflated inner tube tied to our waist by a 7-foot (2-metre) rope. Draped inside the tube was a mosquito-net cage into which any fish we caught were dumped. Catching the fish was fun, one person would hold an open plastic bag near some crevasse or rock while the fish were frightened—hopefully—into the open bag. Most would shoot off another way, but some were caught. There were all colours and all kinds of fish, plus many other sea creatures, such as shellfish, sea horses and sea plants.

GOD PROTECTS AGAIN

"We who are strong ought to bear with the failings of the weak and not to please ourselves. Each of us should please our neighbour for their good, to build them up" (Romans 15:1, 2).

By 1975, when Papua New Guinea gained independence, I was back in the Highlands as president of the Eastern Highlands Mission. It was the largest mission or conference in the Australian field, having a membership of about 17,500 people at that time.

Camp meetings were numerous and because many of the people could not travel to us, we travelled to them. Each meeting was usually three days long and one or two of the office personnel had to be present at each. This meant a lot of hard driving over almost impossible tracks. One day I only covered 6 miles (10 kilometres) in six hours, the road was so bad. Then, after I arrived I found myself sitting for three days on a seat made of a round log, with no backrest.

The wonderful people did their best to make things as comfortable as they could for their visitors but the seats were hard and meetings went on for many hours. The food was whatever they had available, supplemented by a few biscuits or something I had taken with me.

The real value of the camp meetings was the fact that we were with the people, to share and share alike. That's what Jesus did. He became one with us. Had He arranged a softer bed or softer living than the rest of us, He would not have succeeded as He did. There are many who have gone out as "missionaries" who tried to live as they did at home, and were disappointed in the results of their effort. But I don't imagine that Christ would have had much influence if He had resided in a palace and lived a luxurious life.

When God Calls, Expect Adventure

A much more serious inconvenience was constant inter-tribal fighting. In Papua New Guinea, I got the feeling that tribal fighting was like a national sport. In a culture that embraced the principle of "an eye for an eye and a tooth for tooth," it was every man's responsibility to avenge any violence inflicted on his "one-toks" (relatives). The system of payback did not require that revenge be inflicted on the person who started the problem. Revenge could be meted out to any member of the enemy tribe.

Sometimes tribal fighting was more show than war. I have stood looking down on tribal fights from time to time, watching them racing from one cover to another, all the time yelling and shouting just like a football game. As the sides came around or raced past where I stood, they would give me a great grin. Other missionaries have told of times when they have walked between the warring sides, only to have both sides stand back while they passed through, then resume the fighting. However, the fighting could also be deadly.

One day, a huge tribal fight was raging across the hills from the Asaro Valley over to the Watabung/Chuave Valley. Houses were being burnt and whole villages were going up in smoke, and gardens were being systematically destroyed. The battle had been raging for about two weeks and supplies of arrows and food were critically depleted. Then one enterprising individual left the field of battle and made his way to the local radio station, where he broadcast a message suggesting that they stop the fight for the weekend and begin again at 8 am on Monday. And that is exactly what they did. Everyone went home to have a good feed and a good sleep, while the women and older men prepared a fresh supply of arrows. On Monday morning, the battle re-commenced resulting in a constant stream of arrow wounds.

Sadly, since that time matters have deteriorated. Guns are now used and no longer is tribal fighting a "sport" with relatively few fatal injuries. Nor is the fighting so clearly a tribal matter practised according to strict custom and laws.

God Protects Again

The gospel was advancing in leaps and bounds. New churches were rising all over the place. As one would expect, Satan was also busy. Many times things happened which were aimed at hindering the work of God. Often the incident seemed to be aimed at the national missionary, as a person. And many of these missionaries were volunteers for the simple reason that we could not get enough trained workers.

One young man—Benjamin—had been asked to care for a group of new believers in a remote area near Mt Michael. It must have been the Lord who prompted us to go and visit him on a certain day.

It was a long, rough road that took us hours of bone-shaking driving. As we neared the village, we were informed that someone was trying to find Benjamin to kill him. It was the father of a girl and this father had been told that Benjamin and his daughter had met on a grass "road" where they had talked for a time. It appears that the meeting was not planned. But the father's interpretation was that they had met away from the village and broken customary standards of what was acceptable.

I was told the direction Benjamin had run in a desperate attempt to flee for his life. So I drove around that way and found him as he desperately tried to evade those pursuing.

"Get in," I commanded. "Quickly!"

We put him in the vehicle and locked the doors. I drove back to the village where a large log had been laid across the road to stop us. An angry crowd surrounded our vehicle. I got out and re-locked the door.

The anger was palpable. I tried to reason with the people but they were enraged and it was impossible. They would not listen.

With dismay, I saw that those in the vehicle had opened one of the doors. Benjamin was hauled out and led away by a group of fierce men. I raced across to try to save him, noting that they already had him bent over from the waist while one man lifted a large timber to strike him.

The one holding the stick intended to bring it down on Benjamin's neck or head. Instinctively, I jumped in and stood where it would have had to come down on me, not on Benjamin.

Thwarted, one of the angry men came at me with a large bush knife. God was there for sure. I wrested the knife off him and talked to him more severely than I had ever done to another person. That is not natural to me and God surely had to give me the words.

When God Calls, Expect Adventure

Slowly the situation calmed a little but I still could not talk sense into anyone. Finally, I simply took Benjamin and we got into the vehicle and drove at the log, which was pushed aside by the weight of the vehicle.

Thank God, the village men stood and watched us leave. Clearly, our work was not over yet!

While on furlough, I had worked with an evangelist in Sydney. One night, he had shown the film entitled *I Beheld His Glory*, which depicts the final events in the life of Jesus. I wanted to take that film out to Papua New Guinea—but it would cost more than $400, a price way beyond our reach. Then a friend in Australia sent us a large donation. Combined with some funds we could scrape up, this allowed us to buy the film.

The first time I used it was in a mountain village in the East Simbu district. We had a small Honda generating plant, which we placed as far away from the little church as the wires would allow. We projected the film onto a white sheet for a screen. This was the first time most of the people had ever seen moving pictures.

When it came to the crucifixion scene, I heard sobs from the women. Later the sobs grew louder and louder. When the film stopped the sobs died down, but no-one left the room. They simply sat there as though deep in thought. The men finally began to file out quietly. They expressed great interest in the film, asking for a repeat showing. All talk was quiet and thoughtful. Then the women began to come out, making similar expressions of interest.

But one woman came to me and made a statement that has remained with me always. She said in her local language, "I have heard about Jesus, but now I know Him. I saw Him die on the cross. I saw it myself, and it made me so very sad." That woman expressed the thoughts of most of them. For them, it was not just actors playing parts. They believed they actually saw the life and death of Jesus. For them, He had become a living, life-and-flesh person who had lived selflessly, generously and purely. Now they could really see Jesus!

I am sure this film did as much as any missionary ever did to make Jesus a real person to those people. I thank God for that film. We must have used it—mostly by request—many times.

WHEN GOD CALLS . . .

In 1980, we decided it was time to leave the Pacific islands permanently. We felt honoured and privileged to have served the way we did. There would be other adventures, including postings in Australia and volunteer placements with the Bangkok Adventist Hospital in Thailand, in remote Lord Howe Island and also in New Zealand. A wise man once said that God's workers don't ever retire, they just stopped getting paid. It's true! And I wouldn't have it any other way.

Psalm 63:1–8 says it beautifully:

You God, are my God,
earnestly I seek you;
I thirst for you,
My whole being longs for you,
in a dry and parched land
where there is no water.

I have seen you in the sanctuary
and beheld your power and your glory.
Because your love is better than life,
My lips will glorify you.
I will praise you as long as I live,
And in your name I will lift up my hands.
I will be fully satisfied as with the richest of foods;
With singing lips my mouth will praise you.

On my bed I remember you;
I think of you through the watches of the night.

When God Calls, Expect Adventure

Because you are my help,
I sing in the shadow of your wings.
I cling to you;
Your right hand upholds me.

The Lord has granted us a wonderful life, a life we could enjoy, serving others with medical missionary work and seeing many souls brought close to the Lord in strange and amazing places. God, you see, is everywhere! There is no land, no culture, no place, no heart where He is not at work, trying to reveal His grace and bring life to lives. We look forward to meeting these people in heaven, as we praise the Lord for His many blessings and His constant leading and protection.

I am an old man now and have spent many years reflecting on the medical missionary work Freda and I dedicated ourselves to. Without doubt I can say this: when God calls, expect adventure. There is great joy in the Lord's service!

AFTERWORD

by Brad Watson

Seventh-day Adventist missionaries have had a profound impact on the people of Papua New Guinea since Septimus W Carr (an Australian) and his wife Edith (a New Zealander) landed at Port Moresby in 1908, with Benisimani Tavodi (a Fijian). More than 100 years later, official church membership has exceeded 240,000[1] and a Papua New Guinea census has reported that 10 per cent of all adults are affiliated with Adventism.[2] In 2011, the Adventist Church in Papua New Guinea was providing education to 21,000 students in primary and secondary schools, operating one of the nation's six universities—Pacific Adventist University—and one of its vocational colleges, plus offering a wide variety of essential services, including air transport, medical clinics, remote aid posts and dispensaries. The Adventist church is respected as an important service provider.

The rapid growth and broad impact of the Adventist Church is remarkable considering its modest beginnings. Work in the British Protectorate of Papua began in 1891 with a small shipment of religious literature conveyed up Australia's east coast and across the Torres Straight to Port Moresby on a London Missionary Society (LMS) boat.[3] The small vessel was named after John Williams, a LMS missionary who was killed and eaten by cannibals in the New Hebrides (now Vanuatu), and it serviced mission stations along Papua's 1600-kilometre (1000-mile) coastline. When the *John Williams* delivered its small cargo, Adventist church membership in Australia consisted of just 492 persons members led by six pastors.[4] The founding of Avondale College by Ellen White was still several years away and the capacity of the Adventist church to send well-supported missionaries to Papua New Guinea was still being developed.

Where the LMS pioneers were assisted by eight Loyalty Islanders and a troop of Samoans,[5] the first Adventist missionary from Australia to Papua was assisted by his wife and just one Fijian convert. Eventually,

Afterword

Adventist missionaries in Papua and New Guinea were supported by colleagues from Fiji, the Solomon Islands, Cook Islands and by several indigenous couples from Australia. In the early years, Adventist missionary work was characterised by chronic staff shortages, limited funding, inexperience and the disadvantage of being a relative latecomer among much larger denominations like the Anglicans, Catholics and Lutherans.

The first Adventist missionaries found their pioneering work challenging. The first hurdle to overcome was the fact that the British protectorate had been divided into "Spheres of Influence" for existing missionary societies. Various governors had refused "to cede land anywhere round the coast to missions other than the parties to the compact."[6] Unable to gain work on the coast, Carr was able to lease 150 hectares (370 acres) of land from the government inland on the Sogeri Plateau for agriculture, education and mission. Ironically, this land had been sold to the government by the Koiari, who believed it was home to evil spirits.[7]

With a great deal of hard work and hired labour, the Bisiatabu mission house, church and farm took shape. Although 800 rubber trees were successfully planted to provide income, Carr's evangelistic efforts were less successful. The Koiari people had not invited his presence and they resisted Carr's efforts to share the gospel message with them. Carr's only baptism in six years of pioneering service ended badly when the boy's angry father intervened and withdrew him from the mission.[8] When Carr departed in 1914, it was likely with a sense of disappointment.

Six long years passed before a second baptism occurred in 1920. Soon after, Pastor and Mrs Griffiths F Jones were appointed as missionaries to Papua. In contrast to his predecessors, the energetic and adventurous Jones embarked on a walking tour of 27 isolated villages in the remote Astrolabe Mountains. It must have been an unusual experience for a man accustomed to sailing the Pacific on mission boats, but there he healed the dying son of a village chief who gratefully promised to send two boys to the mission. Under Jones's leadership, the mission school at Bisiatabu finally opened with a grand total of 26 students. Reporting on this achievement, Jones wrote, "The school is doing well considering we have a lot of untamed, undisciplined, savage, larrikin youth."[9]

When God Calls, Expect Adventure

Illness took a toll on the early Adventist missionaries. When Beni died from snakebite in 1918, local sorcerers were delighted and interpreted the death as a triumph of their sorcery.[10] In 1925 Ratu Tevita Daivalu and his wife Liviana began work at Bisiatabu School. Sadly, Tevita died of blackwater fever in 1928, and again this was interpreted by local people as a triumph of sorcery over Christianity.[11] The historical ramifications of Tevita's death continued to reverberate for almost 80 years when in 2008, descendents of Tevita's family met with the Taburi clan for a reconciliation ceremony they had remorsefully requested.

Jones's decision to establish small mission stations in villages such as Efogi, on the Kokoda Trail, and William Lock's arrival in 1924 resulted in positive outcomes. Before long, the Efogi School "was much admired by government officials, who urged the Adventists to commence work along the coast in both directions from Port Moresby."[12] Such work was difficult. Travel to Efogi required the traverse of 10 mountains and crossing as many as 90 rivers and streams.[13] Expansion along the coast would require mission boats and experienced sailors.

It is difficult to account for the slow growth of the Adventist work in the years prior to 1924 and the passing of time leaves us to speculate. It is notable that until the Adventist missionaries in Papua provided schooling and medical care in remote communities, growth was slow or nonexistent.

During the 1930s, a number of small mission outposts were built along the Papuan coast. Mrs Alma Wiles—widowed in the 1920s when her husband Norman had died from blackwater fever in the New Hebrides—served at Aroma prior to World War II, approximately 250 kilometres (170 miles) east of Port Moresby.[14] During this period, Adventist missions came to be known for the quality of their education and medical services. By 1940, the Adventist Church in Papua had been active for 32 years and claimed 1780 converts.[15] Church growth was interrupted by World War II, which resulted in the evacuation of almost all expatriate missionaries from Papua and the former German colony of New Guinea by 1941.

The return of missionaries to Papua and New Guinea in 1946 and 1947 was to a changed situation. Large portions of the northern coastal fringe had been occupied by either the Japanese or the Allies,

Afterword

and indigenous people had witnessed, and become engaged in brutal conflict between the armies of industrialised countries. The fantastic material wealth and power exhibited by military forces led to the emergence of cargo-cults in some regions. Further, the rapid influx of missionaries in the post-World War II "mission rush" to the Highlands would result in significant competition between some Christian groups. The Australian government was given the task of overseeing both Papua and New Guinea until independence in 1975.

It is in this context that Lester and Freda Hawkes arrived in Port Moresby. Inspired by the words of Adventist pioneer Ellen White, they embraced her claim that "Christ, the great medical missionary, is our example. . . . He healed the sick and preached the gospel. In His service, healing and teaching were linked closely together. Today they are not to be separated."[16]

The stories in this book provide a fascinating account of their personal sacrifice and commitment to the Great Commission in which Jesus instructed His followers to "go and make disciples of all nations, baptising them in the name of the Father and of the Son and of the Holy Spirit, and teaching them to obey everything I have commanded you. And surely I am with you always, to the very end of the age" (Matthew 28:19, 20).

Half a century before the Millennium Development Goals were adopted by the United Nations Development Program to reduce poverty, missionaries like Lester and Freda were building schools, providing primary health care, training medical workers, improving water sources, educating mothers about safe motherhood, curbing violent tribal conflicts and mitigating against cultural practices that are contrary to our contemporary idea of universal human rights. Seventh-day Adventists can be proud of the contribution of missionaries like Lester and Freda Hawkes, who sacrificed greatly in a personal quest to transform lives through education, health care and Christ-like service.

---

1. General Conference of Seventh-day Adventists (2010), *Seventh-day Adventist Yearbook*, Review & Herald Publishing Association, page 315.

When God Calls, Expect Adventure

2. National Statistical Office of Papua New Guinea (2000), *PNG Census 2000*, <www.spc.int/prism/country/pg/stats/2000_Census/census.htm>.

3. M Hook (not dated), *Lotu Bilong Sevenday: Early Adventism in Papua New Guinea*, South Pacific Division Department of Education.

4. General Conference of Seventh-day Adventists (1892), *Seventh-day Adventist Yearbook*, Review & Herald Publishing Association, page 79.

5. B Schwarz (ed) (1985), *An Introduction to Ministry in Melanesia: A Handbook for Church Workers*, The Melanesian Institute, page 25.

6. J Garret (1982), *To Live Among the Stars*, WCC Publications, Suva, page 231.

7. J Anderson, "Seventh-day Adventist Fijian, Cook Island, Australian Aboriginal, and Solomon Islands missionaries in Papua, 1908-1942" in A J Ferch (ed) (1991), *Journey of Hope: Seventh-day Adventist History in the South Pacific, 1919-1950*, Signs Publishing Company, page 129.

8. Clapham, N (not dated), *Seventh-day Adventists in the South Pacific 1885–1985*, Signs Publishing Company, page 211.

9. Anderson in Ferch, page 132.

10. ibid, page 131.

11. ibid, page 134.

12. Clapham, page 211.

13. ibid.

14. Hook, page 21.

15. Clapham, , page 211.

16. Ellen White (1948), *Testimonies for the Church*, Vol 9, Pacific Press Publishing Association, pages 170–1.